The Business of Digital Publishing

Responding to the growth of digital products and the commercial imperative to build new digital businesses, *The Business of Digital Publishing* offers a comprehensive introduction to the development of digital products in the book and journal industries.

This textbook provides a background to the main technological developments that have influenced the growth of digital publishing, introducing students to the key terms and concepts that make digital publishing possible.

Exploring four key publishing sectors, professional reference, academic, education and consumer, this book explains the context for the digital developments in each area and looks at the growth of new business models and the future challenges faced by each sector.

It also addresses the key issues that face the industry as a whole, outlining current debates, such as pricing and copyright, and exploring their impact on the industry through relevant case studies.

The Business of Digital Publishing is an invaluable resource for any publishing student looking for a starting point from which to explore the world of digital publishing.

Frania Hall is a Senior Lecturer at the London College of Communication, University of the Arts London. She has worked across a variety of publishing sectors and conducts training courses on editorial, commercial and digital publishing, as well as conducting research in the area of collaboration and partnership around digital projects.

D1319412

The Business of Digital Publishing

An introduction to the digital book and journal industries

Frania Hall

Routledge
Taylor & Francis Group

LONDON AND NEW YORK

First published 2013
by Routledge
2 Park Square, Milton Park, Abingdon, Oxon OX14 4RN

Simultaneously published in the USA and Canada
by Routledge
711 Third Avenue, New York, NY 10017

Routledge is an imprint of the Taylor & Francis Group, an informa business

British Library Cataloguing in Publication Data
A catalogue record for this book is available from the British Library

Library of Congress Cataloging-in-Publication Data
Hall, Frania.
The business of digital publishing : an introduction to the digital book and journal industries / Frania Hall.
    pages cm
1. Electronic publishing. 2. Electronic journals–Publishing. I. Title.
Z286.E43H35 2013
070.5'797–dc23   2013003439

ISBN: 978-0-415-50728-8 (hbk)
ISBN: 978-0-415-50731-8 (pbk)
ISBN: 978-0-203-71268-9 (ebk)

Typeset in Sabon
by Cenveo Publisher Services

Printed and bound in Great Britain by
TJ International Ltd, Padstow, Cornwall

Peter Weaver – here my Technique of Lithography and Printmaking

Contents

Illustrations

Figures

Table

Acknowledgements

I have worked in publishing for many years and met many many interesting and inspiring people. They all play a part in a book like this. It has been one of the joys of working in an industry full of bright creative individuals to find them all so generous when sharing their knowledge and experience. Teaching at the London College of Communication has allowed me to learn even more about the industry and to have the continuous pleasure of talking about it and exploring its intricacies with enthusiastic students.

Just some of the people who helped me along the way are Adrian Driscoll of Aimer Media, Mark Bide of EDItEUR, Richard Charkin and Caroline Wintersgill at Bloomsbury, Brad Scott at Brambletye publishing, Sreemoyee Banerjee at Cambridge University Press, Henry Volans at Faber, Claire Round at HarperCollins, Elisabeth Tribe, Alyssum Ross, Deborah Smith and Steve Connolly at Hodder Education, Becca Hargrove at Little, Brown, Mike Barnard at Macmillan, Andrew Welham at Octopus, Andrew Redman at Oxford University Press, Hugh Jones at the Publishers' Association, Lynette Owen and Mari Shullaw at Pearson, David Penfold, Michael Bhaskar at Profile, Rebecca Ikin at Random House, Alan Jarvis at Routledge, Stephen Barr at Sage, Duncan Campbell at Wiley and, above all, Professor Gill Davies.

I am also delighted to have the opportunity to publish the book with Routledge, where I first started my publishing career and where many good friendships started. Thank you to the lovely team working on the book there and doing all that complex work that many people these days disregard; I hope this book will help show exactly why publishers are so necessary.

There have been a number of people who have helped me specifically with reading and comments – they know who they are and they have been invaluable – thank you to you all for taking the time in your busy lives.

Introduction

Writing a book on the business aspects of digital publishing is a challenge. For many the digital world offers the biggest revolution in publishing terms since the invention of the printing press; the stakes are therefore high as publishers need to redefine themselves in light of this revolution. As other entrants move into the marketplace, significantly changing the scenery, defining the area of digital publishing is a question in itself. Not only that; as things are changing on a daily basis, keeping pace can be difficult. How far can a book attempt to keep up? Surely this is one of the limitations that digital publishing aims to overcome, so is producing a book like this in itself an ironic statement on the arena? The area of digital publishing is also extremely wide ranging. How far should a book like this look at the technological developments? Which sectors should be covered? How should the issues the industry faces be tackled, given that the parameters of the debates change all the time?

While these questions might suggest such a book as this is going to be difficult to write, digital products are proliferating and business models for these products are becoming more sophisticated. There are now a lot of well-established models around market-facing products that have been robustly tried and tested and are repaying investment. It is important to have a good understanding of these. And as the consumer sector is catching up, it faces various problems which are also worthy of study, as the market watches for the tipping point and publishers reinvent themselves within a digital age. So while much is work in progress, there are certainly many aspects of digital publishing that can sensibly be studied.

This book can only provide a starting point, setting the scene as the business of digital publishing evolves. It aims to cover the basic background so that readers understand the context which has shaped the way digital publishing has developed. The scope essentially covers traditional publishing and the digital products the industry is developing. It focuses on the way these products have been developed in publishing houses and how they have been monetised in different ways. It seeks to give students a basic knowledge across many aspects of digital publishing, so they gain a level of technical literacy, see how each sector works, are alert to distinctions between, for instance, ebooks and apps, and start to understand the key issues that all sectors of the industry face, whether it be rights management or pricing dilemmas. It cannot aim to cover all these topics in depth, but the book should provide a good foundation from which to explore further.

The book is divided into three parts. Part I briefly outlines the technological context. This is important as it has influenced the way the different approaches to digital publishing products have developed. This section does not aim to cover detailed technical knowledge and is not for the specialist. Rather it is a quick summary of key developments. Students should gain enough background to know what key terms such as XML, metadata and CMS mean in order to understand important aspects of a digital publishing business and the challenges it faces. Having a basic level of technical understanding should help the reader to understand something of the product and strategy issues around the development of digital products and understand the implications of certain decisions in product development. There is only room to cover the basics, but this part does provide the explanation of the technical vocabulary that is then used for the rest of the book.

Part II explores in more depth the way four key publishing sectors have developed: professional reference, academic, education and consumer sectors. Each chapter in Part II looks at the growth of the business models from the first stage of their digital publishing programmes to their current shape. It is important to understand why some sectors have much more developed business models compared to others and what influences these models going forward; indeed it is interesting to see how far advanced some sectors are compared to the more visible consumer sector. Students of publishing need to have a good grounding in what is happening across the industry as a whole as the digital revolution moves forward; this part of the book should alert them to the various determining factors that impact on each sector and how each has responded, and continues to respond, to the digital challenge.

The final part, Part III, takes a look at key issues that are commonly debated by those involved in the industry as it restructures around the new digital environment. Each issue could easily be a book in itself. This one cannot attempt to cover them in any great depth, but it does aim to ensure students know the key points and have a comprehensive grounding in each area so they are ready to explore these topics in more depth beyond the book if they so wish. There are some areas, such as agency pricing, from which the industry is beginning to move on; these still provide important learning for those observing the way publishing is evolving and illustrate clearly the continuing dilemmas the industry faces.

The conclusion to Part I and each of the chapters within Parts II and III include further reading and some useful resources to direct those interested in delving deeper into an area. There are also questions to consider, stirring the debate and getting readers thinking further about an area or an issue. Throughout there are case studies that outline a recent development or provide the background to a current hot issue. There will inevitably be omissions; the book cannot hope to cover every topic and discussion that digital publishing raises, but I hope that it will provide a good readable baseline in order to observe, from the point of some knowledge, the continuing digital developments within the industry.

Part I

Technology context for digital publishing

In this part we will look at:

1 Developments in technology that led to digital production and new workflows
2 Data structure that forms the basic building blocks of any digital product
3 Web development and the implications for digital content
4 Information architecture and content management for digital products
5 The development and growth of e-readers and ebooks

Introduction to Part I

In order to understand the decisions that publishers face with regard to developing digital businesses it is important to have a basic level of understanding about the technology involved. It is useful to see how the technology has developed and what the key building blocks are for publishing products as it can explain some of the reasons why the industry has developed in a certain way. It is also helpful to understand some of the basics behind the technology as it can impact on digital strategies in different ways. It can make it clearer why certain aspects of digital publishing cost what they do, something that is often questioned.

This part of the book therefore outlines the main technical aspects of digital production and digital products. It explains the evolution of some of the main technologies that are key to the creation and distribution of digital products today, showing how this history has influenced the way these products work. It also looks at some of the current technological developments that may well be key to newer digital products, as well as drivers for the industry and its structure for the future.

This part is not very technical but should provide enough information for the non-specialist to understand the basic components of the digital publishing environment. It selects those developments most useful when considering the way the industry is moving in terms of digital products. It does not go into detail about the way the technology works. However, by putting some of the main technical issues into the publishing context it aims to provide a useful starting point for the rest of the book.

A framework for the growth of digitisation in publishing

Thompson, in *Books in the Digital Age*,[1] explores four stages of development in the digitisation of publishing:

- operating systems and control
- digital production methods
- customer and marketing initiatives
- digital products.

The first refers to the operating systems that publishers introduced to allow for the management of different operations from stock control to sales records. The second

1 Thompson, John. *Books in the Digital Age*. Polity, 2005: 312.

stage covers the development of the manipulation of content, moving towards digital production methods. While to some extent these developments took place concurrently, the key point is that these production systems became much more integral to the operation of most publishing houses at this point in time. The third stage focuses on the proliferation of sales and marketing activity that could be clearly observed in the late 1990s and early 2000s as the web began to be fully exploited, both in terms of the growth of online retail and for marketing and advertising through websites and online catalogues; this has continued to develop with the growth of social media for marketing purposes.

Thompson then identifies the fourth stage as the production of digital products themselves, the delivery of digital content in a digital environment. Again it is important to see that while digital products existed (early reference works, for instance, had been available in digital format for some time), the impact is only now being felt more significantly. Digital content development is continuing to evolve within the web environment, with the application of social media to source and curate content, and the growth of self-publishing opportunities.

It is useful to bear this model in mind when examining the key technical developments of the last decades. This part will not deal with all these areas, but rather will focus on the technologies enabling management of the content (and its output into print products) and then track the development of digital platforms that could be used to deliver the content digitally. It is important to remember that technologies at every point are moving at different speeds. Increased processing capacity, broadband strength, mobile networks, new authoring tools, storage capacity, data protection are all driving changes in the development of the digital environment for publishers. Publishing needs all sorts of technology from authentication to compression, not just digital outputs and workflow systems. However, we will not consider every aspect of technological change, important though these are, but rather focus on those primarily to do with the development of the content in order to produce digital products.

1   Developments towards digital production

Introduction

Publishing has been operating in a digital environment for decades. The production of content via digital processes developed alongside many of the key developments in computing for the general user. The digital environment has been the main way of processing information for some time and print products have for many years now involved digital production methods. Some sectors of publishing have advanced more quickly down this route than others and it was those sectors that developed genuinely digital products first, as we will see in Part II, particularly Chapters 6 and 7.

Developments towards digital publishing

What exists today has developed from various strands. These include:

- typesetting
- word processing
- desk top publishing (DTP)
- development of databases

Typesetting

Typesetting systems developed during the 1970s as publishers sought to streamline the time-consuming process of setting type. Manuscripts, previously marked up by hand and then typed into an electronic format, had code embedded in them at this stage to ease the creation of layout. These systems tended in the first place to be large commercial systems with special keyboards that allowed typesetters to label aspects of the layout such as headings, font styles and paragraphs. A variety of different codes developed (such as TeX and Troff) as different companies adopted different systems. Each had strengths and weaknesses for the user depending on the different operating systems and different levels of user-friendliness. The system was not electronic from end to end; to see what pages set this way would look like, typesetters had to output to paper.

Generic typesetting code began to be developed and screens were able to show what the text would look like once set, without the need for generating paper versions. This saw the development of 'what you see is what you get' (WYSIWYG). Large publishers developed their own systems (e.g. Oxford University Press and Wiley).

Mathematical and scientific texts were especially critical in these early stages of development as it was this content that required complicated page layout; streamlining this complexity therefore would have clear benefits.

Word processing

In parallel to these developments advances in word processing were growing rapidly during the 1980s, and ways of creating or generating text within a digital environment therefore were growing alongside the manipulation of the text by the typesetting systems. Early word processors were being developed by a variety of companies, using different hardware and software, so offices often had dedicated word processing machines to replace their typewriters, possibly with linked printers (usually of poor quality). Typesetting from these was tricky as the variety of systems meant it was difficult for a typesetting program to cope with them, and printouts were low quality, so while work could be authored in a digital format, the text was still often rekeyed at the typesetters' end.

Proprietary hardware for the consumer market broadly disappeared and the range of consumer computers reduced in number essentially to a choice between Mac and PC. Operating systems suited to personal computers began to settle around a few main companies too. As personal computing grew, so word processing packages were developed as part of a suite of software for PC and Mac hardware. Mac developed more advanced systems for showing a user what their work might look like on the screen (and today the Mac is the designer's choice for its more sophisticated software in this area); as you could see what you were doing on screen, it was easier to make corrections on screen too. PC, however, gained popularity as a desktop option for business and individuals.

Desktop publishing systems

There followed developments in desktop publishing systems, which could manage a variety of layout issues and allowed for the creation of templates that made publishing easier to manage on screen. Publishing became easier to do in-house without using external contractors for the page make-up. This was helped by rapid improvements in the printers available at a consumer prices that could generate high resolution prints. As with the original word-processing packages, a wider range of new DTP systems developed, of which only a few survived, leading the market finally to coalesce broadly around QuarkXpress and InDesign. One other key development towards digitised production processes was the growth of postscript files – the system by which a file can speak to a printer. This allowed content to be output to postscript files ready for printing.

Database

Database developments formed a further strand in the growth of digital technologies for publishing. Databases had existed for a long time as a way of storing information. The issue was getting information out of a database in order to send it to production, and in doing so embedding the relevant typesetting codes in order to format it as necessary. The aim was to produce material that did not need rekeying from the database – as entries were always the same, content was more likely to retain its integrity if it did not have to be manipulated more than necessary; it only had to be input once and extracted as needed in whatever format was required. *Lloyd's List* was an early example of the use of a database for publishing.

Technological developments towards digital printing

With technology enabling the faster and more efficient production of material various developments in the publishing process became possible. These developments also were able to change the business model around some aspects of printing. We will see later (p. 10) that the ability to hold information in one format but produce it in many formats was being developed, but even if the output was just to be print (rather than any sort of digital product) it was increasingly possible to print much more precisely in terms of both quantities and timing.

This coincided with the development of the digital printer. This has brought several benefits:

- cost
- small print runs
- timing – just in time and print on demand
- lower stock holding
- lower shipping costs
- local printing options

While the offset or letterpress printers are cheaper per unit cost for high print numbers, the time it takes to get them set up for small print runs is not commercially viable. The digital printer has developed so that, while it produces copies of lower quality (though this is improving all the time), it can be cheap where print runs are small. So as print book markets declined and print numbers reduced (for instance the academic monograph market), first 'just in time' printing and later 'print on demand' were opportunities available to publishers with the digitisation of the process.

Publishers can reduce the risk of holding large quantities of stock if they know that the material is in a digital format from which it is relatively easy and quick to print copies. Some companies have been set up predominantly for use by publishers (such as Lightning Source) but print on demand technology has helped fuel the self-publishing industry as well. Authors can now afford to pay for their own print runs, and there is no need for them to incur the cost of holding stock as they can reduce their risk by printing low numbers of books; entrepreneurial websites have developed to help those wanting to publish their own books themselves and these are using digital printing options.

An additional attraction of digital printing is that the set-up time for digital presses is extremely quick; where publication of a book needs to be timely there is the opportunity to manage the print stage quickly, for example for reprints. Offset printing for colour work can be expensive and so is often carried out in print works in the Middle East or Asia, but shipping times mean long lead times need to be built in. With the development of digital presses some of the printing that previously was taken over to China and Hong Kong is coming back into Europe. Being able to print shorter runs also makes it more possible to print locally for local markets and some companies are avoiding bulk shipping costs in this way.

Changing production processes and workflow

Many companies have been reviewing their workflow in light of the changes in production methods with the growing levels of digitisation within the process. Companies will design their production systems in terms of workflow, analysing different processes a product goes through from raw manuscript to final product. In pre-digital terms this was reasonably straightforward as a manuscript passed through various stages of copyediting and proofreading, through typesetting and to printing. It was broadly a linear, single-layered workflow which led to a final product, delivered in one format. Figure 1.1 illustrates a very simple workflow. Each stage would involve various checks, responsibilities and supplier relationships. As the digital environment has developed, various stages have become more complex. Figure 1.2 outlines the way various activities take place concurrently and are collected ready to output in various formats.

Workflow has expanded to accommodate two main issues:

- the ability to adapt the output from just one input – so that from one 'manuscript' many formats can be produced
- the need to streamline effectively various parts of the process, which can lead to cost savings, where certain activities are less necessary, or time saving, where content can be managed quickly through the workflow with as little intervention as necessary

One input many outputs

In the first instance, the aim is to prepare the content in such a way that the format is neutral in order for it to be readily used for a number of purposes. There are many format options, the common ones being:

- a print paperback (these can vary in size and binding)
- a print hardback (these too can be in different formats)
- ebook files of various sorts for different devices
- a PDF, which is often necessary for search inside mechanisms such as Amazon and Google
- ebook files that can then be manipulated further to form an enhanced ebook or app
- a file format that can be taken by aggregators to fit into their complex proprietary library databases

It also needs to be in a format which can be repurposed in the future in different ways (for instance in an anthology or in email bulletins or summaries of abstracts etc.). So the content is managed through the editorial and production processes to have structure added that allows different programmes to understand and output it in different ways. We will look more closely at structure later. The workflow is designed to ensure all the stages necessary to get the material into the right structure, whether text or artwork, happen, and do so, where they can, concurrently.

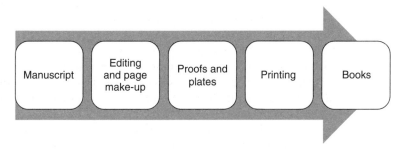

Figure 1.1 Simplified linear workflow.

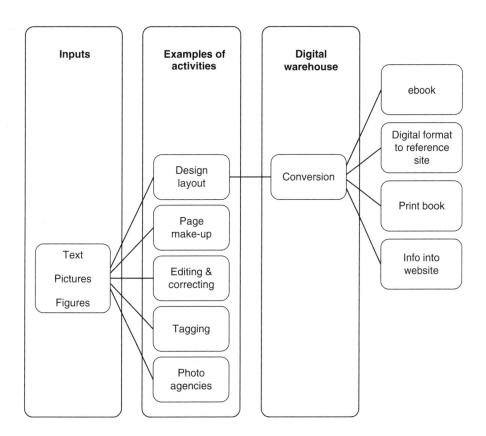

Figure 1.2 An example of a changing workflow to accommodate many outputs.

Savings in cost and time

Where savings in cost and time are benefits, this has led to a variety of changes. The developments in digital typesetting and digital printing continue to progress at a fast pace. In the arena of typesetting there has been a large amount of automation, allowing publishers to make less use of external suppliers. Typesetters, therefore, have to work hard to reinvent themselves in a new highly technological environment. More and more of the typesetting processes are becoming automated, using coding on documents, taxonomies for types of content and materials, and standardised style sheets so that very early on in the process the product can be edited to a high quality and then later laid out automatically into templates, with much of the hands-on typesetting role reduced. Typesetters have had to adapt to bespoke systems designed by their publishers and become more specialised where the straightforward work has been taken in house. There is still a need for specialist companies to output from the digital format, to ensure high quality and overcome technical challenges; these companies need to work very closely with their clients to become embedded in the workflow. In addition, while typesetters in the past traditionally stored the film used for the printed books (charging for storage), these costs can be cut out altogether with the digital formats as content can be held by publishers in their own systems.

With printing similar changes in workflow are happening. There will be a demand for print for some time to come and printing is therefore a key part of the workflow, but as digital presses increase in quality, the ability to print smaller quantities as some readers migrate to digital environments is very attractive. While offset litho, as mentioned above, remains the cheapest option for high-quality, high-quantity runs, digital has the advantage of being able to manage small numbers quickly. The quality up to now has let it down somewhat, so print on demand products have tended to be for academic titles that can be run off cheaply as and when needed and in small quantities (even as small as one copy).

However, as the quality changes and as print runs come down (due to ebook purchase and other market influences such as cuts in schools budgets) digital printing is becoming more attractive for short-run printing, maybe as low as 500. Stock holding can be kept to a minimum, saving money, and reprints can be quickly organised. It is possible that the warehouses of the future, as they hold less stock, will build in the ability to print on demand or print short runs digitally.

Data warehouses and data asset management systems

Once information can be created in a digital format the digital environment where the content is stored and retrieved becomes critical. We will revisit this in Chapter 4, and again in the education chapter (Chapter 8), but essentially a data warehouse is the storage space or archive for digital content. From here titles can be easily retrieved for reprinting or sections can be extracted and repurposed. One of the debates for some publishers is what should go into the warehouse; when some of the older titles that do not exist in digital format (or indeed any format other than the book itself) need to be digitised it can be a costly business, even if it is just a one-off activity. Yet extensive digitising of the print archive may be important for some publishers to ensure the completeness of the data warehouse.

The digital warehouse can simply store the book in the structure necessary to reproduce it in any format and/or style required. But this can go further where a digital asset management system enables the elements of the content assets to be used more effectively and continuously. So, for instance, artwork of all sorts, from illustrations and cartoons to maps and charts, as well as photos and diagrams, can be stored and easily accessed to be used again. This, of course, saves money and maximises the use of materials already paid for and owned by the publisher. Additionally, textual materials, specific collections of copyright-free photos that have been bought in and commissioned video footage, for instance, can be stored to be accessed again for enhanced ebooks or resource-rich websites. This can be an important resource for producers of heavily illustrated books that may also involve a large amount of commissioned artwork or photos that the company owns. These can be used again or even become an income stream with the development of a commercial picture library (such as the one by DK, for example).

A considerable amount of investment is required that only the larger publishing houses can afford. But with these data warehouses in place it is hoped that the benefits strengthen their position as publishers as they are able to manage the material/content they commission and own as effectively as possible; they can develop an important resource from their archive, building up their content assets in order to compete effectively with global internet companies and 'publishers' such as Google and Amazon. Cost savings and efficiencies, as well as content, are therefore stored for the future.

Conclusion: changing publishing structures

Workflows are being redesigned to encompass these changing activities. More work can be managed concurrently and stored appropriately in sections, ready to be consolidated at the final stage and output as required. As this is done the roles of suppliers and activities in house change and are re-evaluated. The skills and roles for managing the different aspects of the process are evolving and different companies are adopting a variety of structures to accommodate the growing digital parts of the production work.

One area of development is the increase in outsourcing for particular activities within the workflow. Typesetting and printing have traditionally been outsourced, but as more specific roles are developed along the workflow, so more activities have been outsourced, from coding material to data warehousing. A large specialist publisher will typically have offices in countries like India and China, not just for carrying out sales and product development work for their local region, but also for work like programming and tagging for the company as a whole. Publishers are re-evaluating working methods and publishing structures around these new workflows and we will look more closely at these in later chapters.

2 Structure for data

Introduction

Organising data, the raw text that goes into a digital system, effectively and efficiently is important for all aspects of publishing. It provides the digital building blocks from which both print and digital products can be produced. Imposing a structure on data allows it to be used flexibly depending on what you want to do with it. This structure needs to be used consistently and be read by different machines for different purposes, so various systems and protocols have developed to ensure this takes place. This chapter will not cover all the various systems and languages that have developed but provides a brief overview of those that are most central to publishing activity.

Tagging, mark-up and the growth of XML

We have looked at the development of digital production methods. In order for these to take place more fundamental developments in digital technology were necessary. The pre-press editorial activity where copyeditors marked up text was one of the areas that started to be undertaken on screen. Developments in working with and managing data on screen were therefore necessary.

For documents to be formatted they need to be coded or tagged (mark-up). These codes are picked up by the formatting program so they can be put into the correct format for the different sorts of outputs, whether for print or digital products. This marking up needed to be formalised to make it easier for everyone to work to the same procedure and so tagging schemes developed that would allow for systematic mark-up for text. Various systems developed and they began to merge as it became clearer a more standardised language was required. This led to the development of SGML (standard generalised mark-up language) based on the GML (general mark-up language), a coding system developed at IBM. It is a 'meta' language. This means SGML is not strictly code itself but is a way of writing/finding coding systems.

SGML provides a structure for data: it is about describing what sorts of data there are (e.g. what is a name, what is an address, or what is a heading, what is a paragraph of text). It is not about the appearance of data (i.e. about the way a book page looks). The term structured data refers to these codes embedded in the data that define structure and relationships. The more structure there is, the more the content is enriched as more detail can be extracted.

SGML became an ISO standard and was the predecessor to XML (extensible mark-up language). XML developed in the late 1990s and was similar to SGML but more flexible by being more precise to use, yet also less complicated for users, and it could work as a transfer language to the web. XML applies certain codes to describe what the content is (a heading, for instance) and then, when you want to output that data, a program shows what the format is to be for the section of content that has that particular code.

So with XML you can create a structured document: in other words, a document that has embedded coding that both describes its structures and defines the relationships between different parts of the data (e.g. a name that might link to an address). Structured files can be created in various ways. The two main ones are:

- XML files created as part of the workflow, which can be used for simple text layout
- files created in a package such as InDesign or Quark first and then converted to XML – which is necessary for more complex layouts

The aim is to get to a tagged document that carries information only about structure and not about the output, format or presentation. That way the data is ready in a neutral state, as it were, and can be used and output in all sorts of ways and formats, just as the publisher wants, now and into the future. So what this means for publishing is that the source is the one database, or data warehouse, but the output can be in many formats and products, from print books to websites.

Imposing a format

To impose format the XML file is used with a style sheet, and using the appropriate XML style sheet language (XSL) it can be converted into whatever format is wanted. The program you choose depends on what sort of output you want; this could be, for instance, a web page using HTML5 or an EPUB file for ebook or a typesetting program for a printed paperback. In that way XML can be regarded as the basic input, while the various programs used to format that content are as varied as the outputs required for that content. Data can be extracted and repurposed, archived until needed or transformed into different, new formats as they develop, which may enable further accessibility.

Where XML is particularly important for publishing is in its ability to enable the quick and easy search and selection of material, not just for finding and reusing material in different ways from the publisher's point of view, but for the usability and user-friendliness of the end product. If you, as a researcher, are searching for articles across a database of journals, for instance, the XML provides the structure for you to reach the information you want quickly and, most importantly, accurately.

In order to define the structure of a document that you will code using XML, you use a document type definition, or DTD. Depending on the sort of documents you use and the way you want to use them, the DTD specifies certain types of data fields, or elements, of the document or series of documents. Schemas, which are also ways to define structure, are often more detailed.

XML is not limited to publishing uses. Publishers use it in a reasonably narrow way simply to output – but it is the structure that is behind, for instance, e-commerce systems. For something more complex, such as an e-commerce system, a schema might be used instead, which allows a lot more information to be defined and validated.

One of the advantages of XML is that it is easy to use on an ordinary keyboard and it is text based so easily accessible by any system in the future (unlike databases with proprietary or highly customised systems). XML is particularly useful in that it is reasonably simple to use. What you *see* when you view content with the XML codes is what you have *got* and it can be edited reasonably easily. You do not need lots of additional programs in order to read it so it should be future proof as far as possible.

So XML is at the root of all digital production today and it continues to be developed. One example of the sort of current improvements is around systems that can auto-check. So, for instance, if a code indicates the start of typing for a heading, the system knows the code it needs to put in place to close the heading once it is complete.

Metadata: data about data

The fact that data is held in a digital format means that digital products can be developed more easily, particularly when using the web environment. When dealing with databases and places where digital documents may be held it is also important to understand the basics of metadata. Metadata is essentially data or information about things or other data. The technical definition is more complex but at a basic level it can be seen as 'data about data', rather like a label about something about the thing, rather than the thing itself; in other words, metadata might describe or define parts of a document that are not actually part of the data itself. So, for example, directories might be regarded as forms of metadata. If you have a business directory it might arrange data in certain ways, by type of business or location; this information would form part of the metadata. Similarly, in library catalogues the book title is the actual data but the location of the title on the shelves is held within the metadata. XML, as explained above, provides a good way to apply these labels about the data and embed them within the document itself. Information systems that can read XML can then translate that information. This is becoming more important when trying to locate information on the web and help computers process information more effectively.

In publishing the ISBN is a form of metadata. In itself an ISBN is not that useful to a user but it is a piece of data that has other information attached to it, such as the title of a book, which can be useful. The ISBN is a document object identifier (DOI); it is a character string that does not change; the location of the document and other metadata about it may change but a DOI will stay the same, just as the ISBN will refer to one particular edition of a title only (even if in different databases the position of that title may change).

So metadata makes information easier to find and more manageable. When creating databases this means that a user can extract relevant data more accurately. The difference between using metadata and a simple search engine is that the latter focuses on the use of keywords, while more precision can be developed using metadata; so, for instance, rules can be used to connect pieces of information and draw links which may allow the user to pinpoint more accurately the information they require. In the case of publishing this is clearly seen in a large library journals database which can enable a researcher to search across a variety of terms from publication year to type of article. It can also be seen in the information you might get about a book on an internet retail

Case study: The importance of metadata for discoverability

In the context of ISBNs, the importance of metadata for publishing can be seen particularly well as metadata is important for discoverability; the more detailed the metadata is about a book, the easier it can be to bring it to a customer's attention as they carry out a casual search. As a good illustration of this, Nielsen, which manages Bookscan in the UK, produced a white paper emphasising the importance of metadata to publishers, with a detailed analysis of the correlation between the level of metadata provided for a book and its sales pattern. This simple correlation obviously does need to be considered in light of wider issues such as market changes, different genres of title, etc., but the overall analysis showed that the more detailed the metadata, the more chance the customer has of finding what they want, and therefore buying it.

The ISBN, as we have seen, is a form of metadata with several other pieces of data related to it: these can cover not just the book's title but the category of book, cover image, product form, etc. This can be used in an online search for a book by a consumer but also for systems used by booksellers when selling through bookshops (offline, as Nielsen terms it). One level of data is regarded as essential to meet a basic BIC (book industry communications) standard to ensure an efficient supply chain, and these elements include a cover picture. There is also an enhanced level of metadata elements (promoted by BIC), which includes short and long descriptions and table of contents of the book. By comparing titles that had smaller amounts of metadata (e.g. no shot of the cover) with those with complete records (e.g. with full content information), the statistics showed that in practically all cases a richer data record would see a direct response in increased sales. This would make sense for discoverability, which is an issue in online retailing, and it is useful to note that good, well-prepared metadata is the basis of this. The full report is worth reading for details, including statistics that point to the fact that a cover image for a fiction title is important for sales or that short descriptions are more important for children's books than long ones.

site, as the ISBN will have other information attached to it about the book, from price to content.

Taxonomies and schemas: organising metadata

Metadata is important in terms of the way data is stored but this does not necessarily mean specific data can be found; the metadata needs to be organised in a way that can be accessed again. More and more individual users are becoming aware of the need to codify and structure information in order to be able to find it again in a digital environment. An example of simple tagging is on photo storing websites, where users can randomly tag pictures with whatever keywords they think are useful when searching. Another example is of a user in Twitter who may add a hashtag with anything they like, to see if a current thread can draw together variety of views and comments; they can then follow themes as they emerge and subside again. However, these 'folksonomies' are not organised in any particular way. This means:

- definitions of words can vary
- use of terms can change
- tags are not necessarily consistently used, particularly between sites

One only needs to look at some of the Twitter hashtags to see very different things linked randomly together, so diluting the use of that tag. But there are much more structured approaches, with taxonomies or automated indexing systems aiding definition and use of specific terms; these need to be used consistently to organise the finding of information effectively.

For metadata to be effective you need to decide which structural approach to take. The definitions of terms such as taxonomies and thesauri are not necessarily scientific and fixed but there are some loose distinctions. For publishing they can be important in that many large projects such as reference works need to be carefully set up to ensure the metadata is sophisticated enough for the data itself to be used in all sorts of different ways by different types of user. Publishers that work in the area of large reference databases will often have groups of people specialising in developing and updating taxonomies. Commonly used terms are:

1   **Taxonomy**: loosely can be seen as a structured list that is formed into a hierarchy; broader terms can exist at the top of the tree, while the list continues to drill down in more detail. Working out a taxonomy for, as an example, a sophisticated database of legal information can be a very involved job. Getting the definitions right for chunks of data, using terms accurately and consistently, ensuring there are no clashes or repeats of terminology are challenging tasks and the logic of the hierarchy must be clear. However, there are also links between different parts of the taxonomy which need to be clear and terms can appear in different places in certain cases. Web designers also used to use taxonomies as the term for the mapped structure of the website.
2   **Thesaurus**: is essentially more sophisticated again, with more interrelated terms and more examples of words, phrases and similar terms that may help a user locate the particular concept or term they are looking for. So it is structured like a taxonomy but has lateral connections and an index underlying it which may show you other things like terms to use, terms not to use, related terms, narrower and broader categories; in this way it covers scope and relationships between terms, so helps you find things and makes links for you, while taxonomy is focused on the classification.
3   **Ontology**: is more sophisticated again and important in allowing computers to interact with each other, helping programs crawl around the web in order to find things. Information needs to be marked up in a way that allows it to be found and ontology finds related things (like a thesaurus), but with more defined terms for a concept, item or relationship.

RDF: dealing with different types of data

One development in the last few years has been the widening range of types of media created and held in databases. Early developments in the web were based around the creation of documents, held in silos, which could be interrogated in order to find what was needed; the basic piece of data was still the document, such as an article or other piece of text. However, data is held in other formats and these are growing in quantity as more individuals are able to create them for themselves – video footage, for instance, or visual material, maybe audio files. All these too need a way to be organised and recognised in order for searches to include them effectively and to ensure searches are as rich and deep as they can be. These different types and sources of data need to be linked effectively so that, for instance, a piece of video information about a famous tourist site could be linked to a GPS system to locate it – hence the development of linked data.

The problem to be faced is the wide range of incompatible standards for metadata syntax. With different data sets using different systems, the linking between them becomes much less productive and enriched compared to a system that aims to produce consistency between all sorts of data types. RDF is a language for representing information about resources on the web. It provides interoperability between applications; they should be able to exchange information much more effectively. This is not just relevant for finding information or publishing it; it is useful across internet activities from e-commerce to collaboration services (like SharePoint). It provides a standard for exchanging metadata and schemas so that integration can happen much more quickly. It looks at the semantics of metadata, not just the structure and syntax, allowing it to make more powerful connections between things.

Everything expressed in RDF (which is an application of XML) means something; any resource can be described: it could be a fact in a document or it could be a piece of visual material, and it has, as it were, an address that makes it readable by a machine. A framework for describing resources allows relationships to be understood, which, in turn, means that other items can be inferred or integrated.

Essentially RDF is made up of three parts describing relationships:

- the resource itself – usually stated as a uniform resource identifier (URI) – which is the thing, such as an article
- the properties (or attributes) of it, i.e. an author or a title, which all articles have
- the property values – i.e. the specific data of those attributes – like the author's name and the actual title of the article

The idea is based around statements about resources in the form of 'subject–predicate–object expressions'. So, as an example:

1 The resource (or subject) is grass
2 The property (or predicate) is the colour
3 The value (or object) is green

Where you might have a sentence such as 'The sky is the colour blue', RDF should be able to make some sense of it.

Recognising resources in this way helps link documents in a way that forms the basis of the semantic web (which we will look at in Chapter 3). With these three elements you can start to link different things. For instance, you can link all the different values to the one thing, or you can link all the same properties together and bring up all the related things. By using a controlled vocabulary or list of terms with assigned meanings, everyone is working to the same definitions, which makes things easier to find. As outlined above, these controlled vocabularies include things like taxonomies.

So RDF provides the basis for creating vocabularies (such as web ontology languages, OWL) that can be used to describe things in the world and how they relate to each other.

Topic maps

While RDF is limited to the model that describes one relationship between two things, topic maps can provide a more sophisticated level of interconnection as they are not limited to mapping one relationship at a time. Topic maps are also a way of organising sets of data and the relationships between them, together with any other information about the data. A topic map represents information rather in the way a concept or mind map does, but it does it in a standardised way to make the information findable. It is a form of semantic web technology. This, like RDF, essentially classifies information using a basic three-part model:

- topics (the things – from documents to concepts)
- associations (describing the relationship between topics and the roles each topic plays in the relationship)
- occurrences (which connect a topic to information related to that topic)

Some have referred to them as the GPS of the information universe, in that they facilitate knowledge management by describing knowledge structures and associating information resources with them.

Other key developments and frameworks for structured data

There are other types of systems which may be used where RDF can be limited. So you may hear about systems like INDECS and ONIX which are used for certain types of data such as rights information. ONIX is the international standard for representing and communicating book industry product information in electronic form. Rich product information can be provided to any part of the supply chain. However, as it also provides the template for the content and structure of a product record, it is useful for forming the basis of many internal information management systems for publishers. The same core data can be used, for instance, by marketing or for a customer-facing helpdesk or by production. This standard therefore already provides a good data source for additional data uses. And as there is less manual intervention at each particular point (instead of, for instance, updating a price across lots of records and different databases across the company) the information is more likely to be consistent and accurate across the company and its suppliers.

INDECS is a system for enabling semantic interoperability so that one computer can understand the way another computer might use terms in relation to pieces of intellectual property. It is important for building e-commerce systems around content of this sort, so deals that are carried out around the sale and use of intellectual property can be matched between computers. ACAP is a global protocol that describes copyright and conditions which has been set up by the publishing community to provide a standard framework that can be used across the industry to manage copyright and permissions. It is an important community for establishing that copyright ownership cannot be forgotten within an internet environment.

The importance of frameworks like these is that they focus on interoperability from machine to machine in such a way that the sort of business model a publisher uses, the type of business they carry out or the varied legal protocols within which business is conducted can all be accommodated.

Managing rights and digital rights management

Managing rights is a particularly knotty problem in the electronic environment. DOIs (a form of metadata, as mentioned above) are critical to ownership of content. Owners can describe the intellectual property they own and link rights and controls to it. Digital rights management, or DRM, describes the access controls that can be built into or around the use of an electronic product. This term is used somewhat loosely and can mean anything from encryption (e.g. in the days of CD-ROM, when you might need a user key to gain access) to the system managing rights across a variety of data in terms of controlling access, tracking usage and collecting revenues. The technology can be cumbersome and can annoy customers. Nor does it necessarily offer much protection for the owner as DRM can be reasonably easily broken by someone determined to do so. However, in the wider context it can allow for control of where and how content can be used, and we will explore it in more detail in Chapter 10.

Conclusion: continuing advances

The advances in frameworks like these meant that publishers could develop digital businesses and in some areas were able to move quickly. For instance, in the journals area the use of DOIs to identify a document or article has particular relevance in allowing publishers to make content, particularly chunks of intellectual property, findable. Industry-wide initiatives such as CrossRef are additionally important for providing the links from the references in a journal article to the cited article. As we will see in Chapter 7, the journals industry has been one of the fastest to migrate into the digital environment and initiatives like these have helped that process, something which has been much more cumbersome to manage with regard to books.

One final development that is currently of interest in relation to structured documents is that of natural language processing (NLP). NLP is interested in the interactions between computer language and humans (and their natural language) and ways for computers to make sense of human language. For these purposes it provides an important way to code up data automatically. Archives may not always be tagged – in order to tag them you can use natural language processing, which uses various approaches from artificial intelligence to cross-referencing with other databases, as well as algorithms and pattern recognition, in order to understand documents and code them appropriately. As the system works it can be trained and learns more, so it builds up a vocabulary and becomes more accurate as it goes. Developments like these become very important when working within web-based environments which we will consider in Chapter 3.

3   Working with the web

Introduction

Structure of documents is important for any sort of digital output but there needed to be a catalyst for the rapid growth in digital products. There had been database products available for some time but CD-ROMs formed the first big wave of digital products in the early 1990s. However, it was the growth of the web that became the main driver for rapid development in digital products from publishers.

The web and HTML

The internet itself developed as early as the 1960s as part of a US government initiative and grew by the 1980s, creating a network of computer networks. However, the way internet sites talk to each other and link together most commonly takes place via the World Wide Web, which developed in the early 1990s. The web exists because of the development of hypertext mark-up language (HTML), which is the formatting language of the web; it allows documents to be linked via web pages and, from that, information can be accessed across the web by anyone with a web browser.

Essentially HTML allows information to be understood in a web browser. It is how something appears on the web, not what it is or how it is structured (XML is key to that) but how it looks. If you have an article in your data warehouse, HTML coding will mean that the article can be pulled into the web environment and displayed in the appropriate way within the website (e.g. with headings as headings, sections of text as sections of text, etc.). It is a text-based coding system and it does not cover pictures; however, you can call a picture in to display using HTML. It is important to realise it is not a style package; you use style sheets to define your own style on the top (though it has a default style), but it describes the appearance so that the computer knows how to format the information for it to appear on the web.

In order to define the style you want, a cascading style sheet (CSS) is necessary. This is the style sheet used to describe the presentation of material held in a mark-up language like HTML. It is most commonly used for websites and this holds the information about font, layout and colours (for instance) for the web page design that is to be applied to the marked-up content to create the desired website appearance. A CSS can be adapted for different sorts of rendering (e.g. on different size screens, or into print). A marked-up document can have a CSS linked to it, but a user may have a CSS on their machine that will override it, which can cause problems sometimes and can need checking where publishers need to be sure the content is accurately presented.

Once the internet developed in this way, publishing companies could deliver products direct to customers, whether linking to a database of journals with a front end or opening up specially designed web pages for content. This made a significant change to the publishing value chain as physical products (even electronic ones such as CD-ROMs) did not need to be produced and distribution mechanisms changed as the product could be delivered to a computer over the internet. We will see how these products changed and developed in the subsequent chapters, but here we will look at the current web technologies relevant to the development of these products.

HTML5

HTML5 is the latest incarnation of HTML. HTML has been revised to cope with more complex websites and more easily encompass multimedia, which forms much more of the experience on the web now. It is not yet finalised but is usable.

The key benefits are:

- it can cope more effectively with the wide variety of multimedia
- the audio visual elements can be easily integrated, as can drawings, which can be created in the new canvas-defined areas
- it can be read across by a variety of computers and devices
- it can incorporate other applications more easily too, like clocks or currency converters or geo-location, etc.

The importance of this development for publishers is that it is should be much easier to insert video or audio material without relying on other pieces of software (plug-ins) to be bought into the website in order to play or make use of that video and audio material. A key case in point is that Flash, a common piece of software that can be used to play video, is not supported by Apple, so users on iPads (as an example) are not able to see certain parts of a website which might display a video using Flash. HTML5 should overcome this problem. There is flexibility to do more with a website more easily, something to bear in mind when developing a new product.

Other aspects of HTML5 that are benefits over the older systems are:

- it is better at handling errors
- greater attention is paid to the fact it must be independent of any specific device, given that it is in the area of devices that so much development has taken place over the past few years
- it is also better for offline storage
- it has a lot more flexibility to create form controls such as systems for automated form filling
- it can cope with more new content elements (such as footers, headers, etc.) that allow for more subtle structuring of pages

All of this makes the development of web pages much more flexible: for some products it may be that the development of an app is less necessary if the web pages can be made to be as powerful. And, crucially, it aims to preserve the level of user-friendliness of HTML so it can be used by anyone.

Web 2.0 and social networking

HTML5 is the language used to create the web pages. However, there have been more fundamental developments in the World Wide Web. Web 2.0 saw the development of user-centred design and interoperability, allowing individuals to interact much more directly, whether creating and distributing their own material or creating or participating in social media environments; it has changed the way we can communicate and collaborate, and has empowered us to make more use of the web with user-generated content (as opposed to passively consuming websites and the products held on them). In publishing the biggest opportunity here in the first instance has been to generate much more online marketing activity. Publishers have made use of sites such as Facebook, YouTube and Twitter to create conversations and develop relationships with certain customer groups, growing brand image as a whole as well as generating PR for particular titles. We shall explore the relevance of user-generated content within the new web in Chapter 13 when we explore self-publishing.

The semantic web

The newest stage of web development currently is the progression to the semantic web (sometimes called web 3.0). This next stage of the evolution of the web is aiming to increase the ability to connect different sorts of formats and data types by including more semantic information within data in order for machines to process information more effectively. The growing sophistication of metadata is important here. Some data is difficult for a machine to understand, contextual issues might need to be considered or different sorts of data might have been used to create a new single tool (like an app). A more sophisticated way of understanding this data is therefore necessary; the idea is to move on from the current position where data is held in silos of different data types; these need to be much more integrated, creating a web of linked data.

With the semantic web therefore it should become easier to find and link very different sorts of data sources because the relationship between them is described in such a way as to facilitate these links. Common formats help this integration of data types and taxonomies, and ontologies provide a basic structure. In many ways it should mean that keyword searches become less important as there will be much more sophisticated ways of searching across different sorts of data that are context sensitive, so users are more likely to reach the precise sort of information they require. Additional aspects of this include storing data in formats that will be future proof, and it should allow users of the data to integrate and reuse data more effectively rather than simply view it (something that may give rise to more copyright issues).

Linked data

Linked data allows the publishing and connecting of structured data on the web and is a central aspect of these developments. If the early web was based around documents, structured and fixed in databases, phrases such as the 'web of data' try to describe the way the semantic web links open data sets together. Structured data is essentially any data that is organised and searchable. Documents have, in general, been made available as masses of raw data, but even with XML and HTML mark-up much of its structure and semantics will have been lost. Where both documents and data are linked, the web of data enables new types of applications. You can browse data sources and then move along links in those to other data sources, rather than moving in and out of fixed data sets; in this way linked data sits on top of an unlimited global data space consisting of all sorts of data types, from blogs to scientific trial data, from music to video footage. An example of all this would be the ability to link something that was said by a professor in a video to marks (i.e. writing) made on a whiteboard and with a chapter in a textbook as well as a few diagrams and formulae from yet another source. Linked data will be particularly important going forward.

Conclusion: the more flexible web

What web development like this can mean for publishers is that they will have a more effective way of building products, with the added value of enriched content and much more sophisticated searches. But it can do more than that: it is a way to extend the power of a search. The results from a search do not simply have to be listed back to the customer with a percentage based around likelihood of relevance. They could, in the new semantic web, be presented to the user in a visual format, showing all the connections and so maybe making it easier to reach the key information wanted.

It should also allow publishers to design and reuse their content effectively so that, for instance, they can exploit the workflow of professionals wanting certain sorts of data presented to them in different ways, with differing levels of interactivity, depending on their particular use at that particular time in the day. This is possible now but the semantic web is potentially able to increase the opportunities here. Publishers can look at more ways to develop new products and build different businesses, creating tools out of existing data sets, for instance, or building new commercial models after data mining or integrating other forms of data (from video to raw statistics). The reuse of data of course will have key implications for the issues surrounding copyright, as we will see in Chapter 10, but for the moment it is important to recognise how fertile a development this can be for publishers.

4   Organising and storing content

Introduction

Publishers can source, edit and structure content but in order to deliver it to customers effectively the way it is organised needs to be considered, particularly when presenting content to the customer. Information architecture is used to plan the way content can be structured for the consumer, most often in a web-based environment. Similar principles apply to other forms of digital products. In order to deliver the content effectively, there are also issues publishers need to bear in mind around the content system itself where the information is stored.

Information architecture

If a publisher holds its data in a structured way and has an idea for a web-based product the first stage in developing that product is to consider the information architecture required. Information architecture is the discipline of creating the structure of a website (or other digital product); the term is applied in different ways but essentially it covers the way to describe and understand the dynamics of a website, database or content management system (CMS) in terms of the following:

- function
- structure
- labelling
- navigation
- interactivity
- user experience
- search
- access
- visual design

It is about getting the information held in the data to the user in the most effective way. When putting together a website it is important to outline the information architecture – in this sense it is a design document which forms the basis of what you want to do with your product.

For any digital product it is important that the publication or service must be easy to use, making it straightforward so that users will want to return. Even in print products there needs to be organisation of the information that makes it useable (e.g. in the layout or the typeface), but with digital products, which may take users into a range of different content types and services, the specifications regarding what the user needs to do have to be very carefully defined.

The process

So the process of designing information architecture has to take into account a variety of things. Typically a design document may include the following elements:

- product rationale
- user profile/user specification/use scenarios
- information audit/content audit
- product design and functional specification
- visual design requirements
- resource analysis

To start with, the project outline needs to be clear, with attention paid to the scope and business opportunities:

- What are the aims of the project?
- What product is being produced?
- Why is this product being produced?
- Who is the audience?
- Why would they want this service?
- What competition is there?
- If it is to make revenue, how will it do that?
- How much risk is involved?
- What is the budget?
- What is the timescale?
- How will its success be measured?

This is much the same as developing a rationale for a published product that might be presented to a publishing committee. Research should underpin all these aspects, with particular focus on the audience.

When designing the product it is important to have a close understanding of the potential user and in particular how they might use the product. The audience needs to be defined and user profiles can outline the sort of user the product will have. Use scenarios can be created to look in detail at the way they may navigate a product – what might they be looking for on a website, for instance, and how will they reach what they need?

The content also is analysed and the functional requirements explored, bearing in mind the potential user. An information audit at this stage allows a company to assess what information it has and the capabilities that exist within it. Requirements can be drawn up and assessed in terms of the resources that might be needed, from cost and time to the level of skills necessary to create the product on this basis.

This content stage needs to be quite thorough: content needs to be clearly mapped out, grouped into categories, the hierarchy laid out, the format of the data outlined, together with the taxonomies that might be used in the structure of the product.

Diagrams showing the way different web pages link to each other might be created, as well as analysis of the number of clicks a user might need to reach their goal. Other considerations include the visual look of the site, conventions for icons or labels, as well as the pathways from page to page which different users may take.

When the design has been clearly mapped out and the information architecture is in place, this is the stage when software designers, programmers and graphic designers will begin to get involved to follow the specifications and start to create mock-ups and designs. Here the product can finally take shape. Various checking stages, feedback loops and quality assurance procedures need to take place throughout. This same process can be used when developing an app, a game or a piece of software. The key is to establish an effective requirements document that can be used by the developers when creating the product. This process is by no means fast. Though the final programming can be done reasonably quickly, the stages leading up to it need to be carefully managed, and formal project management procedures are usually applied to ensure successful product development for anything from a database to be used internally to a saleable digital product.

Content management

We have looked at the way content can be processed through the workflow and held in a data warehouse. An important aspect of managing data is content management and the systems used to do this: a data warehouse in this context can be regarded as a content management system (CMS). Content management originally referred mainly to the management of content to appear on a website, but it tends now to have a much wider meaning as it encompasses anything from a simple website to a database full of assets. Content management systems are essentially ways to collect, edit and publish content, allowing for collaborative involvement with some workflow elements.

Publishing is a content industry and its expertise at managing content is developing all the time. Effective CMS ensures that the content is made available in the appropriate way to the appropriate users, is targeted or customised to suit the user, and can deal with structured and unstructured content, probably in large volumes. The CMS needs to be able to handle a full infrastructure, from the storage and archiving of content to the retrieval and delivery of content at the right time, and here content can be both documents and other types of media. It also has to take into account issues such as how often new content is supplied, how often existing content needs to be updated, what sort of output it is to become and what range and diversity of content there are.

Ultimately, a CMS is about realising the value of the content. One important aspect of it is the guarantee of the content: the quality and accuracy as well as legality of a piece of content need to be assured for it to have value. A publisher's content management system therefore needs to be flexible in various ways. For instance, it is important that content can be:

- used as new devices and applications are developed
- licensed out if necessary
- broken up into small chunks
- easily integrated into an application
- integrated into other internal systems

In the last case, for instance, a program used by the publishers to deal with production planning and publication dates becomes even more useful if it is linked with the marketing database so that changes in publication dates can be made seamlessly and fewer mistakes can slip in between systems.

Some considerations for CMS

Data warehouses and content repositories have been developed by publishers and integrated into their workflow for many years, particularly in the research, academic and professional sectors. By now some of these systems are extremely complicated – a legal database can often require constant updating, with old sections taken out and archived, to be replaced by new sections, regulations and statutory instruments. Control is key: content needs to be accurately put into the system and it is important that the CMS is robust to ensure safe storage. Content must not be likely to get corrupted and the CMS needs to be regularly backed up. Protocols about correcting information where there are errors need to be put in place.

But content also ultimately needs to be findable; granularity in the system and the effective use of metadata are important to ensure content can be found. However, the more detail there is embedded in the data, the more costly the processing of the content becomes, so it is important to consider issues around the value and the amount of return to be gained from the content.

Efficient document management which allows effective use and repurposing of content is becoming ever more critical as users begin to interact further with the content management systems: for instance, lawyers might use the information to generate bespoke forms for their own businesses or researchers may be comparing versions of material as it is being developed. Security therefore is important not only to protect the content from unauthorised uses but also to protect users and any data they may be inputting about themselves in order to use the system effectively for their own work. Data protection issues need to be considered as content management systems become more sophisticated.

Enterprise content management

Content management systems tend to refer primarily to the content which is to be sold or used in some way: a publisher might be selling this content, a teacher may be storing teaching resources in a system of this sort, but it is essentially the content that has the value. But content goes wider than the actual content processed by the publishers ready for sale. Information within publishing can be found in various places; for instance, the actual metadata itself, which is an increasing area of value that publishers are building up for themselves, and also information held within production management systems, information about the distribution and supply chain, market information and financial information. This is all knowledge held in various ways within an organisation, whether by staff or by software programs.

Enterprise content management encompasses all the above types of information, extending the CMS further, as it essentially covers the management of content through all its stages and processes and integrates other organisational information that might have a bearing on the content. So it will cover the content from capture, search and networking to digital archiving, to document management and workflow, to marketing and delivery.

Systems of this sort are increasing in sophistication. For instance, as the content is used, so more metadata about that use is added to the content; this further enriches the information about the content and stores information about its possible use for the future; it can also capture information from things like emails, linking them to the decision-making aspects of an enterprise. Digital asset management is a form of enterprise content management; so, for instance, if you have a photo in your asset management system, you can see how many times it has been used, how popular it is and what sort of use it is put to; you may then be able to make use of that value, by monetising it through rights sales.

Knowledge management and storage issues

All this can also encompass knowledge management. Any company developing new techniques and systems for its content needs to have some mechanism and strategies for identifying, managing and distributing its knowledge and experience; it is particularly beneficial to map this knowledge in developing and adopting new technologies. How knowledge is imparted to people also has a product development aspect: for instance, as publishers seek to develop the way they provide information to their customers they may adopt knowledge management strategies in the structuring and delivery of their information to their users.

Storage of content of this sort is moving, as well as allowing smaller companies more flexibly and cheaply to manage their content and to overcome some of the security issues in having content based on the client. Historically information was most often held on the client and communicated to the server for the service they needed; this is changing now, with information stored on an application server (at the server end) and also remotely in the cloud. Essentially the software that once would have been held and owned by the client/server network is now held in the cloud and supplied, as it were, like a service, with a licence to use the software for the time it is used. This allows for some flexibility when planning new products.

Conclusion: CMS development driving opportunities

Developments of this sort in the planning and organisation of information are continuing all the time, and publishers need to keep abreast of these sorts of developments as they plan their content management and explore ways to adapt and deliver it to customers. This is particularly relevant in the specialist areas where large databases already exist and which need constant development; however, it is becoming increasingly important for those operating in the consumer market to adopt content management systems as the products they are developing grow in complexity.

5   The context for ebook formats and e-readers

Introduction

We have looked at the frameworks in place for developing digital products, from workflow and structured documents to the web and information architecture. Developments here have been in progress for some decades. However, there is one section of the marketplace that has taken off more recently and that is in the area of consumer books. We will look much more closely at the specifics of that market in Chapter 9 but here we will focus on the technological developments behind the growth of ebooks and e-readers.

The development of ebook formats

The technology for books to be produced in digital form goes back a few decades but, in terms of the more general consumer, the early ebooks were essentially available from the late 1990s. Various ebook formats existed, including PDF, developed by Adobe, which had the advantage of preserving the page as it appeared in the printed form and protecting it (unless one had the software to change it). Open source software distributed with it allowed the digital book documents to be read by anyone with a computer. Other formats were developing and various companies developed different systems, making it difficult for publishers to choose one to work with. This also meant that different devices or reading software were required and so the market continued in a fragmented way.

In the late 1990s a consortium was formed to develop the open ebook format. This was so that publishers could provide a single source document that could be used by different software and devices. This used an XHTML, CSS, some multimedia and an XML schema to list the components of a given ebook (such as a table of contents, cover artwork). This open format then formed the basis of the conversion of various books into an ebook format that was open. Google, for instance, used this in its mass conversion of titles (see the case study in Chapter 10). These formats continued to evolve further, and while many different formats still exist today there are two main ones that have become dominant: EPUB and Mobi. As the ebook formats crystallised around these two main systems, so the conversion of titles, already in a digital workflow of some sort, were able to be extracted and converted into ebook formats for use on the early e-readers. They were ready so that once ebook readers became usable and affordable the market could start to buy ebooks in ever greater numbers.

EPUB and Mobi have different benefits and limitations. One challenge, for example, is around illustrations: black and white pictures can be produced but they cannot be placed very accurately within a text. The latest developments in these formats are focusing on making them more flexible. EPUB 3 has recently been launched, based on HTML5, aiming to overcome some of these issues. It provides a much wider range of options, improving navigation as well as the rendering of audio and video material; it is altogether more designer and publisher friendly. Devices can only use it, however, if they have EPUB 3 capability.

An additional issue within the market is the use of proprietary versions. Amazon used its own version, based on Mobipocket, AZW, which is the system its older Kindles use; this has Amazon's own DRM embedded in it. Amazon will usually take a publisher's Mobi file and convert it into its own AZW. There is now a new file format as Amazon's launch of tablets required different capabilities; Amazon has developed KF8 for its Kindle Fire, which supports HTML5 and CSS. This provides more styles, structure and functionality for Amazon's tablet readers. Apple uses a version of EPUB for its formats which is incompatible with open ebook formats. Its iBooks Author has a system based on EPUB which does not allow material created in it to be reused elsewhere. These formats are constantly being developed and various levels of DRM or functionality (for instance) applied to them.

As one might guess, all this causes problems for publishers. While they can produce various file formats suited to different devices and have developed workflows usually to cope with this, there are still problems around ensuring consistency when files are rendered across a variety of devices, and this involves costs in checking each version of the file works. Nevertheless, with ebook formats becoming easier to use and more flexible to adopt, it has been easier for publishers to develop ebook workflows.

The development of e-readers

The increasing number of titles automatically produced in e-format reached a critical mass that coincided with the dramatic uptake of e-readers in the general market. While ebooks were available in the early 2000s in PDF and early ebook formats, they were generally for use on computers or laptops; this was not really the way most readers used books, particularly in the consumer marketplace.

A book has certain aspects built into its physical incarnation:

- it is reasonably light to carry around wherever one is, so it is portable
- it can be read almost anywhere – from in a bath to on a train – so it is easy to use anywhere at any time
- it is reasonably cheap and in some cases cheap enough to be regarded as disposable (certain genres, for instance)
- it is also easy to read again, lend to others or give as an affordable, tangible gift
- it does not require battery power or charging up

In terms of product design, the page is easy to read, clear and flexible layouts are possible, with easy reproduction of highly visual material where needed. In contrast, computers are back lit, so reading on screen could potentially be tiring in comparison to reading the non-reflective printed pages of a book. So to make an inroad into the print market, some sort of digital reading product needed to match these benefits of a book, from cheap prices to portability.

Using a computer as a reading device did not in any way match these book USPs (unique selling points) and it was clear an alternative was needed. Towards the mid-2000s there were increasing developments in hardware to produce dedicated handheld devices that could be used specifically for reading books. These devices were developed with certain key features:

- they were portable
- they had battery power that lasted a reasonable length of time
- they could hold many thousands of books at once
- they used e-ink technologies that meant they did not need to be backlit, which reduced the emphasis on battery power and allowed, potentially, for an easier reading experience
- they often had additional features, like the ability to change font size

Interestingly the e-readers adopted the same size as a paperback, kept page layouts simple like a straightforward book, and of course the e-ink made the device read as much like paper as possible.

Sony launched the earliest e-reader using e-ink in 2004 and developed its Sony e-reader by 2006, which was sold exclusively by Borders at launch for the first six weeks. The Kindle then launched in 2007, produced by Amazon. It was this device that really started to move the market. Amazon already had direct contact with a huge book buying customer base through its well-established e-tail environment, which, significantly, other players like Sony did not have. A cheap price for the e-reader, combined with easy set-up and then access to a vast library of ebooks and extremely good customer service to ensure a seamless consumer experience, drove Kindle sales. The advertising campaigns for the early Kindles were based on price and the ability to download books immediately at any time (and from anywhere if you chose a 3G device).

The relationship between the price of the Kindle and the price of the ebooks has some strategic implications for the sales of the device. If a customer has had to invest in the device, should the books be very cheap? And if the publisher has made savings on printing and distribution, who should benefit from that saving? Selling the device cheaply can help to drive the sales of actual ebooks but, in the same way, cheap prices for ebooks could drive the sales of the devices – with the Kindle appearing to customers to open up access to a market of cheap books. We will look more closely at pricing in Chapter 12 but, in terms of the device, Amazon appears to have adopted both strategies (pricing the device cheaply and pricing the books cheaply) at different times to continue driving the growth of the Kindle; the move to agency pricing for ebooks has dampened down the race to the lowest prices for those books held by publishers.

Ultimately, the fact remains that the Kindle, from release, sold in tremendous quantities in the US and opened up the digital market. Amazon continues to roll out the Kindle programme to other countries, and in some countries, for instance the UK, the Kindle dominates the e-reader market. In the US the strength of the book chain Barnes and Noble has helped its e-reader, the Nook, take some market share from Amazon for e-readers and at various points it has been able to outsell Kindle. Others have entered the market, notably the Kobo, with a focus on flexibility alongside price: it does not include proprietary DRM so EPUB files can be transferred more easily and books can be bought from various online stores; devices like Kobo, unlike Kindle, can be useful too for those wanting to access library services providing ebook lending programmes. Nevertheless despite these entrants, the Kindle still has the largest market share in the US (around 60 per cent) though it is much less dominant than in the UK. With the growth of e-readers sales of ebooks have been able to grow year on year. We will look much more closely at the development of ebooks in the consumer chapter (Chapter 9).

Tablets and the new readership

E-readers may well be used by existing book readers, those already reading quite a few books a year: this is a market that is moving increasingly into a digital format for its books, whether alongside or as a substitute for print. However, there is another aspect to the growth of the digital market for books. The ebook market was additionally spurred on by the launch of the smart phone, first by Apple in 2007; smart phones provided the opportunity to develop apps for downloading books that could be read anywhere, so ensuring portability and ubiquity – two essentials for driving the market for ebooks.

However, the development of the smart phone potentially takes the market further. While those interested in reading widely might purchase a Kindle, there are sectors of the market which do not want to buy a specific single-purpose device such as an e-reader; however, if they have a smart phone anyway, they may well download a free e-reading app that will enable them to read books on their device. To drive sales of smart phones, the more they can do and the more applications they have, the more attractive they are; books are just one part of the offering, but a reasonably attractive one; and the more content that can be provided for a smart phone, the more attractive it is, and the more downloading can take place (ensuring a greater need for packages allowing internet access).

Apple did not set the ebook market alight with its smart phone but it did add to it, and made the argument for ebooks more compelling. We will explore Apple's response to the book market more closely later (see the case study in Chapter 8, as well as Chapter 9) and will also consider its impact on the textbook market; while the starting point for Apple has been less focused on market share in the books market compared to Amazon with the Kindle, it is gaining momentum as more attention is focused on iBookstore.

E-reading apps became even more compelling with the launch of the tablet. Apple's iPad was first launched in 2010, with others following and even Amazon launching the backlit tablet already mentioned, the Kindle Fire. While ebook readers can reproduce some designs in black and white they are not very useful for highly visual books. Smart phones did not have the screen size to be very useful for books with a complex layout. The full-colour high-resolution screens that tablets have are much more suited to illustrated books for all sorts of markets; in order to gain ground in this market, where higher prices may be charged for the products, the market is set to move on quite considerably as products become available. The tablet market too has grown extremely quickly; as with the smart phone, tablets' attraction for customers is their ability to do a variety of things; while books are not the main reason to purchase a tablet, the ability to download books and interact with them is a compelling additional feature of the iPad. They also put books firmly into the entertainment environment, something which has attractions for ensuring the longevity of books, in one form or another, alongside other forms of entertainment. So a distinction is being drawn between single-use devices such as Kindles and other devices that have a multitude of uses, of which reading is one.

Conclusion: the changing view of the book

While book reading is not the prime use of a tablet, and a book has to compete with all the other forms of entertainment that a tablet can support, nevertheless there is an attractiveness in well-produced, visually exciting, potentially interactive content that the tablet can render effectively. When considering a book-based app, the line between a book and other forms of entertainment such as games and video is becoming more blurred in the tablet environment, and there are at least some opportunities for publishers to develop newer markets here.

Conclusion to Part I

In Chapters 1–5 we have looked at the key technological developments that make the production of digital products possible. We have seen how publishers have had to reorganise themselves in order to accommodate new digital production methods and data storage, as well as the devices that are driving the consumer market forward and the new opportunities that may lie ahead. In Part II we will look at each of the main publishing sectors in order to see how they have developed digital products and what the key issues are for their future.

Further reading and resources

Books

There are many detailed technical books on each of these subjects for the specialist. There are also many very general technology books on topics like Web 2.0 and HTML5 which do not specifically look at the publishing industry but provide interesting context. Below are just a few useful references that do focus on publishing and are suitable for the non-technical but interested reader, together with some websites that it is very useful to follow.

Bullock, Adrian. *Book Production*. Routledge, 2012.
Dykes, Lucinda and Tittel, Ed. *XML for Dummies*. Wiley, 2005.
Kasdorf, William (ed.). *The Columbia Guide to Digital Publishing*. Columbia University Press, 2003.
Register, Renee and McIlroy, Thad. *The Metadata Handbook*, 2012; available at www.themetadatahandbook.com/2012.
Tittel, Ed and Noble, Jeff, *HTML, XHTML and CSS for Dummies*. Wiley, 2011.

Websites

jwikert.typepad.com – an interesting blog from a publisher thinking about the future of publishing
toc.oreilly.com
www.bic.org.uk – Book Industry Communication, the organisation for the UK book industry, which undertakes a variety of activities such as best practice, standards, classification systems and accreditation around the book industry supply chain, covering anything from digital production to e-commerce

www.bisg.org – Book Industry Study Group in the US, which oversees a variety of activities, including standards, best practice and policy

www.crossref.org – for information on CrossRef

www.editeur.org/8/ONIX – for information on ONIX

www.futurebook.net

www.idpf.org – the standards organisation behind EPUB

www.nielsenbookdata.co.uk – follow the link to the white paper by Nielsen on metadata mentioned in Chapter 2

www.w3.org – World Wide Web consortium for information on HTML5

www.woodheadpublishing.com/en/ChandosHome.aspx – Chandos Publishing has a range of books that explore developments in the web in relation to library and publishing practice

Questions to consider

Chapter 1

1 Thinking of Thompson's framework for developments in digital publishing, why did it take longer for digital products to be developed compared to other digital developments?
2 Print on demand is helping keep some products financially feasible, such as monograph publishing; however, if those markets continue to decline, what further developments might be needed to make these products sustainable?

Chapter 2

1 Why is XML so critical to the development of digital publishing?
2 How might you explain the importance of its metadata to a publishing house?

Chapter 3

1 What features of the growth of the web and Web 2.0 have had an impact on publishing?
2 Why is the semantic web an exciting development?

Chapter 4

1 What sort of information would you need to construct a detailed specification for a new digital product and how would you go about getting it?
2 What can a good CMS bring to a publishing company? What sort of benefits and problems might this mean for a small organisation?

Chapter 5

1 What has led to the 'tipping point' in sales of ebooks?
2 Some predict that the market for a single-use e-reading device will become saturated as it is mostly of interest to keen book buyers; what impact will that have for the growth of ebook sales?

Part II
Publishing sectors

6 Developments in digital professional reference publishing

In this chapter we will cover:

1 Reference and the benefits digital opportunities can bring
2 Early digital developments in professional reference
3 Issues around migration of customers into a digital environment
4 The changing relationship with customers and how this has influenced the growth of digital products
5 Ongoing product development
6 Pricing and sales models
7 Future developments

There are many sectors of professional reference publishing, from medical and technical material to legal and financial content. This chapter will focus on the development of legal professional reference publishing but the other areas can be seen to operate in similar ways.

Introduction

One of the first and prime uses of the internet is for finding information. The ability to search across an array of online material, tap into a variety of sources, follow links to further information and ultimately pinpoint exactly what is required has been one of the central features of the rise of the internet since its inception, with the additional benefit that much of it was and is available for free. The use of the internet for reference information therefore has challenged publishers of material which was costly and time consuming to collect, organise and distribute via print. Not only can users seek answers across large databases of information at the touch of a button but users are also involved, since the rise of Web 2.0, in the creation and maintenance of more and more reference material, such as on sites like Wikipedia.

General reference publishers have found it a struggle to maintain their expensive reference information even in database form, as information can readily be accessed for free; this free information may not be especially high quality but it is reasonable enough for the general user. Publishers of dictionaries and encyclopaedias, like *Britannica*, targeted at the general consumer have found it difficult to maintain anything like their previous market share. There are still markets for dictionaries and encyclopaedias, particularly those with strong brand names and a long heritage of providing high-quality information created and endorsed by experts. Nevertheless a significant part of their print market has migrated to use free online sources. These businesses have had to find models to help them survive; for example, they may decide to target more niche specialist markets or license information or simply manage around tighter margins. These consumer market titles will continue to face the challenge of offering something different from the free sources available via the internet.

However, in this chapter we are focusing on reference within the professional arena as an example of the way more specialised reference material has developed complex and now well-established digital business models. Prior to the growth of the internet, reference information was mostly available within published print sources: this might be freely distributed (such as government information) or, for something more specific, bought by individuals, libraries or companies. What characterises this sort of reference material is that it is used by specialists. This chapter will be focusing on the developments in legal information as an example of professional reference: in this area publishers are finding rapid migration to online information and in some notable cases have pared their print down to only a few high-profile titles while concentrating their efforts on developing online platforms. This sort of development can be seen in other areas of specialist professional reference material, in the provision of news services and in business to business publishing.

The move online is of particular importance as the logic around what reference material is means that the online environment provides a much more effective space for it; easy, fast searching through large silos of material, together with unlimited storage and ease of access are obvious benefits. In this sector more than some, therefore, print has been viewed as having a limited life cycle. Meanwhile the relationship between the publisher and user of content has become even more embedded and this relationship with the customer is driving the future opportunities within this sector.

The benefits of digital publishing for reference

It was clear very early on in the development of digital publishing that the digital environment offered many unique features that could improve the use and consistency in quality of the specialist material needed for markets such as the legal market.

The key aspects of digital products that are of major benefit to customers can be summarised as follows:

- searching across large quantities of information
- searching more deeply across information
- up to date/real time
- availability of additional material – grey paper, raw law
- automatically updated
- ability to access from desktop – not just in a library
- capability for several users to access the same material at the same time
- cross-referencing with hypertext links
- links to other resources
- shelf space reduction

This list of benefits is similarly compelling for other sectors such as the academic sector. However, there are some additional benefits too: it is important across most sectors that material is up to date, but in the professional reference arena the material itself can be in a constant state of updating. The digital environment makes this easy and it is a particularly attractive feature of the digital product for specialists.

Early developments in specialist reference

The reason professional reference publishing was one of the earliest sectors to move into a digital environment is due to several factors intrinsic to the nature of the material itself. Even before electronic publishing became so prevalent, large quantities of reference material were held in databases that had particular value for certain customer groups and from which various products could be produced. Electronic environments made immediate sense as a way to store information effectively, extract it in different combinations and add to it continuously. In some cases this information was captured and stored in some sort of digital format very early on, even though the output to the customer was only in print form.

These sectors developed expertise in managing data files of reference material and the legal publishing industry began consolidating around the core competence of managing large databases of legal information in the late 1980s and early 1990s. This was not yet focused on the user of the information so much as a way of collecting, managing and storing information in an early content management system.

There are several aspects that are central to the use of professional information that helped to drive the products online and which we will explore.

Continuous integration and organisation of updates

Particular updating needs helped to drive the development of digital systems. In the area of legal publishing there are certain products that focus on the fast and efficient updating of legislation as new regulations and statutory changes take place. The digital environment was an ideal way to start continuously updating material as soon as government information became available. Indeed, core legal material is available for free, since it is produced by the government for the public domain, so arguably a user does not have to buy it. But what the publisher adds is a quick and accurate way of organising the raw legal information that comes from government so it can be readily used by the legal profession in various targeted ways. It is easier to integrate updates regularly into products within a digital rather than a print environment, and doing this quickly and efficiently is a key selling point.

Search

Added to that, the nature of reference material is such that the ability to search quickly and effectively for the particular piece of information required is central to its use and application. Organising material effectively and ensuring it is user-friendly is one of the aspects of publishing reference works on which publishers have always spent much effort. So the ability to find information in a vast database of material is improved instantly if the search can be carried out electronically. The move to an electronic format for the delivery of content to the customer was critical as early as possible as a way of maintaining a competitive edge over other publishers.

Automatic compilation of updates

Since governments continuously revise and adapt laws, many legal works were in the form of print looseleafs; an individual or, more often, an organisation purchases a subscription and then receives at regular intervals updates which have to be filed in the looseleaf, while the out-of-date sections are extracted. This is a fiddly and time-consuming process for both the compiler and librarian/filer. While a looseleaf is, more often than not, a product of legal and financial publishing, the issue of keeping a product as up to date as possible in an area that might be moving quite fast is an important one. An online database that is up to date as far as possible in real time clearly saves time, effort and cost.

Timeliness

When updates are due it is important that they are enacted immediately, yet with the print service (as updates were called) being issued at intervals there could well be periods of time when the product was out of date with current law. This too could be overcome via the online environment.

The early electronic products: CD-ROMs

Some companies started to use databases for the production of print products but many products were still being developed in a traditional way from manuscript to typescript files. Given the compelling reasons above, however, publishers were looking for ways to deliver an electronic product to the customer. As with other specialist reference publishers, the early forays into electronic publishing were in the form of providing CDs that were developed from the production files and which supported the print product. These CDs of course were still not updateable within a real-time specification: CDs were only issued as frequently as the print products. However, they did have four key benefits for users:

1   They improved the search for the user. Being able to type in one keyword to search across a product, and in some cases a range of products, was a benefit.
2   The actual updating was at least done for you rather than having to update print by hand yourself.
3   Access was made available to a wider number of users depending on the number of licences a library bought. The idea behind this was that the work could be used by several people at once and for key works, instead of buying lots of print versions (and updating them all by hand filing), libraries could have one main print work and several site licences to the CD. The print costs could be reduced for publishers (essentially to fund CD development).
4   As an adjunct to this, libraries could manage their shelf space more effectively and supply their legal information direct to the lawyer's desktop. This was mainly managed for the market-leading titles. The move to a digital environment in this case matched demand for libraries to move online.

Problems with CD-ROMs

There were production limitations to the success of the early CDs. The main issues were:

- **CD production packages:** they were often cumbersome to use and, in the early days, may have used off-the-shelf electronic publishing packages that were not especially sophisticated, leading to a poor search experience. These conversion packages scanned in text and overlaid search criteria, but these were ultimately rather too simple for specialist usage. New CD-ROMs often had to be issued with the updated sections integrated, and that process was complicated and could lead to errors.
- **Limited space:** there were also problems with the size of the CD, which only has space to hold a certain amount of data.
- **Changing systems:** the developments in XML, coding and metadata provided a more sophisticated route to converting print material into digital products. However, early on companies often found that they had invested in one particular type of system for digitising and then had to move away from it and use a different system.
- **Access controls:** CDs could also be cumbersome to load onto a library system, often with complex access control and frustrating DRM to limit the number of users. Particularly frustrating was the DRM that shut the CD down once the subscription period was over.
- **Existing comfort with print searching:** customers who were used to print could find their way around it quickly by hand, flicking through the table of contents, or leaping to well-thumbed sections. CD-ROMs meant that users had to spend time learning to use the new environment.
- **Cumbersome CD searching:** the CD search could be unwieldy and pull up a lot of unwanted references. It might not be especially clear which part of the work you had ended up in. An early criticism was that although the customer knew a particular reference was within the work, the actual keyword search did not bring it up, maybe due to data error or the complexity of search protocol around paragraph numbering. This meant that unless a search on key terms or case references, for instance, was very specific it did not work effectively.
- **Not very up to date:** another early problem was the fact that the works were not as up to date as they were expected to be. A CD, for instance, was only up to date for a short time, essentially a similar time to the print service.
- **Costs:** customers felt the CD prices were not transparent enough and were too complex.
- **Inaccurate coding:** where databases were being used (rather than off-the-shelf packages) this could be a problem; something could get lost in the database and fixing this was time consuming and costly. The cost of the initial infrastructure was high; taxonomies and protocols had to be developed quickly but still thoroughly. It took some years to iron out the system for the archive, and then change workflow in order to contribute to the archive. The development of real-time, up-to-date works therefore took some time to follow as well.

Database products

However, these CD-based products were built essentially around key print book titles; off-the-shelf packages or small specific databases. Alongside these, large legal databases from which material could be extracted were being developed. Big publishers such as West and LexisNexis were building expertise here and companies were being bought that could bring technological innovation in developing database platforms to existing print legal businesses. Thompson, for instance, which owned Sweet and Maxwell, bought West in 1996, developing its platform into Westlaw and building key content it already owned into it. Reed Elsevier bought LexisNexis in 1994 in a similar way. Both West and Lexis developed full-text searchable databases around particular areas of legal information such as legal cases in particular states in America (and in the case of Nexis, a service launched by Lexis, a news article database). This data proliferated. In the case of Westlaw the information it holds in its American-based datacentre is so large it has its own power plant as a back-up generator to ensure it can keep going in the event of a failure of the grid. The products that emerged as these databases grew will be explored on p. 52 but they mark the beginning of the transformation of the reference arena into a fully digital publishing business.

Once information was being regularly processed into the data warehouse, properly checked and corrected and coded, and the main archive was up and running, the continuous addition into the databases became easier to manage. At that point in the development of the digital product, the focus moved onto creating effective front ends to the databases. These select and extract whatever content is most relevant for the target market sector. In addition, publishers can allow for more customisation for individual accounts (if they are large enough) as well. So the development became much more focused around creating good, effective, branded front ends.

Once the major infrastructure had been set up and workflows developed the next area for product development was to build the author into the picture more directly. Content management systems based around file sharing platforms have been developed to provide a seamless environment for the collection and management of content, including review and editing, so that authors can be commissioned to write and post up their content, review and discuss their content in chat room-style environments with appointed experts; then the content can be copyedited, coded, checked, etc. and sent to an online publishing platform, where it is published, when ready, and so the site is continuously evolving for the user (in many ways following a journals publication programme). Products such as these are not always as seamless as they might sound, but they do ensure the timeliness of the material even for a non-journal product and a constant supply of new information is available to the subscriber.

Infrastructure requirements and organisational change

To manage reference databases of this sort various structural changes have to be made. These were not, in the early stages, around the product offering but around the building and maintenance of effective information architecture. These companies soon developed relationships with suppliers in countries such as India and China, where inputting and coding of data could be managed effectively and cheaply. In some cases a further layer of data management was established where employees more expert at particular aspects of law are necessary to check the legal data is input correctly and ensure the updates of the law are inserted in the right place. This differed from those editors managing the products for the market, but required some specialist legal knowledge in the effective development of the database itself.

As products developed, these companies quickly developed departments where project management techniques could be implemented quickly to ensure infrastructure projects could be built; they could be involved in managing anything from the development of a generic platform to hold information (which might well require the employment of outside suppliers) to the design and architecture of particular products; from the delivery of a product to the consumer to the user experience of the product itself. Technology departments grew with a variety of experts who had various skills in creating coding systems, taxonomies, protocols and standards, etc. for technical information, thus ensuring that the database was developing in a way that would ensure it could be used in all sorts of conditions, anything from output in print form to customised products for key customers.

With this, other departments became necessary, such as helpdesks for customers and for internal users of the database; there could be specialist units to manage particular services such as daily news bulletins, as well as trouble shooting units and departments supporting the internal IT services for hardware and software. And new systems were needed to manage, for example, the correction of errors, or the flow of information from one part of the organisation to another, or for quality assurance and functionality testing.

As technology projects developed at different speeds, so organisationally there was a change; certain expertise might well have to be brought in for a period of time, with growing relationships with specialist technology suppliers. As projects developed, however, there were certain times when more inputting was required, while at others more testing was necessary. Developing organisations that can expand and contract as technology projects are set up has necessarily been a significant change; for the launch of a major work additional people may be needed, while at a later stage only a few people are necessary to maintain the system. The ability to develop a largely flexible workforce may be becoming more critical to product development strategies.

The data asset

So the focus within these publishing sectors was on the effective and efficient development of the database itself. The database becomes a very valuable asset as the content driver for the company. The quality of the database, the taxonomies it uses and the flexibility in the way it can be used are important for the competitive edge of a publisher; there is intellectual property invested in the taxonomy it may have developed as well as the database itself. Therefore there is extensive value in what it owns.

This makes it, as we will see, a very different proposition from the consumer market. The publisher has ownership of something it has developed; authors may well play a part but the publisher owns a database that can be used in a variety of ways going forward as it responds to market change and gives the market the content it needs in the format it needs it in. It is an important aspect of this sort of publishing that the brand name of the publishing company is well known. The brand of a consumer house may be of less relevance to the customer than the name of the author, but in this sector the customer is usually aware of the brand name of the database product they are using and it is an integral part of the publisher's relationship with its customer.

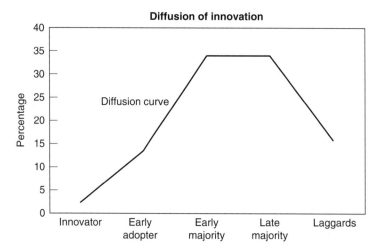

Figure 6.1 Diffusion of innovation.

Migration issues as digital products are developed

The drive for migration from print to digital

When digital products were first developed in a major way for the market, publishers needed to explore how far these different groups of customers were moving online in order to assess the balance between the need for the print product and the need for the digital product. Printing and distribution costs in this sector of the market are high, as are the costs of database development; keeping both formats available is expensive, so it is an important factor to consider when publishers are devising publishing strategies. Some of the key questions still remain around whether it will be necessary to keep the print product, and, if so, for how long. Some publishing companies have moved away from the print market altogether: Butterworths sold a large amount of their print product (to a management buyout originally and now under Bloomsbury Professional), while other companies have seen a significant reduction in print sales.

As new products developed, publishers in the legal area regularly tried to research the market in order to assess how fast customers were moving online. This could be done by directly talking to customers about their needs and their migration strategies, and also by observing the behaviour of customers they could not research as they watched their buying patterns.

Figure 6.1 presents a version of the standard theory of diffusion of innovation, as originally espoused by Rogers[1] in 1962, to illustrate the stages of adoption of a new technology. In many ways companies can be seen to fall into the categories illustrated according to how quickly they move into using digital platforms regularly for their reference content as well as how far they have left print behind altogether.

In the early years of the adoption of online products customers were often loath to relinquish a print version of the product. For some users the ability to search quickly in

1 Rogers, Everett M. *Diffusion of Innovations*. Free Press, 1962.

a physical product they knew well made them reluctant to take up the online product. But the capability for users to access the product from their desktop without a trip to the library and the capacity for several of them to access it at once were clear benefits. So, in the early stages, libraries tended to reduce the quantity of print products they bought, buying instead a licence covering a number of online users. Very few, however, would relinquish print altogether.

Early sales activity

At first publishers often developed the product and pushed it to everyone who had the product already in print, being rather ambitious about sales targets and predicting a much more rapid demise in the purchase of the print product. However, publishers began to look a little more deeply in terms of diffusion in order to assess the speed of change. Market research projects could sometimes profile customer groups according to whether they were likely to be early adopters or follow on behind; by scaling the sort of customer profiles across their customer base, they could identify those that it made more sense to tackle first with deals via their key accounts development, so ensuring they could maximise their sales effort effectively. As they analysed patterns they also saw that their expectations of complete migration from the earliest possible stage were misjudged; this had an effect on pricing issues. Similarly, the continued use of print mixed in with the online product was also not immediately recognised, again affecting pricing. These issues were not always due to the slowness of the customer to take up the online products: as we have seen, the quality of the product was also a factor.

Price and migration

One of the reasons why understanding migration patterns becomes important is that the pricing of the print and online product need to remain, in some way, in line, but the unit cost of producing the print product increases as the number printed decreases; this cost needs to be supported by the growth in online sales. The online sale initially for many products was developed as an add-on to the print product (where it was a direct version of a print product), though with the expectation that this relationship might swap later and the print product change to become the add-on to the online service; in this circumstance the idea was that the print product would become something a publisher charged a premium amount for. This situation has not yet quite materialised. The pressure has been to keep the prices of the print product reasonably in line with the existing and well-established price ranges for print despite the decrease in quantities; though the decline has perhaps been less rapid than some might have predicted for certain types of product.

Some of the online products did not have this problem, having been developed essentially as a new way to access legal information that was as real time and up to date as possible; the large legal databases such as Westlaw or LexisNexis fell into this category. Here there was no particular print legacy to accommodate. The migration of customers to an online environment nevertheless still posed problems in that the cost of developing these large databases needed to be supported by the consistent and strong revenues coming from the print products. Ideally, libraries needed to buy into new legal databases of this sort, which were essential to their business, on top of their existing spend. In practice, of course, while some initial additional budget would often be available to buy into the technologies necessary, some other area of the budget would need to be reduced in order for money to be directed to the new product.

Encouraging migration

There are ways to encourage or force the process of migration. For instance:

- **Forced migration**: forcing migration in some cases made the transfer from print to online more possible, though publishers risked alienating customers who did not want to move. For smaller products which might be in decline anyway, forcing the migration, maybe by providing CD-ROMs to start with and later online access, did at least give those products a chance to survive; savings could be made in the longer term by stopping the print versions. In other cases, migration was forced in order to be able to charge a higher price, a price necessary to support the cost of the online product. Models such as these were not always popular but were another early way to move the more reluctant customers online.
- **Educational pricing**: migration was also supported by a policy of special pricing for educational institutions which ensured the products were widely available in universities and colleges. As new members of the profession enter, having used online products in their courses they would inevitably expect them to be available in their companies.

Other influencing factors

One of the critical migration issues for the legal market was the range of customers using the products. It was often assumed that customers would want to move to the online product given the USPs and that the print could be cut out of the equation very quickly. However, there was a large number of users who preferred to use the print that they knew very well as they found that navigation was much quicker and easier than learning a new protocol through the online version. Older members of the legal profession did not want to have to change. That continues but the make-up of the user base will alter as students enter the profession and are not accustomed to using print. This illustrates how carefully the industry needs to observe the behaviour and work patterns of the profession in order to manage their publishing mix.

Changing relationships with customers in the specialist sector

Key customers

Publishers of information for professional groups of customers have always had a close relationship with the various segments of their market and are in direct contact with their customers in different ways on a regular basis, so they are very knowledgeable about their customers' needs. Their key customers, often early adopters, are particularly important in the development of digital services. Large corporate or institutional buyers spend significant sums of money on their information needs, so publishers have worked with them closely when negotiating packages of products or have supplied libraries with regular subscriptions. These key accounts will have developed long-term relationships and will be used to pricing arrangements specifically suited to them; in certain cases, the overall price will be negotiated on the basis of a percentage rise in relation to their last year's spending, rather than on totting up the prices (with discounts) of the products themselves. For some, standing order arrangements may be in place: for instance, some firms may pay a regular subscription and get a range of reports sent to them as and when they are written: rather than knowing what the content of the reports might be, they trust the publisher to produce interesting and relevant products for them. Some companies might be large enough to request a particular sort of product and the publisher can develop it for them, whether customising something it already has or creating something specific for that customer.

The new online products have allowed these key relationships to grow and become even more central to the sales business of the organisation. Online products can be grouped together in a range of ways and different levels of service can be provided, so ensuring that a much more complex set of product offerings can be produced; titles and services can be mixed and matched to provide the perfect library for a key account holder. As a consequence the product range has developed to be extremely flexible; while some technological work is necessary to select and structure the product, this can be crafted to quite a detailed level for a particularly important client. Thus publishers in professional fields such as law have become much more integrated into the work of their key account firms, supplying them with some sort of bespoke information that is necessary for them to work effectively.

The pricing for online products therefore becomes much more about issues of size of company, number of users, value of the information for those users and customisation than about lists of specific products with attached price tags. The firms need the publishers, who are expert at organising the information (expertise they developed with the print forms), and the publishers need the firms to purchase these works, which are expensive to produce and even more so to customise.

This symbiosis can have dangers. The importance of these customers is critical so publishers must maintain a good relationship with them; one of the ways of doing this is to ensure the other aspects of their service are good as well, not just their product offering. The ability to fix technological problems and provide additional service supporting use of the products, for instance, is important, as may be the way the way the products are integrated into the business. Some areas of professional publishing will have experts who go into companies to advise them on their information needs or create bespoke taxonomies or archiving systems for them. The latest issues are around integrating the use of information directly into workflow, something we will look at a little more on p. 58.

All this can mean additional revenue (though there are related costs as well in terms of time and skill), but where a company changes in some way, so can its budget; firms of this scale rarely entirely fall out of the market, but mergers and acquisition can leave a publisher vulnerable to a reduction in spending as companies consolidate resources, or downturns in the economic climate can lead to large areas of budget spend, such as for information needs, being threatened where cost cutting is required. The relationships with these customers therefore have become more entwined than before.

Medium-sized customers

Professional publishers may only have a certain number of very large customers that merit this sort of attention, so a more standard set of reference packages is available that medium-sized customers may well buy. Sales effectiveness was an area that needed more careful development in this sector. Key customers already had a much more personal service, and while reps covered these medium-sized businesses, the usual fliers and direct mailings in between reps' visits were not enough to sell complex products. Sales leads development might lead to a sale in a print product but an intermediate stage with demonstration and training became part of the sales process for a digital product in the early days.

Flexibility in being able to design product offerings that match well to customer groups is important as there will be less opportunity to customise these. These packages have to make sense for the customer so that they do not have to buy into material they do not really need; early mistakes were made in packaging up selections of titles for this sector of the market. Pressure on libraries within medium-sized companies means they will look carefully at the pricing options as well.

Other customer groups

There are customer segments that contain buyers that are:

- specialist users – they operate in a niche where they depend on key works but may not need to purchase many to satisfy their needs; they may well be early adopters
- individual users – where the average value of what they buy is low and they may be a mixture of early and later adopters

These customers, when added together, may represent a lot of money and can easily have been loyal for many years, but individually do not merit a lot of work developing relationships and bespoke customer service as described above. These customers can be more difficult for a publisher to manage effectively. One of the traditional ways to keep some sort of communication going with them has been developing newsletters that are sent out regularly either with regard to a specific product or about the business environment in general, allowing for a marketing relationship with this group. The advent of new online products has allowed publishers to develop these connections much more quickly and easily to keep in touch with a customer base and try to provide a more customisable service on a wider scale for customers who are not necessarily commanding a large amount of budget.

Ongoing product development

Market research for product development

Market research is essential to developing high-value products and in the early stages of digital products there were some problems building a useful picture of customer needs. At first getting commentary from customers on what they wanted in a digital product was difficult given that many customers did not feel they understood what they might be getting. Now this would seem unlikely as everyone has had experience of the internet, which has become routine in their lives. But in the early development of digital products in the early to mid-1990s the internet was new and customers did not necessarily know how they might use it or what the limitations might be to a desktop product. Expectations ran high, which did not help the rather simplistic early products.

Different approaches were taken to solicit information, such as conjoint analysis to understand decision-making behaviour when choosing and building up packages, but these could be too complicated for customers new to the area to understand. These worked better for corporate librarians, who were already sophisticated users of databases and did understand the options; closer work with them, understanding the way products were used, was important.

Learning about how the market research process needs to work has been important, as has the scope of research in learning what is necessary to adjust selling and marketing techniques around digital products. However, research activity is now much more embedded in the continuous relationship between customers and new product developers.

Approaches to product development

The products that were developed over the last decade could be summarised as taking two main approaches:

1 **Horizontal approach**: where products of a similar type were brought together (often based around central databases and data warehouses), such as all case law or all updated statutes or archives of news articles. Comprehensiveness was the key issue here, so a customer wanting to ensure they had access to a wide range of cases across many legal areas could buy into a case law product section.
2 **Vertical approach**: which took a particular area and supplied a range of different materials that could be integrated to provide a one-stop shop for all information requirements for that particular area. So, for instance, you could have an intellectual property site, which would have statutes and legislation, case law, annotated law (i.e. law selected and critically examined by experts), news, journal articles, etc. Similar approaches are taken in other professional areas such as finance or regulation. Understanding job roles and functions more precisely is important here as complex digital products are built up for different uses.

Pricing and sales models

Early pricing problems

In the early stages of these products the pricing often reflected a naivety about the electronic version, partly because of the migration expectations, as we have seen, and partly because of the added value provided by the digital version. The idea was that customers would substitute their print product for the digital – but would be willing to pay a higher price given the benefits of searching, up-to-dateness, etc. that the electronic version provided. With this in mind prices were generally at a standard percentage higher than the print version. Thus publishers hoped that the premium of the electronic version would allow for them to extend the value of each customer account without necessarily adding new product lines. That would help support the cost of the development.

While libraries did not necessarily assume that the development of digital meant huge cost savings for publishers (they knew the value of the information itself was the critical factor in the cost of a product), they still did not automatically expect to pay more for the product. Customers often stuck to the print version on that basis as it was cheaper, contained the same content and was without the failings of the early electronic version. In any case, many libraries wanted to keep a copy of one print version as the main reference, with the electronic version essentially enabling easy access for multiple users, saving space.

Pricing the bundle and subscriptions

This led to a growing sophistication in the price offerings as the bundle became more critical to the sales forces than the expectation of direct migration. The advantage of this approach was that the digital version became more integral to the total package and actually eased migration, given it happened more slowly and in a more integrated way, once it was accepted migration might not be total. The main complexity about this issue was that the package had to be unpacked in some way or other in order to calculate the VAT that was due on the electronic aspect of the bundle.

Subscription pricing was already well established in the legal reference market for regularly updated materials so the concept of pricing for a subscription for an electronic service was not a huge leap (unlike in other markets, as we shall see in Chapter 8). However, there were some issues. The early CD-ROM pricing mechanism was more complicated, as essentially to get an updated CD you had to buy the whole electronic product again each time so it was up to date (whereas with the print product you bought the main work just once, and simply subscribed to the service afterwards); this meant service charges for ongoing CD purchase, once you had bought in to the product initially, were higher than many customers expected. The development of online systems finally ended this problem, which could stimulate many customer complaints. However, it is an important lesson in understanding the way a product's structure or format can determine an approach to pricing which in the end is counter-intuitive to the market. This is something that continues to recur throughout the industry as pricing remains a knotty area for digital publishing.

Licences and pay per view

The initial sales often focused around licences, with complicated fixed price menus of pricing and discounting based on numbers of users that were paid on top of a base price. While everyone understood the importance of transparent pricing, pricing was inevitably getting more complicated with the alternative ways of buying into what was at heart the same product.

There were also discussions with regard to pay per view options compared to buying a subscription. This essentially arose where the expense of buying a complete subscription could well be beyond some customers whose rate of usage was as yet undetermined, so pay per view options were built in. Some of the issues here were really around the newness of the products to customers who could not at that stage be sure how useful the product would be. This also stabilised once the customers started using them, as they could get a better feel of the value of the product to them and so develop a greater sense of what they might be willing to pay.

Customised pricing

These pricing issues largely settled around subscriptions packages with pay per view or pay per use options. The e-commerce and access management technology developed quickly enough to be able to accommodate flexible options, and the products today can be used and paid for in a variety of ways. However, one can quickly note that when searching for prices on a specialist publisher's website it can be difficult to find a clear fixed price. Pricing is perhaps less transparent than it was, despite it being more flexible, as pricing has become much more tailored to the customer. This builds on what was outlined at the start of the chapter in relation to the sorts of customers for these products and the value these customers place on them.

Large corporates can normally be sure a large database will get used somehow or other and so accept it is worth paying the publisher for this information. The question therefore for publishers is less about the need to make prices attractively low in order to capture a market (though of course competitive pricing is still important) and more about determining value in the quality and usefulness of the information in digital and print formats to those companies. They do not want to underestimate its value nor price it to jeopardise print revenues. So analysis of the way companies use the information and review their current library practices is important in order to assess prices. The size of a company, the number of likely users, global reach, etc. all have to be taken into account when agreeing a price. As the purchase decisions are based around much bigger bundles and customisation, customers also need to get a better idea of their own usage (helped with the analytics provided by the publishing company).

Customers and publishers have had to get a better sense of how to value the information they provide and, as such, have arguably become much more closely knit. It used to be the case that if something new was bought by a library it might have to cut something off its list. Now packages can be designed that maybe include less critical information for free as a taster for the main deal. In fact understanding the financial make-up of a large company has become important, as the overall spending is often looked at and a publisher might target an ideal percentage uplift on the value of that account year on year, regardless of what was specifically included in the package; it can then adjust the package, add in more, etc. to gain the deal. Of course, as with any negotiation both sides need to be happy with the deal, so it was not always one way but a collaborative approach to negotiating might evolve. This is similar to any library purchase for a large database-style product, but at the high end of the corporate market the opportunities for customisation become more key to a deal.

There are lower prices for smaller customers and package deals with fixed prices and discounts for those who are not able to command large budgets or may require the more specialised vertical products as well as the educational prices noted above. Differentiated pricing had always existed but it has become more critical.

Future developments

Building on existing products

The ongoing cost of the support and development of a database that is only ever expanding is an important one for publishers. They need to ensure they are satisfying their customers as far as possible in order to ensure the necessary revenue is still coming in. This requires a programme of continuous improvement for the products and services.

Add-ons

With the core digital products one of the obvious ways to develop the product is to build add-on services either which form part of the core product (making it all the more central to the customer by becoming 'have to have' material) or for which they can charge a top-up premium. The digital environment allows for suites of add-ons to be developed from email alerts, selected digests, expert commentary on newsworthy events, even easy ordering for print on demand for transcriptions.

Access levels

Access is also something that can be manipulated to add value to products. Customers can pay extra for additional levels of access, maybe for particular resources they only need at certain times; or they can be allowed to search across a wider range of databases than they currently have direct access to, and pay for additional material they find they need at that point.

Tailored products for market segments

One of the benefits of structuring the documents and the database carefully is that content in the data warehouse can be exploited in different ways to develop new products. In order to do this, further segmentation of the market is becoming more critical; to tailor products effectively the publisher needs to understand the requirements of each segment and target new products appropriately. Pricing and content can be very carefully managed to suit exactly that market. Growing subtlety in segmenting markets is becoming important. In many cases publishers have been simplifying the marketing of the offering, consolidating their lists around key brand names (such as Lawtel or Westlaw) rather than breaking it down into lots of smaller separate digital products. Some of the material will be the same behind two different branded products but directed in different ways for different types of user.

Flexibility of use

Large digital databases offer clear benefits for those looking for a comprehensive approach to legal information, but there are still parts of the business that focus on books. The print versions of titles continue to be successful for highly specialised customers who many not want online packages of products. Simple ebooks replicating the print products are usually available too. Large online databases are also cumbersome to use on the move and ebooks in app-style formats are being developed to make them more useable.

Products are being developed to be used in particular ways according to the sort of material they contain. An example would be an ebook designed to be viewed in an app environment where it is easy to bookmark pages, add comments, highlight significant cases, gather key information together as well as allow for easy searching anywhere, any time. Here publishers are getting closer to understanding the exact way content is used (rather than what the content is for) and designing a product with that in mind.

Case study: The White Book

The White Book is an example of a major work that presents civil procedure rules for lawyers and barristers, written by experts and established over many years as an essential and authoritative source of information. In terms of migration to a digital product a rather specific issue around migration emerged as there was a convention of referring to the print product during a court hearing. When the first digital versions of the White Book were under development, neither online access nor controlled digital access was allowed in court. Knowing the peculiarities of your own market therefore becomes critical as print versions can still play a critical part in some aspects of user behaviour.

Alongside the print version, there is online access available on Westlaw as well as a CD version. However, the way the book is used is significant. In many cases users will want to add their own annotations, mark in highlights, refer to particular sections regularly, stick in Post-It notes and tabs to mark sections; portability is also key, which can make internet use of the work more cumbersome. This very physical way of using the book is important so the publishers have developed a professional grade iPad ebook which allows the book to be used in a way that mimics this with digital interactivity. They also dealt with the portability issues as an iPad was lighter than a heavy print volume. The book therefore is available in a wide variety of formats, some with different additional materials to add value to different degrees and allow customers a range of options to choose from so they can have a package that exactly suits them.

Newer digital products and the old dilemmas

Print and price still continue to pose challenges. While developments in apps and other ebook formats are growing in number, the pricing here is, as in the early days of the online products, not yet settled and may require refinement as the new offerings are taken up. For instance, a large print book product bought as an app product (which allows for portability and interactivity) can be offered at the same sort of price as the original print book, bought instead of the print; if this is the case, are the additional benefits being undervalued as there is no uplift on price, or, since the essential content is the same, does this matter? Meanwhile, the digital version can be bought as an upgrade on the main print product; if these prices are not calibrated carefully with the print-only and digital-only prices it can seem as if the deal is actually about having the print as the add-on premium to the digital rather than the other way round. So the pricing questions continue.

The dilemma of print also continues. Publishers are reducing their print offerings but see that there is still an extremely high-value market there. Publishers are continuously re-evaluating their print markets and the current migration patterns to online. The cost of the online products may also mean there are challenges in supporting the print side of the business, and more structural changes may need to take place as the old print-based departments may need to be reinvented as content development departments.

One problem for a publisher is that, broadly speaking, it can only offer what it has. The major players own proprietary systems that work with their data warehouse and maintaining the quality of those warehouses is critical – adding to them continuously and developing new content silos. It is important to be comprehensive in your offering so customers do not need to go outside. Where this is not possible information can be licensed in and smaller specialist publishers may be able to benefit in that way. Big customers will usually have more than one of the biggest services, and understanding the strengths and limitations of each is important. Nevertheless the drive to comprehensiveness may have an effect on the market. The larger players may have to buy companies to gain ground in a particular field in order to be competitive – whether a discipline or a market sector – and the market may then consolidate to a small number of companies.

Providing information services

Publishers in the professional arena are beginning subtly to change their emphasis. The following reflect these developments:

- **Workflow:** use of the content has become a feature of the current developments. Information such as this is used in certain ways at certain times within the development of a law case or a planning appeal. Seeing how the information is used gives publishers new ways to structure information in the best way for the user. The more it can be integrated into the daily work of the user, the more valuable it becomes.
- **Chargeable useage:** another aspect of understanding workflow means that, as with chargeable work, being able to identify when and how something was used in a case means that the price for that use of legal material can be charged to the legal firm's client appropriately.
- **Convergence:** as publishers build their content more closely into the workflow of individuals there is a convergence between the content and the daily activity of the user so that the information and the application of it are more tightly tied together. The boundaries between information and its use are blurred, and the publisher and user are therefore becoming more embedded.
- **Integrated CMS:** complete customisation is difficult and costly to do for every customer, but for larger customers bespoke work can be done, tailoring information to their needs, building it into their content management systems, allowing for collaborative work and integrating it into their charging systems.
- **Information consultants:** what this means is that publishers need to work even more closely with their customers and in many ways begin to act as information consultants with the in-house information experts to ensure they get the best use out of their content. They become part of the competitiveness of a firm – if they can get the job done the best way possible, which includes using their information effectively.
- **Other businesses:** from this sort of integration it becomes easy to see other opportunities, such as the development of training packages providing continuous professional development (CPD); the effective use of information itself is becoming an important part of CPD. Other opportunities include providing boiler plate materials for daily use in constructing documents. In this way some publishers are reinterpreting themselves as wider service providers for the industry.

Conclusion

For some, the development of digital publishing has been a catalyst that has reignited the specialist reference sector, opening up a lot of opportunities in a marketplace that had become more static around core print products. In every sector the digital environment is leading to new approaches to the role of the publisher as relationships with customers change and products become more flexible, taking publishers into new directions. In this case the larger publishers have been developing extensive and sophisticated databases on which to build new products. The advantage for the specialist reference sector is that the publisher has always had a close link with its customer and has had highly valued expertise at developing content for the market. This will continue to be vital for the sector in the future.

Further reading and resources

www.outsellinc.com – a consultancy supporting the information and publishing industries, particularly in the professional and education arenas, providing useful reports and surveys

It can be useful to explore professional reference publisher sites to examine their digital product ranges. Here are some examples:

www.bmj.com
www.informabusinessinformation.com
www.lexisnexis.co.uk
www.lexisnexis.com
www.nature.com
www.sweetandmaxwell.co.uk
www.westlaw.co.uk
www.westlaw.com

Questions to consider

1   What challenges will publishers face as they develop increasingly sophisticated platforms for their information and how might they overcome these?
2   Some see publishing as moving towards becoming an integral part of the way a company that it serves does business. What are the opportunities and challenges for the publishers who move in this direction?
3   Will there be areas of the market that might lose out as publishers develop more bespoke expertise for their large professional clients?

7 Developments in digital publishing for the academic market

In this chapter we will cover:

1 The academic publishing context, focusing on the way publications play a part in the research process
2 Development of digital products and why these first evolved around journals
3 What current digital products look like and the challenges they face, first looking at journal services and then at monographs; this section will look in particular at the issues of open access
4 Future developments of digital products, exploring the themes that will influence the academic publishing market going forward.

Introduction

The area of academic or scholarly publishing is another sector where the digital product is well established and has, in some areas, entirely supplanted the print product. Indeed, the area of academic and scientific research was the arena in which the internet and, subsequently, the World Wide Web first developed. The application of digital technologies to research was therefore an obvious step to take to improve and add value to content that was previously only available in print.

Research needs to reach across boundaries in order to be useful; dissemination is critical to the purpose and continued dynamic of research, and the World Wide Web in particular enabled that to happen much more quickly and effectively than ever before. Easy access to material for researchers, whether raw data or fully validated research papers, is critical, and print had obvious restrictions to the efficiency of access, limited as it was by shelf space and physical access to a library. So the digital environment was an obvious way to ensure these key precepts of research such as access and dissemination could be realised and research taken into new realms.

Context: the research environment

In this section we will explore the characteristics of research publishing, including:

- what research publishing is in both STM and HSS contexts
- who the customers are

- peer review and the role of publishers
- who owns the content
- the publishing dilemma for research

What is research publishing?

There are a few distinctions that need to be made around the area of scholarly publishing and the publication of research. These definitions are not strictly applied, and may be subject to debate, but it is important to be aware of areas where terms overlap, albeit loosely, as there are some differences in publishing strategies depending on the area of focus. Scholarly, or academic, publishing will generally refer to publishing based on research from academic institutions; research takes the form of academic papers published in journals as well as in book form. Scholarly or academic publishers will also produce textbooks suited to the higher education market as well as supplementary works that are more specialised than core textbooks, crossing over between the curriculum and the research of an academic institution. For the focus of this chapter, it is the research aspect of these publishers and their output that is key (we will touch on higher education textbooks in Chapter 8). However, research is not undertaken only within academic institutions, so publishing of this sort also encompasses material produced by research institutes, maybe governmental or private sector research organisations, as well as companies such as those operating in the pharmaceutical sector.

Drivers of the market

There are three main issues around research that influence the publishing environment:

1 **Dissemination:** research needs to be spread widely in order for more research to build on it
2 **Distribution:** scholarly publishing is global and the distribution needs to be too
3 **Storage:** research needs to be collected and stored in an accessible way for easy access later on down the line

Publishers were able to do this effectively in print formats: as global businesses they developed the relationships necessary to spread information widely and in a targeted way to ensure appropriate dissemination; they could also help libraries archive it as far as possible. Digital publishing clearly provides ways to solve these problems even more effectively.

Journals and monographs

In many cases the primary source of published research material is a journal and that has been the focus of many of the digital developments in recent decades. However, there are also monographs, extended pieces of writing exploring and presenting a thesis in more depth, as well as collections of articles written specifically for a research book that are by a range of different authors, perhaps following a conference. These all form part of a scholarly publisher's range of publishing.

The publisher/academic circle

Thompson, in *Books in the Digital Age* (2005), explores the nature of the academic publishing field and the field of academia itself. These fields exist together, both needing the other, but with a different emphasis at the heart of their activity. Figure 7.1 illustrates the symbiotic relationship between research and publishing.

Academics want to disseminate their research and spread new knowledge effectively. Publishers have, until recently, provided the most effective way for academics to do this, so academics depend on scholarly publishing organisations to validate their work and ensure it is spread widely. Academics depend on them too for the materials they use for their research; they want to read what others have published in order to advance their own thinking. In addition they gain more credibility and authority the more their own work is cited in new research, so the mechanisms publishers have in place to monitor citations are also important for their career development. Publishers meanwhile need a constant supply of research material to publish, need to ensure it is of high quality and need academics to encourage their libraries to buy this material. For both sides of the bargain quality and validity are important, for the prestige of the publisher and for the authority of the research for the academic. So the relationship is interdependent: an academic will choose a publisher or journal based on the authority of that journal; the publisher wants high-level academics to contribute to ensure the prestige of the journal.

There is also an additional angle to the journal publishing field as there are many institutes and learned societies that own journals that are published by scholarly publishers. Publishers tender for the rights to produce the journal for the society and need to ensure that the particular ethos and mission of the organisation in question are supported in their publishing practice. These organisations have needed publishers as producing journals is an expensive business, and publishers can also maximise the commercial opportunities: journal publication is often a significant source of revenue for these societies.

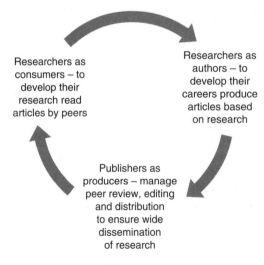

Figure 7.1 The publisher/academic circle.

STM *and* HSS

It is important at this point to draw a distinction between STM (science technical medical publishing) and humanities and social science publishing (HSS – this acronym is not always used extensively but I will use it here). These are both fundamentally scholarly publishing arenas but aligned around different sectors of the academic market. Definitions of these markets vary but it is important to recognise that there is an element of STM publishing that has a strong overlap with the professional arena of science publishing (i.e. as undertaken by medical research companies, for instance). Some scientific journals have an extremely wide reach beyond academic institutions; an example would be *Nature*, which is a large publishing operation in its own right. Of course there are practical applications of areas of social science, law, education, finance, etc., and journals will feed into the more professional markets of these areas, but the main fields of humanities publishing tend to be centred in the academic environment (one exception being humanities titles that might cross over into general interest).

It is useful to make a distinction between STM and HSS areas within the arena of scholarly publishing as they have developed a little differently within the digital environment. Both sectors publish journals and monographs but the nature of research in each bears a slightly different emphasis. Historically the HSS markets have lagged behind the STM markets in moving into digital environments, particularly where, in the STM sectors, some journal publishers have moved away from print almost entirely. STM markets, for instance, are more significantly driven by:

- a more immediate need to spread scientific research in real time
- the ability to access scientific research quickly and easily in order to build upon it in a timely way
- the fact that the older the research is, the less useful it can be within the STM disciplines

For these the reliance on journals as a primary way to disseminate findings was already well established.

These are not insignificant issues for the HSS arena but there are some other nuances in the publishing business here:

- there is a strong tradition of the research monograph where academics can extend argument and develop understanding within a longer narrative form
- older journal articles or monographs can still be current within the context of a debate
- historical reference to earlier research sources will very often still be critical to the development of current thinking
- HSS academics are likely to be returning to older sources and research more often than their STM counterparts as this is critical to building a rounded picture for debate

For these reasons monographs are an important aspect of HSS publishing and that leads to more potential for a live backlist. This can be important for many publishers as a long-term revenue source; the writings of particular people such as famous economists or psychologists, for instance, may later become paperbacks as key texts move into the teaching curriculum.

So there is a difference between HSS and STM publishing which has meant that scientific journal publishing has, up to now, been ahead of the humanities research monograph in terms of migration to the digital platform. HSS has been catching up but it is still worth noting a slightly different approach as we look at monographs later. It is also important to note that there has been a faster drive towards English as the main language for all published material in the STM sector than in the HSS arena.

Scholarly research customers

In the market for scholarly and academic publishing there is a distinction between the user and the buyer of the material. The libraries buy the journals and research works, following recommendations from the academics using the library, and these libraries are large institutional purchasers responsible for considerable budgets but, of course, under pressure to get value for money as a public institution. They may well form consortia to increase their purchasing power and they will be regarded by publishers as key accounts, with highly tailored sales packages planned according to their needs.

The libraries will have various concerns as they manage their books. They will be wanting to ensure they get access to the works right so that titles or journals are easily available to students and researchers; this needs to be managed with the popularity/importance of the journal in mind, yet they do not want to restrict the lesser used journals too much, thereby limiting the possibility for their researchers to access everything they might need. But their budgets are not unlimited so they need to balance the titles they take between popular, '*have* to have' journals and '*nice* to have' journals. They will, in most cases, spend the full value of their budget, so if a new title comes along, they may well need to reduce their stock somewhere else in order to afford it.

The publishers need to bear various issues in mind for their library customers, such as effective customer service, fast distribution and, of course, pricing, as well as recognising the competing draw on library budgets (for instance to supply technology for use in the library or buy other resources such as DVDs). Shelf space is also a growing issue for some libraries as well as the ability to manage ever-increasing archives. But publishers also need to be satisfying the users – ensuring the titles are easy to use, well designed, high quality in terms of the content, and properly referenced and indexed to ensure the information is as easy to get at as possible. These issues have always been important and are critical in the move to a digital environment.

Peer review and the role of publishers

The importance of validity has already been mentioned and the main way this is achieved is through peer review, whether as a journal article, through a peer review process, or as a monograph or thesis where influential readers will have considered the work for publication. In the journal arena, of course, this is an ongoing process that forms the backbone of journal publishing. As new articles come in for consideration the peer review process is continuous and thorough. If peers accept the research it is regarded as validated and sound. This also reinforces the nature of authorship as researchers can lay claim to an area of research; copyright in the material once published further protects their material from misuse such as plagiarism. One of the central tenets of copyright is the protection of authors so that they can expect to be recognised as authors of their material while allowing it to be applied where relevant to further research initiatives; with recognition for their work, authors are inspired to continue research and so creativity and innovation continue to be nurtured. With copyright comes citation and this forms part of the area in which publishers can add value, by providing citation indexes, for instance, or ensuring work is properly referenced throughout their published output.

The key issues with peer review are:

- it is time consuming
- it requires effective organisation
- it needs to meet high standards
- it comes at some sort of price

The cost of peer review has been effectively borne by the publishers, who, if they manage the publication effectively, hope to recoup the cost through their own sales, and thus support the activity.

Who owns the research?

Research, in many cases, is carried out by people funded in their various countries by the state: universities and research institutes are very often supported by the public sector and research grants will frequently come out of the money paid to the state by taxpayers. So if the research outcomes have been paid for once already should the research not therefore be free to access? In addition to the issue of the number of times the content is paid for, there is the moral consideration which raises the issue that the commercial appropriation of research content goes against the grain of research as open and free for all to use and benefit from. The ethics of disseminating research have come to the fore now that methods of dissemination are much easier and cheaper with the use of digital technology.

This has also enlivened the debate about open access. We should consider briefly the terminology used in relation to open access. Open access essentially means that material is available online and with unrestricted access; research material can be lodged in various places such as a public subject-specific archive or an institution-specific archive. The terms open source and open content licensing are both used in the context of open access. Open source can be used interchangeably with the term open access but in general is used in relation to the release and exchange of software, while content in other forms of media (e.g. published in journals) is covered by the term open access. Open content, while also somewhat non-specific, can be used when referring to content that can be modified in some way, something we will look at along with usage rights when we consider Creative Commons in Chapter 10. These principles have been around for some time now: self-archiving/sharing was originally carried out by computer scientists in the 1980s, with a considerable body of articles available as open access by 2000. Scientific journal articles have led the way. This is especially true of the newer subject areas which have been developing in more recent decades; with less heritage of print journals behind them it has been easier for those titles to step directly into the online world.

We will explore the challenges in more depth on p. 73, but the issue centres on the accessibility of research and the value it provides. The argument goes that if research helps mankind in some way, then if it is limited only to those who can afford to pay what may well be high subscription rates to journals surely that is preventing research from moving as fast as it could in order to continue helping mankind; and does it not also prevent those in poorer countries from accessing it at all?

Ownership of content is being reconsidered more acutely as universities lay claim to the work carried out within their departments; while not denying moral rights of authorship over content (so not affecting the ability of an individual to gain recognition and accolades for their work), universities and institutions where researchers carry out their work may claim copyright over material which could allow them to exploit the material more effectively for themselves as an institution.

These are not new concepts but the freedom and democracy of the digital environment have allowed the relationship between the commercial product and the need to sustain and disseminate well-tested research to be reconsidered. The peer review process is central to the continuing model of research and yet this part of the research equation has not been entirely covered by the academic sector in the past, but supported by the commercial journals market. So if the process of dissemination moves away from publishers as universities and researchers experiment with different forms of access with different models, there is still an issue of the cost of managing a peer review process, which is not negligible and needs to be considered in some way.

The publishing dilemma

From these debates, it could be said that publishers are beginning to seem less important in the process of research publishing. The cost of peer review aside, other costs that had made publishers essential to the research dissemination process are changing. While journals were only available in print, the additional production and distribution costs also needed to be covered by publishers; they could invest in this and build the value chain necessary to do this, so were the only real option for disseminating research information effectively. Digital publishing has led to a re-evaluation of journal publishing as it becomes easier to disseminate information in other ways that do not necessarily need to involve a publisher.

Changes in the publishing value chain are leading to changes in the cost base for books. The costs of printing and global physical distribution are immediate savings that can be made. Given the critical importance of timeliness in spreading information and competing effectively in a research market, which, of course, the internet enables so well, the benefits are clear. While academics and their institutions were not really able to set up a global distribution network for print output, the dissemination of their research on the internet is something that it is possible for them to undertake, thus threatening the position of scholarly publishers. This will continue to be a theme through the chapter.

The development of digital products

In this section we will look at:

- why digital products work for this market
- the early development of products and why journals articles were first

The benefits of digital over print

The digital environment could immediately bring obvious benefits to the scholarly and academic markets. Many of the critical issues that are part of the research environment could be immediately solved. There were many limitations of print:

- timeliness of accessing the research could well be limited if the journals came out bi-monthly or quarterly in print form
- the ease of access for large numbers of people was difficult to manage if only one print copy was available
- users had to be in the library physically to use the products
- shelf space could well be limited
- searching library catalogues could be time consuming and was not always revealing
- dissemination was still limited, particularly in developing countries

These issues could be quickly solved by digital products.

The value of content to the library

Libraries need information in order to manage their collection effectively. Libraries wanting to ensure value for money need to understand how popular and useful a title or article is. A book physically booked out of the library will leave a record but titles referred to within the library are more difficult to trace; while a well-thumbed section of a journal can indicate a popular article, it is difficult to monitor in a systematic way. Yet this sort of information allows a library to establish much more precisely the value of a particular title to them. There could be journals that they do not want to stock in entirety but which have a few articles every year that could be of interest to users; in print formats this is almost impossible to manage. There could well be additional costs in purchasing bound volumes of journals, an important way to ensure durability for well-used titles.

The early development of new digital products

It was clear, therefore, early on in the development of the sector that a digital product could resolve many of these issues. There had been early efforts to move scholarly content into digital environments but the main expansion followed the development of the World Wide Web, and the move to digital platforms for this market started in earnest in the mid-1990s. Publishers began to focus on developing more commercial products and finding ways to migrate their content into digital environments.

As Table 7.1 summarises, adopting technologies for journals was easier to manage than the transfer of books, as the rolling programme of delivering and typesetting articles that already existed allowed for the introduction of digital platforms in a more controlled way; smaller chunks of information such as articles are easier to code and manipulate on a rolling programme, and workflow could be adapted to phase in digital platforms.

The journals market in particular was highly concentrated around a few key players with global scope and financial strength. As they developed more online systems a critical mass quickly developed, which in turn encouraged the market to move relatively

Table **7.1** Differences between journals and books that made it easier for journals to emerge as digital products first

Journals	Books
Rolling programme of articles being delivered	Manuscripts delivered at irregular intervals
Short articles easy to code	Large manuscripts
Structure of articles often written to defined style (e.g. with abstracts, keywords, references)	Different author styles and possible varying series/house styles
Archive easy to build up on a continuing basis	One-off titles that stand alone
Articles easier for customers to read online and customers are more used to an online environment for this style of publishing	Long narratives not always so easy to read online
Shorter turnaround for preparing articles	Longer time needed to get the work ready for digital service
Archives easier and quicker to digitise	Books more costly to digitise and more inconsistent in style
Journal publishing more profitable and so investment more readily available	Books less profitable, and more difficult to find a framework in which to sell digital content
Pricing easier to manage – libraries used to subscriptions	Different sales model required for libraries, while ebook models for individual purchase were less developed
DOIs and other structured systems make it very easy to handle articles	This has proved more of a challenge for books

quickly into online usage. Online journal models developed reasonably quickly and libraries were quick to see the opportunities in buying new services, so providing good models for the smaller players to adopt.

The production of specific journal issues still currently remains the dominant pattern for journal titles (as opposed to continuous publishing making articles available as and when they are ready), but the digitisation of content was more manageable and digital archive started to grow early on, so that now good digital archives exist; for key titles, previous print issues will also have been put into a digital archive. Even the peer review process could be integrated into the digital workflow, with authors delivering into a platform where readers could access review and carry out debates about the material (as mentioned above); manuscripts can be submitted directly to the journal front page within a publisher's catalogue too in some cases.

What current digital products look like and the challenges they face

In this section we will consider journals services first and then explore the different challenges facing monograph publishing.

Digital journal services

The digital products that have been developed therefore broadly take a similar structure: the articles are available in a digital format and users access them through a front end or portal, usually integrated into the library's own system, that allows them to search in various ways (from title and author to keywords) across the digital database to access either an issue as a whole or a specific article. Users therefore can search across a wide range of titles at once and hop between articles easily where links have been created. Additional benefits may include places to save past searches or build a reading list of titles, as well as the ability to explore other archives that may not be part of the full subscription package to see how relevant they may be. Individuals can also access these via portals on the web, and pay, according to their needs, a subscription or a pay per view/use/download price.

Benefits for users

Digital products such as these could clearly offer from the outset five unique features that overcame particular limitations of print:

- timely dissemination
- global access
- searchability
- discoverability
- more flexible use of content

Journal articles can be posted up as soon as they are available (suitably reviewed) online, even if they still have some link to a particular issue that might come out in print later down the line. In addition users can access these articles much more immediately: they do not necessarily have to wait until they get hold of a physical copy in the actual library; they can access the information from their desktop wherever they are. Products are searchable now in an easy to use web browser so reaching specific content or tracking down particular information is quick. Not only that, but discovering content one did not know about is quick too as the search allows for fortuitous discovery of other articles and information that might, for instance, appear in a journal from another discipline that might not normally be stocked. That also means that direct hypertext links can be made between titles, and not only titles owned by one publisher but across a series of titles. Titles can be grouped in different ways according to their users. Furthermore, with the texts accurately marked up and resting in a digital warehouse, they can be used in a variety of ways in the future as they can be accessed and formatted differently according to market needs; customised lists of readings, for instance, can be collected together and this may be valuable for some users.

Benefits for libraries

For the libraries too there are many benefits:

- measuring use
- flexible payment according to use
- fulfilling the demands of their customers
- value for money in purchasing

They can measure very effectively how the products are used. This can lead to different scenarios: they know how well used a journal is so they can justify keeping it on their list; but they can also see quickly what is not used enough and take it off their list. For more obscure journals they do not want to stock, they may be able to pay for access as and when necessary, by pay per view options, saving them money from stocking something in its entirety. They can also fulfil demand much more effectively as users do not have to wait to access the limited number of copies; users can access articles from wherever they are and a library can pay for a number of licences that allow several people to access the article at once. The management and access controls that many of these platforms have can also help the libraries understand their use and their users. Overall the libraries should be able to get better value for their money by buying more accurately according to the needs of their market.

The importance of usage

The production of digital information and in particular the considerable change in infrastructure that it required is costly, however, and libraries are not necessarily saving money as they have to accept that there are charges for obtaining the material in a more flexible format. The publishers also can see quite how critical a title is for a library with usage figures, and so both parties need to negotiate carefully to ensure fair pricing. This has meant deals have become more complex and customised.

The monitoring of use is important for publishers not just for their negotiation with libraries. In a competitive marketplace they need to show that their journals remain leaders in their fields. They will monitor citations, which they can track digitally in order to show which journals are most frequently cited. This is particularly important in the arena of society journals, where journals are put up for tender by their owners (the learned society) and publishers need to show how far they are able to promote the academic authority of the journal both in terms of wide and effective distribution (so that the material is picked up on quickly) and in terms of the quality of the content itself. It is this aspect of journal publishing that is important for academics too, as we have seen, and so the digital environment has made it easier for academics also to measure the success of their published output.

Product sales and deals

Users can buy digital products in various ways. Publishers will produce each individual title with a subscription price, which is often tiered with a print and electronic bundle, or an e-only or print-only option. This is just the start of what can be a quite an extensive menu of prices. There may be prices for institutions (which may indicate access for a number of people), as well as prices for individual subscribers wanting their own copies/access, and there may be prices for individual issues and archived issues; the relationships between these prices have been an active area of experimentation for many years.

However, the price for an institutional purchase is determined by the arrangements and negotiations between the libraries and the publishers. The size of an organisation as well as the type of people using the databases will also be taken into account. Publishers may put together collections of titles in different packages for libraries to choose from (e.g. Elsevier Science Direct). They will provide front end access to their journals so that users can search across them all and they may have premium levels that can, for instance, allow access to other journals on a need basis – so that organisations only pay where the user downloads a particular article. While the prices will be, to some extent, negotiated based on pricing menus, libraries may well end up with titles they do not want in their packages, but it can be difficult and expensive to tailor entirely a package to an individual institution's actual use; buying a package is usually the cheaper option. There will be bespoke options where customers can select from a range of titles within a package, though a minimum order will usually be required. There will be other levels of control around the ability to download entirely or print. Further aspects of added value (these are not necessarily always charged for, but form part of a title's competitive edge) can include:

- email updates about forthcoming issues
- online-first options
- citation alerts
- viewing samples or abstracts for marketing purposes

Some libraries may have their own front ends, to which they connect their different publisher materials, and there are arrangements (e.g. Shibboleth) that enable one main password to be assigned and used by an institution across a variety of products. In addition there is a drive towards multiple-year purchases – three- to five-year deals – and the importance of having access to non-subscribed journal content is growing.

Advances in usage analysis, as mentioned above, can help libraries get a very accurate picture of what is used and not used to enhance their negotiation power. Publishers can use this to their advantage too in sales pitches as they can clearly demonstrate how far journals are used and so prove they remain essential to the package. However, the changes do bring problems. The print subscription price and any special discounts applied to the whole deal were transparent. Prices now may be set with more knowledge of precise use but libraries have to be able to understand a whole range of different pricing mechanisms, and publishers have to ensure their customers are happy with the price and value of the product. But if librarians start to be more selective about their package it can act against publishers, who may be supporting smaller journals, still essential to research, on the basis that they are part of the package with journals that are used more extensively.

Aggregators

The other major way to access journals in digital environments is via an aggregator. They will collect journals together in packages from various publishers and present them via their own platform and front page. Their selling points will be based on their ability to allow searches across different publishers' products, select and package groups of materials appropriate to their customers, provide price benefits where their negotiations with publishers have allowed them to benefit from economies of scale due to their wide customer base, as well as effective management and control tools for librarians. These aggregators include people like MD Consult, ingentaconnect, EBESCO, Pro Quest, Gale – but there are also specific ones serving corporate markets like infotrieve, reprints desk. The benefit of getting the full range of subject relevant titles is clear but there can be problems with these where deals go wrong, and publishers can suspend or withdraw titles from these arrangements, leaving a library exposed. While aggregators are a key part of the market, the larger journal publishers see that by dominating an area they can sell their packages direct to their key market and will be strategically trying to advance their position in the market.

Nevertheless licensing to aggregators and other third parties remains a key part of a publishers' strategy. It is an additional sales channel with the following benefits:

- maximising reach and readership – which is critical also to authors/editors/societies
- allowing publishers to become involved in sales and distribution mechanisms they may not be able to access easily themselves – e.g. into different territories, within new formats, utilising new technologies
- ensuring wide access, one strategy in preventing piracy
- allowing content to be managed in different ways, but always ensuring copyright is protected
- enhancing sales revenue from the main market as some libraries will prefer to use third parties rather than go direct or work with consortia
- accessing new markets – e.g. institutions that may not focus on research but where students may find access valuable; individual consumers; pay per view access for the corporate market
- aggregators are extremely well integrated into libraries and spend a lot of money focusing on the technology which is their USP, so they are a critical market

The challenges for digital journals

Changes from the print business models

So for publishers the business models revolves around the following:

- subscriptions on a title by title or package by package basis
- library and library consortia purchase of titles and/or articles
- bespoke licensing to customers
- licensing to aggregators

This has not changed markedly from the print model, in that subscriptions still form the foundation for the product sales, but there are challenges in these business models specific to the digital context, which include:

- investment in product development
- authoring
- financial strength of smaller journals
- the challenge of open access

The ability to customise, pick and mix and supply to aggregators has required considerable investment in digital platforms and workflow in order to manage content in a way that can be used in these many different outputs. The importance of being able to connect to third parties such as aggregators means the development of protocols has been critical to publishers' successful development of their content, ensuring their content is in a format standardised enough to be used by different people within different platforms. This comes at a cost and requires a lot of development work up front.

For authors (or journal owner such as the learned society) this means a change in various aspects of the process. The way they deliver work is now much more controlled by the workflow system of the publisher, and authors may have to work within new digital environments when they deliver and edit their work. Their material is being accessed in a variety of ways. This can lead to increased royalties as there are wider opportunities for access, and contracts need to cover different types of payments for different types of access (e.g. pay per view, usage rates or volume sales rates). It is worth noting that the contracts for journal articles and monographs in this arena have covered digital rights very clearly for some time, and while early backlist titles do need to be re-evaluated in terms of digital rights, the problems around author rights and contracts have been less than for the trade market.

Assessing success in terms of the financial strength of a journal can be more involved. In print it was transparent, as one could assess success title by title. Now content may be much more embedded in the package deal and assessing the success of an individual title can be more tricky. The profit and loss of a title is more complex and this may change the premise on which some journals survive; this does not necessarily mean the end of small journals: some journals may find that life as a pay per view title on the outskirts of a package rejuvenates them with new revenues; with lower costs for production and distribution they can survive on lower revenue. But equally, as mentioned above, journals may find themselves under pressure if good levels of active usage are not proven: important titles that have niche markets may suffer as their purchase cannot be justified by librarians, and as margins with publishers remain under pressure there is less profit on the larger titles to support the specialist ones. The support a learned society provides for certain specialist journals is critical. This once again opens the debate over whether if the journal is already subsidised it should then be commercially exploited by a publishing company.

The move to the digital environment has been swift in this area, so fast that the print products are declining rapidly and in some cases are no longer produced except on demand. The STM arena in particular has been quick to move. To some extent this reflects the range of product needs outlined above: digital products have so many advantages over print ones. But it also is because the internet was already being used in this way by researchers – unlike some professional markets, where users might still very often show a preference for using print, the scientific community had already converted to working and using material in an online space. Critical to creating the products was the workflow, which was digitised relatively quickly, and libraries, as the main customers, had already evolved into highly computerised spaces so could migrate to digital products quickly; this meant that print has become less important for users. As early as 2005 online revenue for one publisher surpassed its print revenue; for another, print titles are simply print on demand now.

The open access challenge

Ensuring research is freely accessible over the internet has become an issue that journals publishers are increasingly having to face, the remit to disseminate becoming more compelling now that it easier to achieve. Copyright systems have evolved seeking to further enable the electronic dissemination of research (as we will see later in this chapter and in Chapter 10) and open access has become a key topic for debate among scholarly publishers and research institutions.

One element of this has been the growth of self-archiving. Institutions have developed their own archives where their researchers lodge their work. There is a register of open access repositories of this sort. These institutional repositories may well have self-archiving mandates ensuring that their researchers must archive work undertaken while working for that institution. There are various organisations that are involved in this aspect of open access, ensuring continued access to these archives is available.

In theory, therefore, research like this is openly available and anyone can access it for free. But, as we have seen, peer review is important for journal articles. Articles cannot simply be lodged in any form without some sort of assessment of quality and accuracy. Here, therefore, remains a barrier to research being openly available immediately. Some sort of peer review needs to take place. In many ways this becomes the critical arena where publishers can add value. Where self-archiving happens, the actual article does not have to be the final version, as might be produced by a publisher, but does need to be post the refereeing stage, so it could, for instance, be a final draft before it is officially published; this is important as it still allows for a publisher to play a part of the process even where there is self-archiving. The fact the material is free at some point in its life cycle goes some way to answering those who suggest that research needs to be available for all to use and benefit from.

Open access models

Self-archiving is only one element of the picture. Open access has developed along two main lines: Green Open Access (green OA) and Gold Open Access (gold OA). Green OA is essentially the self-archiving outlined above: it is important to note that the repositories used can also be centralised (such as PubMed Central) and there are many well-established ones that are not necessarily associated with a particular institution. The issue of green OA is evolving, and in some cases, where a publisher is involved, green OA can refer to journals where a subscription is paid for access to material for a certain amount of time before it becomes available for free. Gold OA essentially refers to an open access journal that is available through a publisher's website. The publisher manages the journal but it is open access at all times and so all articles are available free to all users. It may be that they receive a fee for managing a journal on behalf of a learned society which covers costs to enable the open access, or individual authors or their institutions contribute to the cost.

The challenge has been for publishers to look closely at these models and see how they can still be involved, not just from the point of view of the peer review process but as part of the academic drive towards increasing accessibility, while maintaining some commercial viability. So, for instance, hybrid open access journals will have parts of the journal only accessible via subscription and others that are open access (obviously something only possible for internet journals, where various access controls can be set up to manage this). To fund the open access parts of such journals the author has to pay (or more commonly their institution) if their article is to be open access. This leads to the issue that again the research is being paid for twice – once by the institution which funds the research itself and then again for it to be disseminated. For leading journals, which can be expensive to maintain, a hybrid approach can provide an option for authors to be published in those key journals while fulfilling any open access remit their institution may demand. Publishers can maintain the quality of the journal with these different revenue streams.

Publishers have developed a further model to marry a commercial journal with the remit to disseminate it. For certain non-open access journals which are paid for as usual by subscriptions, licences or pay per view on an embargo basis exist so that articles become open access after a certain amount of time, commonly six to twelve months. Given the speed with which research moves in certain disciplines this can be beneficial to publishers, who maximise this commercial viability up front; by the time research falls into the public domain its value is much decreased. However, with the obligation for research to be available to researchers this model can be contentious as key research cannot be accessed easily or freely until it is becoming out of date.

To develop these hybrid models further publishers are focusing on the concept of serving the author's needs; if authors pay for their material to be included (subject to peer review), rather than simply self-archiving, they can get a wider service from the publisher. For some journals authors can choose the level of involvement, the tiers of accessibility; so, for instance, Springer offers a menu of open access options for a selection of its journals.

There are several benefits publishers can bring to authors over the self-archived systems, including:

- the ability to track citations
- interaction with a high-quality review process
- help in managing their rights effectively
- protection against piracy
- marketing, keeping the profile of the journal high
- effective sales activity, also improving the profile

These last two points are important – keeping a journal's profile high plays a critical part in ensuring wider dissemination of research; these journals, actively and continuously promoted by publishers, may well be much better known than an institution's own archive.

The problem remains with these systems, however, that the peer review process has to be paid for somehow. Not only that, the cost of running journals is expensive because of the technological infrastructure, which needs to innovate continually to provide accessible, easily searchable content across an endlessly increasing body of work. Institutions looking to move away from formal journal arrangements with publishers can find themselves debating the cost of setting up and managing their own easily accessible archives; they may well end up paying a third party to maintain a CMS for them, in which case they have not necessarily moved very far away from the published route.

But there are attractions to rethinking the way journals are managed, particularly in relation to speed. Currently the peer review process is not necessarily speedy, which can delay important time-sensitive research. Authors publishing in journals have to undertake more detailed editorial work, delaying them when they could be concentrating on the next stage of their research. When speed is of the issue can the current journals model really fulfil the researcher's needs? Articles are not in essence any different from the printed version; some interactivity may be of more benefit to the process of research.

While some of these institutions are exploring alternative ways to manage the peer review process, publishers too are having to review each stage of the journals process in order to innovate and satisfy some of these key issues. They need to add value to ensure their well-established publishing mechanisms remain critical to the academic community. Keeping ahead at managing aspects such as citations, impact factors, etc., building premium services with alerts, bulletins, etc., and marketing effectively are important parts of what a publisher can offer.

Governmental drive to more open access

As the debates and business models around open access evolve, there is a growing momentum in the public sector to force the move to open access. Government-funded research projects are increasingly including a requirement for researchers to publish via open access. The EC is currently considering a proposal of this sort with its £64 million research funding programme; pilot schemes and extensive consultation are underway to explore it. The Working Group on Expanding Access (the Finch Committee) in the UK is another example of a government examining the process of publishing academic material; in this case the working group is conducting a review of the way open access could, and possibly should, work for the dissemination of research, further defining the green and gold academic approaches. Green open access is beginning to become a firmer concept whereby green journals can charge a subscription for a limited embargo period with a defined length of time, currently subject to debate; the gold system is in many ways preferred by publishers, who will gain some sort of funding via the research funder, and so make the material available on open access from the start; research funding on this basis would therefore need to include some allowance to cover the cost of dissemination. These debates will continue and the scholarly publishing industry has consistently to establish the importance of its work within the academic community.

The monograph: the scholarly publisher's next challenge

We have looked at the key developments and current challenges facing the journals publisher, but the issue of digital environment for monographs has yet to be tackled as fully as for journals and the industry has been turning its attention to this area more recently. Monographs as a type of published research work have, over the last few years, suffered a decline. Academic libraries, facing the pressure to spend increasing amounts on their digital provision of journals, have made savings by cherry picking more carefully titles for their monograph lists. Academic presses therefore have had to respond in various ways, whether turning their main focus to textbooks or supplementary books that may have a longer shelf life in paperback or reducing their range of topics in order to consolidate on a particular discipline and build expertise there. University presses, which were responsible for considerable monograph output, particularly in the US, have often been put under pressure to become more commercial and have had to reduce their monograph output despite their remit to advance research through publishing. So the market in print form is declining and both the numbers of titles and the quantities printed have reduced. So what impact can the digital environment have?

Print on demand

One solution to the problems monograph publishing faces that has emerged with the advent of digital publishing is the ability to print on demand. While just in time printing was already developing for short reprint runs, the digital environment makes this even easier to manage. Academic publishers were accustomed to building up dues on a title until the numbers reached a sufficient quantity to make it worth reprinting. Libraries had to wait for a reprint, but usually, if they wanted to fill in a gap in their collection, were willing to do so in order to receive the title eventually. Now print on demand is so flexible it can be put in place for every individual who asks for a single copy of something at the point they ask for it. This has not had much effect on the monograph price for the library but does mean that publishers can save money on stock holding and management, and, as such, keep some monograph publishing alive (and indeed supplementary text material) which it might otherwise not be possible to maintain. Print on demand exists for other sectors too but it has arguably been most fully integrated into the workflow of an academic house, and often purchasers may not know if a title has been designated print on demand when they order it.

Increased access for monographs

Researchers see great opportunities in being able to access monograph research material. Mass digitising of books such as Google has undertaken has helped to develop an expectation amongst researchers that they can access older material that previously may have been difficult to find; this has been important for driving usage in research monographs, and participation in book search initiatives like this, which aid discoverability for specialised titles, has been of benefit to some publishers in growing sales of their own titles. It increases the long tail of the monograph. For authors too it is significant as it increases discoverability of specialist works, so increasing the potential for wider dissemination.

Problems for the monograph

The main problems for a digital monograph programme revolve around:

- the archive – the length of time and cost required to build an archive
- different purchasing patterns for a library – the change from an individual purchase to a subscription service

Creating the archive

Creating ebooks for any new titles does not in principle create a problem: digital workflow for new titles coming in is well established. Monographs are available and marketed individually in ebook format and can slot into a library's own e-resources catalogue. However, the older titles, the important backlist, may remain in print form only. We have seen above that the book has taken longer to adapt than the journal to the digital environment. There are digitisation challenges for the longer form of the monograph, which short journal articles do not face. There may be more complex issues of consistency across the text, and effective searching across longer pieces of work and the ability to 'chunk' books is challenging. A monograph is less likely to be standardised across the whole list, but rather designed to have stylistic integrity within itself.

The creation of an ongoing digital archive, due to the longer development times required for a book, is slower than that for journals, while the cost of digitising large numbers of older titles is expensive, particularly given the lack of standardisation across titles. Different production methods used throughout the last century lead to a variety of different approaches needed to turn the book into digital format. The archive frameworks for storing and presenting digital monographs are also not as fully developed as the digital environments for managing journal articles. Different publishers have different approaches to digitising older monographs. One will take the view that if it is asked for a digital version that is the prompt to produce one. Others are taking a systematic approach to developing an archive. Sometimes the only record of the book is the print edition itself, which then needs to be scanned and verified. This covers titles that are held by the publisher and still in copyright. Google's involvement in mass digitising of archive titles is covered in the case study in Chapter 10, but it too has found issues with regard to the quality of the texts it has scanned in, and has tackled the need to verify text that may be unclear from simple scanning in different innovative ways.

The sales model for electronic monographs and portals

There are problems in the sales models too. The availability of ebooks does not mean that libraries will purchase them; libraries will be making decisions as to whether the cost of paying for access to ebooks is worth it, with different criteria in mind from their decisions with regard to journals, where their expectation of migration from print is further advanced (if not complete). Selling packages of journal subscriptions is more effective in terms of sales effort than the selling of an individual book in print or in ebook format, so the market here is less developed in comparison: titles tend to be selected individually, or in small batches, and the purchase once made is not reviewed as it is a one-off payment. Nor is the cost of an ebook monograph going to provide much saving for a library – the cost of the book as a whole still needs to be covered (royalties, marketing, etc.) despite some savings on physical printing and distribution. While for textbooks the availability of an ebook is of more use to a library in providing online access for a number of users at once, this is less critical for often highly specialised research books, which may be of relevance to only a few users.

Meanwhile, for archives, the pricing and the range of content available can prove more problematical than for journals in that libraries may well be expected to pay a subscription to products they previously bought individually for a one-off price, and so owned within their own print archive. Converting libraries to a different business model therefore makes this a more difficult project for publishers and does depend on them being able to offer a comprehensive list as well as depth of output within particular disciplines. However, despite these hindrances, the move is clearly towards more electronic delivery of these products and the sales model is beginning to adapt.

Book-based services and adding value

Publishers have started to create more complex digital products. They have taken a similar approach to journals in that the focus on new product development has been in developing portals to access an archive of digital book content. Similar benefits to journals portals apply, such as the ability to search across a range of titles and pinpoint relevant material within a book. Integrating these with the journals databases too makes a compelling offering. For smaller publishers there are opportunities to join groups in order to make their publications available: Oxford University Press and Cambridge University Press both have programmes of this sort gaining a level of critical mass.

Some of the large aggregators offer such services as well, such as Dawsonera or MyiLibrary, set up by Ingrams and ebrary; these may include an element of ebook and document management services for libraries to maximise their book collections.

Yet the creation of a database of content is potentially an important strategy for academic publishers; as with the journals industry, the value that publishers hold is exactly the fact that they have a large database, continuously evolving, which can be used in different ways, flexibly and future proofed. Putting book content also into a database and treating it almost like a raw data set may be the way to ensure monograph-style material can survive. Making it easy to reuse in different ways (for instance linked to teaching resource material in the form of textbooks or put together in different ways to create new collections) may be an important part of keeping the material live.

For some the development of digital publishing programmes for scholarly books may help rejuvenate the monograph. It can help this declining market in various ways:

- books can live on the long tail and still be accessed when needed, continuing to build citations where journals may well not
- authors will get more discoverability in searches – books can rank as well in citations on Google Scholar as journals
- cross-disciplinary learning can take place much more easily, particularly for more book-based disciplines
- there is wider access to titles beyond the research community

In the longer term there will be increased convergence between journal and book publishing as they will be increasingly integrated.

Future directions: problems and opportunities

Declining budgets

While an onlooker may have considered the digital environment to be one where libraries could save money, as publishers were saving print and physical distribution costs, the key benefits of online access – those of timeliness, accessibility and discoverability – have come at a cost. Though they should be able to increase the value they get for their spending, libraries are rarely able to reduce budgets in any significant way.

The scholarly market faces one main problem around which there are many issues: research output is increasing but library budgets are often flat or decreasing. In some global markets there will be growth, but in the majority of western economies, where research continues to be extremely active, there is increasing pressure on libraries. As the research communities continue to evolve, so increasing specialisation (especially in the scientific arena) requires more specialised journals, thus increasing the number of titles a research institution needs to purchase. This pressure on budgets is not going to go away.

Are publishers necessary?

We have also seen the challenges that publishers face in the light of issues such as open access. Publishers have to justify their role in scholarly publishing and show why, even in the changing environment, they remain critical to the arena. Issues around quality and prestige clearly play a part in this as publishers have developed highly effective processes to manage research. Investment in sophisticated search engines and data warehouses also plays a part. Many publishers also own many important journal archives, which will always make them important players.

However, sales and marketing activity is also key to what publishers can offer. Maintaining the prestige of a journal is important as more journals are developed: the competitive edge of a title is critical to its continued place in the market. Institutions doing their own archiving may find it difficult, and certainly costly, to continue the sort of marketing presence a professional publisher can provide. Learned societies may very well value a publisher's marketing and PR investment and expertise highly as a way to ensure the profile of their society is preserved; that way they can continue to attract excellent contributions and so maintain their prestige. In the battle over which journal's portal dominates, it can be important for a journal that is establishing itself to be accessible and searchable via another key title with that publisher. As publishers develop more integrated platforms (developing integrated books/journal material) authors may also find they want to be part of that.

Philanthropy

One important area that has improved is internet distribution to markets which previously would have found research difficult to access. Developing economies have in the past benefited from various schemes to allow for production of cheaper versions of print products to ensure they can still access research that may be critical for their continued development. However, a physical product still has limitations and full costs that cannot always be subsidised, while online some of these barriers to wider distribution are removed. Various organisations have a remit to ensure research can be accessed by poorer economies, and the proliferation of these in recent years has been a reflection of the ease with which material can be managed in an online environment. Selected journals can be accessed in different ways, and these may involve reduced or no fees for users. For instance, the Hinari programme set up by the World Health Organisation (WHO) enables organisations in developing countries to access health and biomedical research; it works alongside similar organisations focusing on different disciplinary areas, like Access to Global Online Research in Agriculture (AGORA), Online Access to Research in the Environment (OARE) and Access to Research for Development and Innovation (ARDI). These and other organisations are building important relationships with research publishers.

Future research models with public peer review

We know the process of peer review will be an issue that challenges the academic community and there are examples of open access journals that are looking at ways to manage this without the involvement of publishers. These stem from various motives. They are not just a way to manage peer review with a reduced cost base, nor is re-engineering the review process simply a way to improve speed to market; but they also embrace some of the democratic ethics that surround the internet with what is called public peer review. There are examples of journals applying a more interactive peer review process which allows for mechanisms of continuous reviewing and updating until a final article is approved.

What this means is that articles are posted up in a very early stage, with the understanding that they may not be tried and tested fully. Official referees will be designated to review a paper but other people may contribute at any point as well as make use of some of the findings if they choose before final peer review. They could be posted as discussion papers only. This in effect tries to combine a conference and journals approach, allowing for online discussion of material that may lead to improvements of a greater degree than would be contained in a traditional peer review environment (which broadly works on one draft at a time with less ongoing input).

The argument is that this allows for the maximum amount of input and the finished work may be much better than it would have been; the research itself started its journey into the community at the earliest possible stage, allowing for fruitful development by others. Authors too feel the pressure to submit better work as it will be viewed publicly at the earliest stage. Of course there are also criticisms:

- there may be problems with the motives of some of those who review documents
- the potentially competitive nature of the discipline may distort the process
- there may be problems where people cannot distinguish between good research in progress and research that will not ultimately pass the process
- inadequate research may start to be used before it has been properly reviewed
- the final article may never quite be fully formed and finished off

There are ways of managing these issues, but they may require more cost. However, this represents a slightly different approach to research that may be a threat to publishers unless they move forward.

Conclusion

For publishers to withstand these sorts of pressures they need to maintain their relevance to the fast-moving arena in which they operate. So where next for academic publishing? When looking at the future there are a number of directions publishers are exploring and new debates that are surfacing:

- New sales models will be developing around more specific understanding of usage and the experimentation around the open access arena.
- There may well be new ways of working as users interact with systems and the line between writer, contributor and user becomes more blurred.
- Strategic reading/data mining/data access will customise products further – as customers get more access to the raw data warehouse and only take what they really need.
- Content may also change – the individual journal issue may well disappear entirely and the ongoing nature of the review process can be interrogated and accessed throughout the process.
- Sources of content are likely to change, with BRICs economies increasingly providing content as well as buying it. Many companies have had sales and marketing sites across Asia, for instance, but editorial offices are growing in number too.
- A particular advantage of the internet is that definitions of book and journal articles can change – a piece of academic work can be any length and not limited to

a traditional article or book format, so the opportunities to publish material in whatever is the most appropriate way are opening up. Publishers are moving to offer spaces for researchers to publish material that does not have to adhere to a predefined length or format (such as Palgrave Pivot).

- Continuous product development will need to keep pace with technological developments – product development will move on from search and archive to making content useable in different ways – using, for instance, the semantic web to draw connections, linking data and extracting different sorts of data such as diagrams.
- Adding value will need to become more sophisticated as users become more accustomed to expecting certain features as standard (such as email alerts) rather than as add-ons.
- Version control will become critical as there will be increasing time sensitivity around access as research moves into the public domain.
- Integrated platforms will emerge as there is likely to be increased convergence between journals and book publishing as they use the same systems.
- There will be more integration with the wider internet via search engines and a more seamless route to the content.
- Access issues will remain key – ubiquity and mobility. It is not just about accessing content from where you happen to be (e.g. via mobile phone, which will require reworking material to make it useable in small-screen formats) but accessing it from what you happen to be doing; in this way research becomes embedded into the tools you might use.
- There will be increasing debates about economy of attention – how long is information used for? And how long does it have value? Or how does that value change in terms of its longevity?
- Measures of usage will change as libraries look at new ways to assess the value of research products to their work.
- Business models are continuing to be developed outside publishing (e.g. from academia itself, from crowd-funding).
- Public sector pressure on access will also continue to force the sector to make information freely available.
- Timeliness will also continue to be an area for improvement as research gathers pace and readers expect less and less delay.

With all these we come back to the central tenets of research – timeliness, accessibility and discoverability. Ultimately publishers will need to ensure they remain ahead on these key areas in order to maintain their position. The relationship between publisher and academia will remain a special one that will need to continue to evolve and change as the digital economy develops.

Further reading and resources

Books

Campbell, Robert, Pentz, Ed and Borthwich, Ian (eds). *Academic and Professional Publishing*. Chandos, 2012.
Clark, Giles and Phillips, Angus. *Inside Book Publishing*, Routledge, 2008.

Cope, Bill and Phillips, Angus (eds). *The Future of the Academic Journal*. Chandos, 2009.
Mincic-Obradovic, Ksenija. *E-books in Academic Libraries*, Chandos, 2010.
Thompson, John. *Books in the Digital Age*. Polity, 2005.

Websites

Some examples of journal portals and open access sites:
ejournals.ebsco.com – for journals sites
www.credoreference.com – for journals sites
www.dawsonera.com – for ebook aggregators
www.doaj.org – for journals sites
www.ebrary.com – for ebook aggregators
www.ingentaconnect.com – for journals sites
www.jstor.org – for journals sites
www.myilibrary.com – for ebook aggregators
www.ncbi.nlm.nih.gov/pubmed
www.plos.org – for journals sites

Examples of publishers:

journals.cambridge.org
onlinelibrary.wiley.com
online.sagepub.com – for publisher's own site
www.alpsp.org/Ebusiness/Home.aspx – for other relevant organisations
www.jisc.ac.uk/aboutus.aspx – for other relevant organisations
www.oxfordjournal.org
www.springerlink.com – for publisher's own site
www.stm-assoc.org – for other relevant organisations
www.tandfonline.com
www.wileyopenaccess.com
www.wolterskluwerhealth.com/pages/welcome.aspx – for publisher's own site

Questions to consider

1   What are the benefits for a learned society of continuing to work with a publisher?
2   How can a publisher resolve the question of critical mass in relation to the development of a digital service where they might have strengths in some disciplines and weaknesses in others?
3   Can publishers help libraries manage budgetary issues?
4   How might publishers balance the need for stable revenues and profits with the costs of investing continually in publishing technologies?
5   Some experts foresee a further consolidation among the key industry players. What problems might that pose?

8   Developments in digital publishing in the education market

In this chapter we will cover:

1   The educational publishing context, outlining the background to the textbook markets at both schools and higher education (HE) levels with reference to the differences between the UK and US markets
2   Characteristics of the schools market in terms of publishing and development of classroom technologies and learning resources
3   What current digital resources for schools look like and the challenges they face as the business model develops
4   Current developments in digital resources at the HE level, with developments in e-learning
5   The e-textbook for schools and HE markets, including a look at the iBook textbook
6   How educational publishing houses are developing digital assets and the challenges they face going forward

Introduction

The education market quickly recognised the potential in the advances in digital technology for presenting an exciting and interactive teaching and learning environment. However, this market is a much more price-sensitive market than some and so it is a challenge to build digital products that are comprehensive in their application of technology while cost effective. Schools cannot spend a large amount of their annual budget on digital resources, which also require significant investment in technology; students, who are the purchasers of texts in the higher education market, are often burdened with course fees and living expenses, which means that they have little left to spend on textbooks. Yet to make the texts visually enticing, truly interactive and significantly different from a print book is a costly business. One of the biggest problems for publishers is how far the print and digital products remain linked and reflect each other. Pedagogy would suggest that digital products could and should be significantly different from a textbook but this transition is a difficult one for publishers, and indeed teachers, to make.

This chapter will consider these challenges and explore how far the industry has moved towards transforming itself into a more digital-based business. It covers the characteristics of the markets and the development of technology within the classroom in order to understand the environment for digital products. Looking first at the schools market it describes how the industry has developed products, exploring some of the key issues publishers face here. It then looks at the issues around developing e-textbooks in both the schools and HE sectors, including the opportunities and threats surrounding Apple's focus on the education market. While some issues are similar across both schools and HE markets, a further section explores some of the distinctive products available to students and the changing approach publishers are taking to the sectors. Finally, it looks at some of the future directions for the education market as a whole.

Context: introduction to the textbook market

Textbooks in the US and UK markets

When looking at the area of education there are various distinctions to bear in mind. In general the focus of this chapter is on schools publishing. However, education publishing can encompass the production of textbooks for HE and academic audiences. These are sometimes dealt with within the context of academic publishing, at other times as part of educational publishing. Because the focus is on the type of book, i.e. a textbook to be used as part of day-to-day learning, both schools and HE markets will be considered in this chapter. This section explains some of the characteristics of these sectors in the US and UK.

Schools and HE textbooks: the US market

It is important to understand the differences between the UK and US because publishers have to adopt different strategies for each, even global companies such as Pearson. This can influence the way digital products are developed. The US market operates differently from the UK one in both the schools and the HE textbook sectors. Textbooks in the US can command large markets at both levels and, since companies are playing for high stakes, the cost of developing texts in a highly competitive environment is considerable. For both sectors the development process for the book is detailed and extensive; the production is costly as textbooks are long (in order to cover as much as could possibly be needed and so to be a one-stop shop) and are generally published in hardback and full colour. A market-leading macroeconomics text for university students can cost around $150, while a school text can cost $50. The structures in place to sell these books are highly organised as sales people focus on claiming large-scale adoptions; and the costs of texts, whether borne by students in the HE market or institutions in the schools market, are therefore exceptionally high. As we will see, technology has played a part in the ability to supply interactive and multimedia materials to add value around the core text in the form of resources that are used by teachers and students. Nevertheless the cost of these has to be covered in some way by the book itself, so prices continue to be very high in the US market at both the schools and HE level.

The effect of adoptions for schools and HE

Various mechanisms around adoptions exist as a result. In schools it is quite common for texts to be chosen at state level, and so for the successful text an extremely large and guaranteed market exists. For this market the result is that the cost of books is high as publishers aim to produce the most comprehensive and enriched textbook they can in order to win the adoption. So the cost of investing in a set of textbooks to use for a course in school is considerable. Therefore the books schools use often have to last for a long time, which means at the end of their life they are often out of date – something that becomes significant when looking at the potential for digital products.

In universities lecturers sit on boards to select the key texts that are to be used and there is generally a high expectation that students have to purchase them in some way or other. The challenge of the adoption is that the publisher must persuade the lecturers to use their text, but it is the students that must actually buy the text. As Figure 8.1 shows, the student, though the main customer, is only a small part of the cycle and often the one most distant from the publisher's sales effort. As publishers at both levels compete to win what can be a large adoption, the books have become enhanced first in terms of production quality and comprehensiveness of content, then with a variety of other products and services that support students or teachers. Figure 8.2 illustrates the constant developments required to keep competitive. To cover these developments the cost of the books increases, but for lecturers who have got used to choosing

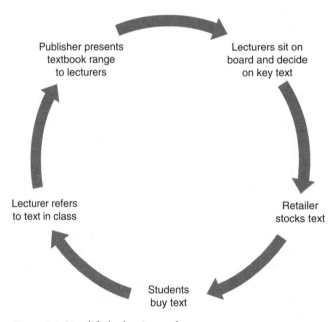

Figure 8.1 Simplified adoption cycle.

| Textbook covers the course | Text gets bigger, more colour, more coverage, more questions | Add more resources for the lecturer | Add more resources for the student | Add more interactivity for both | Lecturers can feel they must adopt the text but the cost of the text is now high |

Figure 8.2 The drive to the bigger, better textbook.

full-colour texts with all sorts of additional web-based resources it is difficult to go backwards; they aim to choose the best for their students and that usually means the biggest and most comprehensive book.

At the HE end of the market in the US the result has been the development of a sophisticated used books market which enables students to realise some of the value in the book once they have no need of it. It also allows bookshops to engage in a second-hand market which holds higher margins for them than new textbooks. In order to preserve sales the publishers have responded by putting pressure on new edition cycles as the first-year sales of a new book are more critical to make up the costs of producing the book; previously second- and third-year sales were more significant to making profit. There is also a book rental market where books can be rented for a semester: Amazon, for instance, do this in the US; a student can then have a new book, but pay a much smaller price, returning it at the end of their course.

As the price is so high lecturers are also aware that value for money is important, so customisation or course packs become attractive as users get exactly what they need rather than pay for material they are not going to use. Companies specialising in putting course packs together, where lecturers can use materials from a variety of publishers, have developed in this market. Similarly, publishers have found it useful to create libraries of material so that they can then offer, for instance, a bank of case studies from which lecturers can pick and mix. Here again, one can see opportunities provided by digital publishing to allow for further customisation.

It is in the US market that Apple has focused its attention on the launch of its iPad-based textbook programme for both higher-level schools publishing and the introductory end of the college and universities market; one of Apple's tenets is that the average US textbook is simply too expensive and yet is failing to do what is needed to provide a good and effective learning experience. We will look at this in more detail later in the chapter (p. 102).

Schools and HE texts: the UK market

In the UK and European markets these issues still exist but they are much diluted. As the markets are much smaller and the money within the market is less, price sensitivity is a more critical driving force in the sector. On average textbook prices are much lower; the same macroeconomics text adapted for the UK market may cost £37, while a schools text that may cover more than one year of a course can be around £17. The pressure on winning adoptions is still there but less so than in the US as the financial stakes are lower, and though sales activity does focus on trying to promote adoptions, there is not such a formalised way of approaching these at either schools or higher education level.

Schools

The UK schools market is not driven by the adoption culture in quite the same way as in the US, though of course it exists; groups of teachers will adopt a text that can be used across classes and levels by different teachers at different times to ensure consistency of approach. However, the prices of books are considerably lower than for the US market and there is a more adaptable approach to the mixing and matching of textbooks (particularly at the primary school level) within the classroom, though, in general, the drive to pass particular courses is central to the development of any textbook programme. The books may cost less but schools budgets are also lower, so winning an adoption is still a critical part of the sales process for a publisher. Well-designed and comprehensive support materials remain an important way to attract an adoption; some of these are expensive, and detailed teacher guides to delivering a course based on a certain textbook are sold alongside the student packs, but there will also be resources available for free.

HE sector

In the case of higher education, while lecturers may recommend texts and, in some cases, work very closely with them in the course of their teaching, the choice of texts tends to be reasonably individual in comparison to the US; there are also somewhat lower expectations that the students will need to have their own copy of the book. With smaller class sizes compared to the US it can be easier for a student to keep up with their studies without extreme dependence on a book. Clearly there are some subjects that are driven more by the need to have textbooks than others, and in the social science and science arena set texts are still particularly important, but the prices are much lower than in the US, even for textbooks adapted from US courses for a UK/European market. Support materials are provided, though on a much smaller scale than for US texts; they are broadly free, however, in order to attract adoptions.

HE courses in any case are structured differently, with less emphasis on large numbers taking similar introductory courses before specialising around specific subjects. In the UK students tend to study a more focused programme of topics around their subject area rather than take some general courses before specialising; courses from the first year can therefore be more varied than is often in the case in the US, where students across a whole campus may all be doing similar course choices in their first year. There is also a greater likelihood of academic publishers in the UK who publish monographs and journals also producing textbooks for university markets; in the US key textbook publishers tend to have consolidated in the HE textbook market.

So it is useful to bear in mind these distinctions between schools and HE market as the drivers in these markets are slightly different. Some aspects of these markets are similar: for instance, in both the UK and US schools do not always have the resources to invest in the hardware needed to support the digital products. However, there are also some differences. The price issue between the US and the UK is an important one which makes the introduction of the Apple textbook product more critical to the US market (see the case study on p. 102); but the US market can command higher investment in digital products as the financial stakes are higher.

Characteristics of the schools market for publishing

In order to understand the reasons why digital publishing has developed for the schools market in the way it has it is important to note some the drivers of the market in general. In the development of digital products there are two important facets to the schools market:

- the curriculum – which drives any sort of publishing for this market, both print and digital
- the technology – which provided the infrastructure to develop digital products within schools

The curriculum drive for publishers

Key to the development of textbooks for the schools market is the curriculum. In primary school in the UK this is focused on the development of a national curriculum, for which books do exist but which can be used flexibly, interlinked with the teacher's own materials. The particular focus of the curriculum is literacy and maths. Literacy programmes in particular are big business for publishers, as using printed books is central to the teaching of reading in the early years: developing reading schemes can take up to around 50 per cent of a primary publisher's budget, for instance. As educational pedagogy changes, different emphasis is given to different aspects of primary teaching, and so products suited to these new pedagogical trends have a role. For instance, the use of phonics is, at times, more central to the teaching of literacy than at other times (when it is used alongside other literacy methods). Educational software companies are also active in this market, producing programmes that can be used to individualise teaching for each pupil or to reinforce learning; as long as there is access to the technology these can be used alongside teaching with texts. As teacher's own materials play an important role in teaching at primary school, publishers also focus on producing resource packs (anything from photocopiable sheets for spelling home-work to online music resources for non-specialist teachers) that support flexible teaching within the classroom.

By secondary school in the UK the national curriculum continues and introduces more subjects: students will generally use textbooks that follow each subject, sometimes designed to build into a three-year programme which takes them through the whole subject up to age 16. There will be areas where teachers can make some selections as to which topics to cover in more detail (e.g. history topics or English texts). From age 14 the curriculum is superseded by the detailed specifications set up by exam boards for each subject leading the GCSEs at age 16. Teaching at 16–18 is completely determined by the specification being followed, whether academic (A levels) or vocational (BTEC or OCR National). This is similar for qualifications in a further education framework or for various vocational qualifications that are available at various ages. So from this one can see that the focus on curricula is important for publishers in this market, and especially the focus on exam board texts.

The trend in the UK has been for more exam-specific texts to be produced. The boards often put up for tender the opportunity to be the main publisher for a particular course book. Edexcel is an example of taking this further: Pearson owns this exam board (part of its remit is to become a key player in the area of assessment globally, which we will touch on again on p. 106) and so Edexcel textbooks tend to be produced by Pearson, though Edexcel will endorse texts by other publishers. This specific arrangement may not last, but the principle is that if there is an exam board text, then teachers have to be reasonably confident of other texts if they decide they are not going to use it; and if they are anxious to ensure that they give their students the best outcome and that they do what is needed to pass, they can often feel they need to adopt the endorsed text to be safe. The advantage of such texts is not just one of focusing very closely on the sorts of questions students will face, but that they represent value for money for the school in that it buys a text which only covers what pupils need to know – i.e. it is not paying for extraneous material that is not required learning. Even where a textbook is not endorsed specifically by an exam board (and some authors are so well known in their own right that teachers will still use those texts above an endorsed one), resources mapping the text onto a specific curriculum are provided. So as exam board texts drive the schools publishing at that level publishers inevitably enter the new edition cycle as driven by the exam board. When the exam changes, the texts will need to change, which requires investment from the schools to buy into the new texts. Even for those levels which do not have exams, the push to keep renewing texts in order to get the most up-to-date one is still important.

Teachers' resources are also important at the secondary level, with books covering a range of support materials such as printable resources, lesson plans, practical exercises and assessment activities in print and online formats. The thrust of much of schools publishing is around the development of a 'course', often branded, as a group of text-books that work through each year, together with support books (maybe working on skills) to supplement each stage and teaching resources in print and online. Pedagogical thinking around learning styles, flexible teaching and ways to cater for different levels go into designing these courses, so schools will often have to buy into packages and be sure that they can get their full value out of their investment.

Blended learning, the mix of styles of teaching and learning from face-to-face to online support, has played a part here; the curriculum now includes more digital requirements (partly in order to ensure increased access to learning), so digital support has become a more integral part of the overall adoption of a textbook. The trend to more blended learning is going to continue and materials are set to become more sophisticated in order to support the digital learning environments, which may well be accessed remotely (and independently) rather than in the classroom with teacher support readily available.

Changes in government policy have a considerable impact on the development of textbooks. So, for instance, when the UK government decided that phonics was the only method to be used for teaching literacy for 5–7-year-olds, it had the effect of changing the market. Publishers had to spend money developing new texts (maybe having wasted money on developing schemes that could now no longer be used), but on the positive side money came into the market to help schools buy new books: the market for reading schemes in this particular instance grew by 75 per cent. The problem publishers face is that government policy can change, and even reverse, on a regular basis and second guessing policy in order to future-proof a publishing programme is a thankless task.

Technology in schools

Technology has been prevalent in schools for some time now. A drive in government funding in the mid- to late 1990s in the UK ensured that technology was integrated into the classroom. This revolved around increasing access to computers and building more IT suites, replacing blackboards with interactive whiteboards and ensuring increased internet access.

Two organisations played a particularly important role in the development of technology within UK education:

- BETT
- BECTA

The British Educational Training and Technology Show was founded in 1985 and is now known as BETT; it is an annual exhibition and trade show which showcases the latest educational technology. It also presents awards for the best-quality teaching resources that make excellent use of technology in the classroom. While it is generally dominated by educational software providers and also covers hardware and IT solutions, publishers do win these awards for their digital teaching programmes.

The other influencing body in promoting technology in schools was BECTA (originally British Educational Communications and Technology Agency and now dissolved), which was set up in 1997. This organisation was set up by the government to 'lead the national drive to ensure the effective and innovative use of technology throughout learning' (www.education.gov.uk/aboutdfe/armslengthbodies/a00192537/becta). BECTA undertook various roles, which coincided with the increase in government funding to schools to develop their IT capacity. These advisory roles included working on projects to help embed the effective use of technology in the most coherent, cost-effective way within schools, encouraging the market to develop appropriate and effective teaching and learning materials to promote the development of IT, as well as share best practice and ensure value for money. This organisation now no longer exists as government funding ceased, but it was very influential in the development of technology for schools.

Also in the late 1990s and early 2000s there was a significant increase in government funding to bring technology into schools and particular efforts were paid to starting the development of digital content for the new technologies. Initiatives were developed, with considerable funding, in order to deliver a digital curriculum. BBC Jam is an example of an online education service; it was launched in 2006 with a budget of £150 million. This was subsequently closed by the BBC Trust due to issues over fair trading. The Harnessing Technology Grant, which set aside £2.5 million for schools to support digital projects of all kinds, was another example of funding opportunities, but this was subsequently cut by the Coalition government which took office in 2010, which again highlights the problems a publisher can face in this marketplace.

Nevertheless, taken as a whole, access to the technology became much easier through these initiatives, allowing publishers and other suppliers to develop digital products knowing that they could be adopted very easily within schools. Interactive whiteboards (large, touch-sensitive white screens that link to class computers and can display material, connect to the internet, etc.) were one area of focus for publishers as they were quickly adopted across the schools sector with the injection of funding. Publishers quickly produced materials and resources for use on these, building on their print programme of teachers' support materials. These materials were also suitable for virtual learning environments (VLEs), which provide a web-based interactive space for students and teachers to access, collecting together various resources, learning activities and student support. The increase in the number of computers in schools was also important and education software companies have also been active in this area; publishers may own, or work closely with, software houses to produce materials that students can use to develop their own learning at their own pace.

Digital products for schools

Background to developing multimedia in schools

With the growth of technology in schools the main focus of product development in the first instance was around supplying teachers with more materials to use on those systems. Publishers aimed to provide additional resources to be used in the classroom to support print texts, but this allowed for the development of interesting and interactive learning packages that exploited the benefits technology could provide.

CD-ROM was the precursor of the online product and many sophisticated CD packages were developed that could be loaded onto a central network within schools and used to support lessons. These tended to involve additional resources and links to the web for teachers to back up their use of the texts. These were then transferred into the online environment, not always an easy process, to form the early web products, around which more sophisticated products have grown.

Features and benefits

It is reasonably easy to see how the digital environment can enhance learning for pupils. The sorts of features that can be added into a multimedia product include:

- video footage
- audio
- animated diagrams and figures
- links to websites
- links to web-based resources (e.g. maps, images)

These features clearly add interest to a subject and mean students can access learning through different media according to their own learning style.

Teaching can easily be made 'more alive' with the integration of a variety of different resources, but there were additional benefits in the flexibility to tailor programmes in various ways. For instance, digital resources can allow for:

- flexibility for teachers to adapt their teaching programme
- customisability – so that teachers are not constrained by the pedagogy of a text
- built-in add-on resources for teachers
- built-in assessment for teachers
- marked assessment (i.e. multiple choice)
- homework options
- independent work options
- the ability for students to progress at their own rate
- more flexibility to cope with different learning levels, including special needs

Overall, the opportunities provided by the digital environment can enhance the education experience.

What do the digital products look like?

The first products did not aim to tackle the issue of ebooks for use by individual pupils, but they focused on ways of enhancing the use of print texts within the class. This has continued to be the trajectory on which products predominantly have developed, cost and access to hardware being the main limitations for developing individual e-textbooks. However, the benefits that the digital environment brings have been embedded further into the products in terms of flexibility and customisation by publishers. They will, for example, take the text itself and put it within a digital environment, developing from there a wide selection of resources to wrap around it. This has the advantage of allowing teachers to work with the texts they know and are accustomed to using. There may even be a visual representation of the actual text page on screen. This, therefore, can then accommodate additional resources, whether video footage of a historical event or an audio file of a section of Shakespeare being read out; teachers can zoom in on photos, hyperlink to glossaries or select the boxes with questions in them. There are additional benefits to such resources; of course the pupils should find the topic comes to life with video footage but it goes deeper towards issues of access: if, for instance, some children have problems with literacy, an audio file can be a great help.

Additional resources and activities for teachers to integrate into their teaching may also be available, and one of the exciting developments around these products is the flexibility that teachers have to pull apart a text and rebuild it for their own use in the classroom. An online learning environment allows teachers to select various resources and elements from different parts of the text and build them together into a new way of teaching a topic, setting everything up in the VLE to be ready to teach the course. User-friendliness of such products becomes key here as teachers do not have long to spend on lesson planning so simplicity is important when mixing and matching elements from a text to produce a customised lesson. Many products will use a similar environment across a range of subjects, tying together numbers of titles (even if the teachers teaching these topics may be from very different subject areas) and making the product buildable for a school.

Problems for publishers

However, various problems arise for publishers when developing these products. These revolve around:

- quantity (and cost) of material
- robustness of the technology
- flexibility and user-friendliness of the program
- school budget and the business model

Cost

One of the problems publishers face is that of selection versus cost effectiveness. Once material can be multimedia there is an endless opportunity to add more and more exciting aspects to the resources, but that can be costly. It can mean the development of thousands of resources; creating the resources from scratch is expensive, though in the longer term owning these resources can be of benefit to the publisher; otherwise getting permission, in itself a time-consuming process, can be expensive, and extent of the permission can be an issue too (if these products are sold into other territories, for instance, the permission needs to cover those territories).

At some point the authors and editors need to decide when to stop adding new material. By basing the products closely on the books or even on the page, this to some extent creates a natural boundary between what to include and what additional material to add in. Also the material needs to be really effective. It is easy to find free resources on the web, but by searching out and selecting key materials the publisher both saves the teacher time and ensures, hopefully, that the material selected is the most appropriate and effective for learning. This may ultimately add to the cost, as the best video footage of, for instance, an historical event, may cost more to include, but it does offer a selling point that can be attractive for teachers, who may not want to seek out permission or identify the most informative pieces themselves.

Technology

An important aspect of these products is their robustness. There is no room for technological glitches when working in a classroom environment. The online product also needs to be adaptable for a multitude of platforms and networks, which proliferate in schools, and support needs to be provided for whatever platform schools have adopted. Schools need to upgrade constantly and digital resources need to be flexible to keep up to date; clearly working within an online environment makes this easier, but some things are downloaded and/or used and customised locally to the school, so these need to be integrated effectively with whatever system is used. The products need to work quickly and easily so there is no delay in downloading materials nor any risk of the server crashing. Helpdesks to support customers are necessary.

Flexibility and user-friendliness

There is also the question of how far these really can be flexible. While they clearly are more so than a printed page, it can still be time consuming for a teacher to plan a lesson using them; they may not have the sort of flexibility to cope with different levels of learner as it is hoped; assessment built in the form of, for example, multiple choice or homework activities may be very limited and may still encourage a rather homogenous way of learning. Debates about how far digital learning has yet to go to cope with these aspects continue, as the pedagogy around the use of technology to improve learning has yet to be fully applied in a teacher's day-to-day work.

The business model and school budget limitations

The underlying business model for publishers of these sorts of resources remains the same; adoptions of print texts bought in numbers for class sizes and used for a certain number of years form the basis for digital product sales. However, the pricing mechanism for multimedia products is more complex than a print adoption. These require a change in mind set around issues such as:

- licences and subscriptions
- duration of subscription
- decision-making around an add-on purchase to the textbooks
- what the school owns in the digital content
- renewal points and potential budget savings
- how a school judges value for money

Institutions need to examine new purchasing models. They may have to buy user or site licences, and a subscription model is often more applicable for an online product given the continuous access to the site (rather than the one-off purchase of a print text).

This subscription element for web-based sites has represented a change for schools in terms of purchasing model; it commits them potentially to paying more further down the line in order to continue the subscription. Publishers have made this transition a little easier. Subscriptions cover different periods of time and often schools can access sites for the duration of the curriculum (or for the course of the life of the adoption of the print text) and it seems that schools have not had major problems with this new way of purchasing material. Prices are set according to the size of the school (number of pupils etc.) and teachers often view the support of good flexible resource material as beneficial as lessons can become much more dynamic immediately with access to the online resources available.

Certain problems are posed though. As we have seen, producing wonderful and effective teaching resources of this sort is not cheap, especially when the print text still forms the basis of the teaching and needs to be bought for students to use in the classroom and at home. Buying electronic products with all sorts of exciting additional multimedia elements presents a different budgetary proposition. A school cannot necessarily simply add to its budget and yet this is an additional purchase. A teacher may have bought a resource pack, usually at additional cost, but the price of these products is usually more and yet a school still needs the actual texts themselves, so these will come out of the budget first. Other costs may take precedence when schools consider their budgets: they need to bear in mind how long the books will last in terms of the curriculum changes due, and if the textbooks wear out, then titles need to be replaced, so that too will have priority; they also get economies of scales when purchasing bulk copies. So the budget that is left is not always that large and they need to ensure they get value for money.

Of course excellent resources encourage loyalty to a text and so it is important to ensure online sites are affordable as that may encourage sales of the textbooks. If the subscription is available for a fixed term, i.e. until the next syllabus, the price will often decline according to the length of time left to run; some publishers are working with this model, though it is not a firmly established pattern yet. Books were owned by the school, but to what extent do they own the resources that are available digitally? These will essentially disappear once the subscription has run out and the school does not have anything tangible (such as an archive).

This method of purchasing material needs to be considered in light of how far it represents value for money. It can therefore be seen as a much more discretionary purchase, one that will be easy to cut should cuts be necessary. The term of the subscription therefore becomes key for the publisher: it wants to ensure long enough access for the resource to become embedded in the customer's daily activity so that it will be considered an essential purchase next time round, while also ensuring that there are not too many renewal points at which the school can decide not to renew.

Sales strategies for these products

Print textbooks are reasonably easy to sell in that customers know what they are getting. They read the marketing literature about them, attend fairs at their school to look over new titles, view inspection copies and quite quickly get an idea of how good the text is. Sales reps know a lot about the schools and the sort of curriculum they are working with, together with the range of pupils, and can direct the textbooks appropriately.

Selling these digital products becomes a little more involved. Demos are available online but it is usually more effective if customers can be shown these products much more closely. The more customers can get to use the products the easier it is for them to see all the benefits. Tying the resources to the textbooks helps of course but the interactivity and usefulness of the products need to be shown more directly, so sales strategies have to be tailored to this. Teachers do not have a lot of time and there are only certain times of year for decision-making in terms of book buying; finding the optimum time to sell in an ancillary product can be difficult. Overall this has led to a trend of building closer relationships with key accounts in order to sell products – something that may be set to develop further.

New product development

While cost is an issue, the creation of online learning environments like these involves a lot of additional development work for the publisher. New material may need to be created in a way that has not been the case for the journals or reference sectors we looked at earlier. While those sectors have focused on the manipulation of material once within the system (and added access to new materials), the actual creation of material has not been a factor for them. For schools publishing (and in Chapter 9 we will see consumer publishing) commissioning additional elements has been key, whether it be photos, interactive artwork, video footage or audio files. Not all of them are created from scratch – we have already touched on the fact that some things will have be bought to use with appropriate permissions but some will be created, commissioning voiceover material or filming parts of a play, for instance. So editors working on these projects need to act to some extent as producers as they commission a variety of resources.

These websites also need to be storyboarded in particular ways to ensure the right additional resources are commissioned. Creating user specifications, understanding the structure of the website and considering the way the product will work for the end user are all important when developing these products. The structure is also important in order to develop the metadata behind the various elements effectively so that those elements can be easily identified and linked together across the digital platform. This requires development of workflow and data warehouses, which are costly for publishers working within a marketplace that is price sensitive.

Higher education and e-learning

The development of digital resources for lecturers and students

For higher education similar market trends are in play as for schools but driven by the fact the end user is the student. We will look more closely on p. 101 at ebooks for both schools and HE markets, but texts in ebooks format, or enhanced ebooks format, have been available for some time and these have been predominantly rendered in a web-based environment as the books are too complex to be presented on simple e-readers. However, the main investment in digital products in this market up to now has been, as with schools publishing, in providing digital resources that support a print text.

Developments in digital products started, particularly in the US, by focusing on building web resource pages for lecturers to use to support the main adopted text.

In order to make their package attractive to professors so they would adopt their book, web resources were a good way to add value, doing something different and exciting. These included additional case studies, video banks, more activities, discussion points as well as multiple choice questions that could be given to students. In this way, sophisticated and enriched web resources have been developed, much like the schools market.

Expansion of these services has continued but there is an increasing focus on the student user, not just the lecturer. It had been easy to forget the student user (who actually has to buy the book), instead focusing on getting lecturers to adopt. However, as publishers look for new ways to add value they have started to use technology to increase student interaction with the text and build on the student package around the product, particularly in relation to e-learning.

The implications of e-learning for print texts

The HE market has been changing in its application of technology, which means publishers need to engage more closely with the way technology is used for learning in terms of structure and presentation of content. It is clear that the nature of the textbook even in digital format is still linear, and this clearly reflects the nature of the curriculum, which is in itself linear. Publishers are aware that the textbook is still very much at the centre of teaching for a course in whatever format, as it can follow the curriculum very closely. Education publishers in both schools and HE sectors therefore always ensure they keep close to the changes and development in the curriculum, and this relationship will continue to be important going forward. But it still generally starts with the print product: a text is written and developed with the course in mind and, as we have seen, the digital product can be developed in tandem; even with an iBook type of textbook, which we will consider in the case study on pp. 102–3, it is still tied to a linear process. It is the adoption of the print title that remains the pivot in the first place for the sale of the digital resource.

However, for many, something much more fundamental needs to happen to textbooks and there is an aspect of digital publishing that is focused on e-learning – where all the learning is done within a digital environment. This area is attracting more attention. For publishers it is an opportunity to embed themselves more closely into education, both at schools and HE levels, exploiting and customising content in a variety of ways, such as providing assessment or creating e-textbooks or collaborating on distance learning programmes.

The definition here is loose but it is important to draw some distinction between digital publishing and e-learning. E-learning tends to refer to the fact that the transfer of knowledge occurs within the electronic environment; it can cover such things as computer-based training (CBT), internet-based training (IBT) or web-based training (WBT) and it may involve some sort of controlled assessment to reflect the progress of the e-learner. This is not necessarily directly the realm of the publishers, though some are moving into these areas more than others.

In this arena the way an education product works often involves some elements of control of the learning process. The linear approach described above can be regarded as limiting. A much more flexible learning experience, that can still build towards a full curriculum in a more intuitive way for an individual user, is possible in a digital space. However, in learning environments it is not always appropriate for a user to be able to jump in anywhere. Just as the curriculum itself needs to be followed in terms of building blocks, one thing needs to be learnt and understood before moving onto the next stage, so e-learning needs to take some consideration of that. This does not necessarily apply to resources under the control of the teacher as in the products above, but there are situations where this does become an issue, in, for instance, effective assessment programmes. The relationship a learner has with the content of their course is beginning to change and this has implications for the print text.

Technological developments in e-learning

Developments in technology are important here. Learning management systems (LMS) are the systems used by organisations for a variety of activities from managing student records to running distance learning programmes. Different organisations will use their LMS for different sorts of things; they do not necessarily have to encompass much learning material, though institutions may have a learning content management system (which tends to be a subset of an LMS), where the actual content used for a course may be held and/or published for students.

There are some standards that have been developed to take this into account when developing learning management systems. SCORM (Sharable Content Object Reference Model), which emerged from Advanced Digital Learning Initiative, is a system that has been used to sequence material; it creates relationships between content that mean that the order in which the content is used is defined, creating a pathway for the learner; this can be particularly important where testing may take place, for instances in a self-learning environment, so the tests can be reasonably expected to test what the user has learnt so far. There are other uses and the critical aspect is that SCORM content can be delivered on any SCORM-compliant learning management system – so creating a level of compatibility across learning objects.

These technological developments are important for the development of more sophisticated products that tackle e-learning. Educational software producers create a lot of products of this sort but publishers are engaging with e-learning more and more as they develop and publish online assessment systems or more sophisticated online packages that can be integrated into a college LMS, for instance. For some publishers this is a particular area of focus as they protect themselves against declining print sales; for others it is a key part of a globalisation strategy where they can bring their material to new online learning markets around the world. The challenges of e-learning clearly affect both the schools and higher education market, but it is the latter where there is currently more activity. US publishers in particular are developing new approaches; this brings us back to the size and competitiveness of the market, which can engender high levels of investment.

Developments in e-learning and e-textbook products

Some publishers have created hubs around particular areas such as marketing where students access the specific textbook they are to use together with additional materials and additional tools to help them plan and organise their work (e.g. MyLab, Pearson), and which can also include access to their assignments and grades. These often have some sort of communications element so students can chat to their classmates about topics, email instructors, get involved in discussion forums, and can also include links to apps of enhanced e-textbooks where bookmarks, highlights and comments can be shared within the book. These sorts of hubs are highly customisable to the course and linked to a menu of textbooks which can be accessed if part of their course.

Overall this sort of development needs to manage the central issue in the area of higher education: students need to be satisfied as well as lecturers – by being able to customise resources around either the lecturer or the student the text becomes more flexible and hopefully attractive to both sides of market. If the student is pleased with it the lecturer is more inclined to adopt it. The student is, therefore, becoming more involved in the process of developing the textbook than previously was the case. In this way, even if the lecturer does not use all the chapters in the book the package can still have value, encouraging students to extend their learning too, and the more that can be shown to the student about how effectively they are learning, the more value they will feel they get from the package. This might then have the additional benefit of more students wanting to purchase the text, feeling like they are getting a complete service for their purchase, something they could not get with a second-hand print copy.

Lecturers can also benefit from the focus on tools to manage the course (and not just the text). Lecturers want to be in touch with their students' learning, and if the text can be integrated more seamlessly into the other aspects of their learning on the course that can be of benefit to the lecturer; if they can monitor the progress the students are making, both parties can be more closely engaged in the student's learning. If the lecturer and the student work can also be integrated together around the core product, the student might feel more obliged to sign up for the product, while the lecturer would see all the benefits an integrated platform might have for the organisation of their course, drawing the lecturer and student closer together in the decision to adopt a text.

Publishers' new ventures and the new players

Publishers in the US such as McGraw Hill have also developed centralised tools providing web-based assignments and assessment platforms that can be linked to particular texts (e.g. Connect). These systems are aiming to take the development of digital learning further, moving beyond simple multiple choice assessment to much more integrated and sophisticated practice exercises. These are intended to work alongside whichever book the lecturer chooses, yet still have an automated marking function, providing a certain level of feedback and suited to the individual student needs – in that they can access this whenever they want. For introductory university and college courses, which have huge numbers of students, lecturers can manage these large numbers effectively. Also, because of the large numbers involved, these tools, which add so much value for a busy lecturer, can potentially command more revenue, which allows the systems to be built to a sophisticated level. Customising these effectively (with technical support at hand to help you do this) is also part of the package, as well as the ability to build it into any VLE or LMS system the college or university uses.

From this one can see how the trend of building distance learning around the texts linked to specific courses can easily grow. Here publishers are really trying to tap into the resources of the university rather than those of the student in terms of the end purchaser. Selling a product at institutional level makes a lot of sense compared to selling lots of textbooks to lots of students. For sophisticated products in any case the publisher needs to make a large-scale investment, so it has to sell to an institution to support the costs. Reps are already meeting the right people in an institution and so the sales strategy is to get more direct value from the institution rather than have to sell the product again to the student once the adoption has been made.

This all means that the textbooks become much more integrated into the workflow of the course for both the lecturer and students. The more embedded they become, the more involved the process of moving on to a new text becomes when lecturers want a change. Continuous innovation in these areas becomes a vital part of a publisher's ability to maintain an adoption. It also becomes a way for it to gain a competitive edge and gain a new adoption by making customisation easy and encouraging lecturers to move to a new platform, which creates new opportunities for publishers to provide something unique where the texts themselves have become more standardised.

For these things to happen critical mass becomes even more important. Consolidation around key players in the US particularly has been an important step for publishers to be able to develop comprehensive content that can then be customised into course materials.

Once publishers develop frameworks such as these it becomes even easier to customise products to a course as well as develop new content to fit. By developing content in particular ways, it can then be mixed and matched differently according to the way it is to be used. As in the professional markets outlined above, new markets can be reached more easily, with the same basic content, if it can be adapted and customised according to different market groups or segments.

And so the dilemma around price becomes even more critical. For publishers there is upward pressure on prices given the cost of developing increasingly valuable resources based on the core product. But this pressure on price has spurred others to rise to the challenge of offering more cost-effective products. Companies entering the market are aiming to bring prices down or, if a course so chooses, make material free.

Inevitably there are other organisations moving into the market. We will explore the significance of the developments by Apple with their iBooks product for both schools and HE markets in the case study on pp. 102–3. However, developed by Apple specifically for the HE market, iTunes U is an app that allows lecturers to create and design courses easily (without necessarily being tied to a textbook of any sort); a lecturer can give students access to all the materials for their course in one place – so they have a bookshelf of items linking their iBookstore and their iCloud in one place, as well as links to websites, videos and presentations (maybe of the lecturer themselves), and assignments, keeping notes, highlights and documents in one place. These can be synced across all their Apple devices (so ensuring continued purchase of Apple hardware). Tools make it easy for a lecturer to build a course around all these elements. This is similar to the sorts of integrated platforms described above, but the step that Apple takes with it is the ability to publish that course globally – so anyone anywhere can access it – and in addition, if you choose, it can be available for free, fuelling the debate around the democracy of education. It may not be the whole course that is available but it could be a particular presentation, and many well-known institutions are using this to develop free materials for anyone to use anywhere on almost any subject. These in turn, where they are copyright free (or perhaps using a Creative Commons licence), can be built into more new courses where lecturers feel they are relevant. This is taking the learning 'anywhere anytime' issue of ubiquity to a new level.

The development of the e-textbook for schools and the HE market

These digital developments, as one can see, extend learning to new levels and involve a considerable investment and consultation. However, the print text still remains in place. But for how long? The next stage of development is likely to focus on ebooks and the individual use of digital textbooks for both the schools and HE markets, and new players are coming in to attempt to shake up the market.

Ebooks and e-readers

In most cases textbooks, at whatever level, that are produced in print are also usually available as ebooks. Up to now standard ebook formats are not the best way to render highly illustrated, very integrated textual layouts. Even for more text-based materials (i.e. without the extensive full-colour illustrations and photos) EPUB formats simply cannot cope with the complexity of a standard textbook at any level; while some work can be done to the files, the main problem is that the school texts are designed into complex page templates, while an EPUB file is not really designed to manage page formatting at all. In addition, EPUB files may be reasonably standardised but they can still render differently within different hardware, so they have to be checked across all possible options. E-readers have not been seen to be of much use for the textbook market.

Many pupils will have their own laptops, particularly at secondary level, and at HE level they generally all will, so they can access ebooks. For schools though, to ensure access for everyone investment in hardware will still be required, and so selling ebooks has not been a focus for this market.

For the HE market the purchase of ebooks is much more prevalent. Sites such as CourseSmart, set up by a group of the largest textbook publishers in the US, provide a one-stop shop for purchasing e-textbooks, making it easy to read in any format, anywhere, with attractive discounts on the books for students. There is also a growing rental market for ebooks, with, for instance, Amazon in the US offering this option on its site (as with its print textbook rental market); this can prove an attractive alternative for students and one that is easy to manage in a digital environment. This could well have a significant impact in the longer term.

Future developments for educational publishers

Building up the assets: digital warehouses

Whether building an online resource or developing a textbook such as the ones available in iBookstore, there is a clear overall trend towards interactive resources and more highly developed visual material and photography. Taking images alone, these could represent quite a lot of the cost of print books. While there may still be a cost to developing the images, the actual reproduction of them within the digital environment is not expensive in comparison to the high-quality printing necessary for physical books. There will still be costs, whether to buy the rights to the photos (these will often need to cover global rights, depending on the sort of DRM/access controls the materials have and their ability to cope with territoriality) or to commission artwork, photos, diagrams, maps, cartoons and other illustrations. There could well be an expectation in

Case study: The development of tablets and Apple's iBook textbook

The growth of the tablet market has entirely changed the potential for the use of digital books within the classroom and could well revolutionise the learning environment at all levels. Tablets can reproduce the high-quality full-colour graphic nature of the textbook while being much less cumbersome to use than a laptop. They offer the opportunity to bring e-textbooks to students to use in lessons, easily and quickly; long battery power and robustness of the systems are also advantages. There are obviously issues about providing tablets to pupils given the expense of providing and supporting so much hardware (not least entrusting pupils with pricey technology compared with reasonably cheap print texts). However, while it is early days, there are examples of UK schools using iPads in class and in the US whole school districts are supporting the adoption of iPads in their schools. The attractiveness of iPads for the HE market is also of critical importance.

The development of the tablet for education use has very recently been accelerated by the introduction of the iBook textbook by Apple for use on its iPad. Apple has identified the education market as one where it can promote hardware sales with the introduction of tools and platforms on which textbooks can sit. These are books (rather than apps), which may be media rich but still follow the format of a basic book.

More critically, Apple has created user-friendly development tools that it makes available for free in iPad Author, in order to encourage people to make textbooks that can only be used in iPad environments. This authoring tool is very easy to use, providing creators with templates to help them upload photo galleries, use html widgets to enhance user interactivity with diagrams, include presentations, manipulate 3D images, insert video or audio files and create tests, while the book itself will provide additional user-friendly tools such as the ability to make index cards for learning from highlighted text.

The impact here is likely to be greater in the US than the UK. One of the aims is that, with more content available, customers are attracted to the hardware, and schools and college markets will feel they need to embrace iPad technology to offer their students the best products. The pricing is a critical factor here. While the prices within the iBooks textbook store are comparable to UK-based texts, they are considerably lower than US prices, which is one of the issues in debate.

The other critical issue for the US is that the opportunity for individuals to develop texts themselves may prove a big problem for publishers used to operating within the system where textbooks are adopted centrally. It is much easier for teachers to develop their own materials, which may start to dilute the big adoptions and allow access to materials that, while they may not be the best, are of reasonable quality, look good due to the flexibility of the Apple software and are considerably cheaper.

Publishers and the iPad in education

Apple is not yet creating its own content and indeed may never intend to do that. Its aim is to encourage people, including publishers, to use its authoring tool to create content and post it onto the store (incidentally driving Mac sales too as Macs have to be used for the Author tool). So Apple launched its textbooks iBookstore with books produced by the key US textbook publishers (McGraw Hill and Pearson) to show that it is not alienating publishers but, instead, is keen to get them to use Apple's tool in order to produce high-quality content. Nevertheless Apple also envisages the tool being used by individuals, such as teachers, wanting to develop their own texts and creating highly individualised teaching materials. While Apple does take a percentage of any actual sales of a book on the iBookstore, an individual teacher's textbook can be posted up free on the iBookstore (with Apple therefore encouraging true internet democracy to self-publish and freely share), which means that competition will therefore be increased, or, at the least, the market diluted.

The problem is that the proprietary nature of the hardware means that publishers face a dilemma when developing products. Publishers have to make decisions as to the format in which they publish. Do they make all their materials available across all platforms and hardware? This will be something we look at again in the consumer market (Chapter 9), but in the case of the iPad, if publishers use iPad Author to produce their texts, they can only be used by schools or individuals with iPads. Even if iPads are very widely adopted, not everyone will adopt them, and are they then excluded? (This is a debate which is all the more pointed when it is about education.) If they do publish for iPad specifically using iPad Author there are certain restrictions on the content that Apple have built in, which means publishers cannot necessarily use everything again exactly as it is in a different format for a different tablet – something that can be a problem if they are looking to produce consistent education materials. Publishers have to be aware of this issue and decide whether to develop their own system and make it available on Apple devices rather than use Apple's own tools. There are some issues around how far a publisher can reuse some of the materials provided within the iTextbook too, which can cause problems.

The advantage of producing digital texts for publishers in places like iBookstore is that they are able to reach a larger market. They can attract global audiences in a way schools publishing hasn't been able to do before. Curriculum-specific texts are unlikely to travel much beyond the remit of the exam board (which may be wider than just the UK but is not generally global), but for some titles, such as language courses or literature texts like Shakespeare, they can tap easily into markets that were prohibitively expensive to reach before.

Even in the tablet environment, however, the books currently developed are still textbooks that follow a clear narrative structure and work from page to page as a normal book would. An iBook allows for the use of beautiful high-definition resources but it is not a hugely innovative or interactive experience compared with the e-learning environments described earlier. And once set they cannot be pulled apart and adapted and customised any further. There are some dilemmas about publishing materials like these. They are not necessarily much more flexible in helping students to progress at different rates than standard print books. They are still bound to the curriculum and new books are needed every time the curriculum changes.

the market for a digital product to contain more of these sorts of elements, so there is an incentive to ensure as many as possible of these features are included in the product, so that the market feels justified in purchasing them.

Publishers therefore have been developing data warehouses and digital asset management systems, as outlined in Part I, where they can store and reuse material effectively again and again. This means they can easily reuse information at the point a syllabus changes; while artwork could previously be redundant or fiddly to repurpose, storing materials in a digital environment means they can not only be reached quickly but reused and adapted quickly and cheaply; given that key concepts, say in geography, will remain the same even when the syllabus changes and the fact that the old texts based on old syllabi are no longer in circulation, the reuse of material makes sense (and is not just cannibalisation of a publisher's material).

However, three key issues are important when developing this sort of system:

- copyright
- standardisation
- structure of the data warehouse

The publisher has to own the copyright in the artwork; in many cases, publishers have been accustomed to commissioning images and owning copyright in them, so this fits well with them.

The material needs to be in a standardised format. Metadata will sit behind the material, whether text or visual, but, with artwork especially, there needs to be standardisation in the creation of the material in order for it to be easy to use again across a variety of different texts. There are problems with this. The design of texts needs to be rationalised so that standard templates are easy to create using a few set styles, otherwise everything becomes costly again if it needs to be customised in some way or other. There will clearly be flexibility around the styles, but they may be limited to a smaller set of style sheets for the sake of cost effectiveness and to ensure content can be created so that it can be used across a range of products. This is unlike the print environment, where different individual designs per book (or book series) would be common and there is a risk of homogeneity. Publishers involved in this development tend to have an aim in mind for the percentage of material that will be reused compared to newly commissioned material, in order to ensure the overall effect is still unique.

The structure of the digital asset warehouse needs to be developed in such a way as to ensure effective use. Once again, this means the application of metadata in order to identify images that may be suitable for a particular project; recording the ongoing use of the images is also important, so that images are not overused and the look of books, while standardised, is not too homogenous.

However, digitisation of their production methods can allow publishers to produce materials cost effectively, which can help towards the development of expensive digital resources for the market.

The role of the author and the standardised text

What does this mean for the author? As the development of resources becomes more standardised, can, or indeed should, the work of the author become standardised too? Will written sections be chunked in a similar way and pieced together in different formats for different occasions? Authors within the education sector have often collaborated to piece a book together around a curriculum. Some work on the whole project themselves and deliver a piece of work that is individual and very tightly constructed. However, some projects are built by a selection of writers who work on sections or different types of resources, mixing and matching skills and piecing sections together in order to work alongside a syllabus. These authors are already more used to working around parts of a book, knitting it together at the end, and this approach can work well within a digital environment. In order to support the costs of setting up, delivering and maintaining digital resources, the ability to rework content becomes critical as a way of managing content cost effectively. Of course, some may feel that this has the potential to undermine the quality of textbooks as they become more homogenised; careful editorial work can ensure this does not happen, but the drive by schools to achieve exam success does mean the market has an interest in producing books that can achieve this for teachers, which does, to some extent lead to a perceived 'standardised' textbook. This debate has become all the more furious in the higher education market.

Other future directions

There are a variety of issues that will challenge educational publishers in the future, though some may provide opportunities. Digital warehouses are key to the future developments but there are other important areas that need to be taken into account. These include:

- budgets
- accessibility (especially in relation to technology)
- curriculum change
- customisation
- new business activities, e.g. assessment and the development of communities

Budgets

Budgets will continue to be a problem for markets essentially funded by the public sector. School budgets will always be tight, and in periods of recession even more so. For schools, as new digital products are produced, their cost is not necessarily likely to be low. If they are discretionary purchases, there will be pressure to prove their worth; if an e-textbook becomes more central to a course, the costs of supporting the hardware can be a problem, and if schools have to do that it may be with the expectation that the actual materials will be cheaper. This puts pressure on the print texts around which some of these digital products have been built. The trend towards working more closely with the institutions, arguably more advanced in the US HE market, may therefore become more important.

Accessibility

Among the issues that will continue to be important, there will almost certainly be a focus on accessibility. Clearly there is an issue with access to the technology itself. Technology is expensive and can need continuous servicing: the more education products become dependent on technology, the more accessibility may be threatened.

There will need to be ways, for instance, to support poorer students who cannot afford an iPad, or schools with low budgets that cannot support the computer services they need.

There are also purely technological problems around access. For instance, materials created using Flash may become a problem as Adobe will not be supporting this in a few years' time. This may mean the re-rendering of materials that used Flash. HTML5 will offer the sort of flexibility to embed multimedia within websites, which may also be future proof as it is a generic standard, but what it shows is that publishers in the education market need to pay continuous attention to the way they create their resources, to ensure they continue to be accessible despite changes in software and hardware, and keep track of where the education market is spending its technology budgets. They cannot second-guess every technological development but will need to be ready to change and upgrade materials where they can quickly. Ensuring the raw format of the material is as flexible as possible is of course a critical aspect of this, but they will also need to review which systems and programs they can and cannot publish for, and allow for additional cost to keep their materials available throughout any techno-logical changes.

Curriculum

Of course the driver of education publishing remains the curriculum. Remaining flexible so as to produce high-quality content quickly at the point of curriculum change is critical to a publisher's commercial success. Print products take time to produce, whereas the digital environment can sometimes allow publishers to reap the benefits of bringing materials to market quickly – as sections can go live as soon as they are ready. This, however, still requires considerable management, particularly when there are major changes in the curriculum across a wide range of subjects; being prepared to manage this will be crucial. Trends around e-learning will become more critical, as technology can deal more effectively with independent learning opportunities or different learning levels.

For both schools and HE levels there is the opportunity to customise products for specific needs and uses. Publishers can work closely with a school to pick and mix materials or services to link into the school's VLE, or they can put together content from a variety of sources to produce an ebook according to the specifications of a lecturer (which already happens in print). Publishers will have a lot of exceptionally well-developed content that is of great value, so offering opportunities to schools and colleges to individualise learning for their own students with bespoke packages will be a way to realise value across their content. Also, most teachers will accept that while they can do some limited self-publishing within iPad Author, they cannot neces-sarily match the depth, range and high production quality of content produced by a publisher.

New ventures

As we have seen, some publishers are experimenting with new ventures and developing more expertise in areas wider than traditional publishing. Taking Pearson as an example, as mentioned above the company has been building expertise in assessment, buying the exam board Edexcel in order to turn it from a charitable organisation (as many exam boards are) into a commercial enterprise. There are problems with this model, not least around the monopoly position Pearson has in relation to publishing textbooks for the courses, and there are pressures on the way this can be effectively managed and organised, but in Pearson's case the link between learning and assessment is important. It is something which drives its strategy in other parts of its business, for instance in language assessment in Asia or professional clinical assessment in the US. This links Pearson to the arena of educational software and knowledge management systems so it builds expertise in areas around the management of education as well. In this way it can become much more embedded in the educational market, supporting a range of technologies within schools, colleges, universities and the professional training sectors. Other publishers are developing different sorts of collaborations that are more integrated into the education sector, around, for instance, e-learning; and on a smaller localised scale it can be seen that publishers are getting involved in helping schools create and support their learning environment. This provides some exciting opportunities but is of course a huge challenge. Like the professional reference sector some of these publishers are in the process of changing the sort of company they are.

Learning communities

There are also developments around creating communities, using content and support materials in a new flexible way based on a customer-centred approach. The community can centre around a topic or subject and get access to support and material at its point of need. For instance, communities for English language teachers have been developed where teachers can ask others for advice, access key authors in webinars, find articles by professionals or source materials on related topics, with self-assessment sections for their own personal development. The benefit to the user is that they can interact with fellow professionals who they may not necessarily be able to meet in any other way, and get answers to much more specific and individual questions. For publishers, it means they have a two-way conversation with their customers and can understand more closely what they want and help to develop it for them. These systems can work on a variety of levels – they can be entirely free sites in order to develop customer groups and build loyalty, for marketing around specific titles, or can become a little more of a standalone service in itself that users may access for different prices (e.g. freemium models, where certain parts are free but others can be paid for on subscription or by use).

Conclusion

So education publishing faces particular challenges in the future. The market is embracing technology but cost is a problem and price can be a barrier. They too, like the academic market, face the criticism that education should be freely available and encounter resistance to increasing prices. New entrants to the market are driving the move away from print books and changing the cost base of the sector. Publishers have to reinvent their role, drawing even closer to the sector and changing the way they work with their customers. Yet some argue that the digital products are still quite limited in their scope and the full extent of what digital technology can provide is not yet being fully exploited. Here both the sector and the publishers will need to move together to create the digital products of the future.

Further reading and resources

Books

Clark, Giles and Phillips, Angus. *Inside Book Publishing*. Routledge, 2008.
Thompson, John. *Books in the Digital Age*. Polity Press, 2005.

Websites

oyc.yale.edu – an example of a university posting up free lecture content; limited in scope but nevertheless providing free resources for blended learning opportunities

pearsonmylabandmastering.com/learn-about an example of a student digital hub for their textbooks and learning

wikieducator.org – an example of a wiki site aiming to aggregate free e-learning content for open use

www.apple.com/education/ibooks-textbooks – Apple presentation on their iBooks textbook for iPad.

www.bettshow.com – for the BETT educational technology show

www.education.gov.uk/aboutdfe/armslengthbodies/a00192537/becta – archive site for BECTA and Harnessing Technology Grants

www.education.gov.uk/schools/teachingandlearning/curriculum – government resource for information about education and the national curriculum in the UK

Questions to consider

1 Do you think that students who have invested in tablets and laptops will expect the price of content to come down and, if so, how can publishers respond?
2 Is there a danger of the homogenisation of textbooks given the development of data warehouses for digital content and how can this be overcome?
3 How extensive is the threat of self-published teaching materials for publishers?
4 What opportunities are there for publishers to work more closely with schools?
5 The cost of producing good digital texts is high. How far can the market sustain rising prices?
6 What can publishers offer in the face of the rising tide of free content and online learning materials?
7 How can publishers best exploit the move towards blended learning in schools and colleges?
8 When will the digital products be less reliant on the print sales of textbooks?
9 What sort of impact might the iPad authoring system have on traditional textbook publishing?

9 Developments in digital publishing for consumer markets

This chapter will explore the following:

1 The development of ebook sales – how this reached the tipping point
2 The ebook business model – the way books are currently sold and the issues this raises for the traditional business model
3 Other digital products: enhanced ebooks and apps, exploring the strategies and challenges of these digital options
4 The impact of digital publishing on the wider consumer environment, focusing on the way social media play a part in digital books and how the sales environment is changing
5 Futurising the book

Introduction

While the professional and scholarly sectors have well-developed digital products and business models, and the education markets have been following on rapidly, the consumer (or trade) markets have been slower to change. As the internet expanded and became more flexible as a rich mode for delivery of content, so specialist markets could all expand too; customers were increasingly used to using digital environments via computers for their activity and publishers had more direct relationships with their markets, which helped when developing and selling new products.

While the internet was accessible to the consumer markets, the activity of reading for the general reader did not really take place on or near a computer. Two main developments had to take place to ignite the market – the development of flexible ebook formats and the growth of affordable e-readers. As we have seen, there were early developments but it was not until around 2005 that the market started to develop, once the technology and hardware became more readily available.

For consumer publishers the technical ability to produce straightforward ebooks has not been a major problem, though some outlay has been required in terms of developing workflow and digitising past titles. The bigger problem has been how to price these products and put a price and value on the content. As we will see in this chapter and in Chapter 12, it is clear that customers have felt that, with savings in the cost of printing and distributing physical books, as well as in inventory management, the price of books should be cheaper.

This is tied up too with perceptions of price established by the big technology players that have moved heavily into other parts of the entertainment industry such as the music industry; there the expectation is that the price of individual items could be cheap, the outlay having been made by the consumer on the hardware. For those players, content has become part of the game of driving the purchase of the technology rather than an item in its own right. Of course there are differences: the act of reading a book, the duration of the activity and the motivation behind doing so are very different. In pricing terms a book is not like a short piece of music, so standard pricing would be more difficult to apply. The pattern of purchasing is different too: customers in general would not usually purchase as many books as they might pieces of music in a given period of time; the price of a paperback book was also reasonably cheap, whereas an album could often cost more.

Nevertheless the industry has to face a changing perception in how a book is to be valued in the eyes of the consumer, whose views are influenced by other types of digital material. The value of that content from the publisher's point of view includes not just an idea of what the market can and will pay but also an understanding of the cost of acquiring the content and producing the product. However, it is more often only the tangible parts of this cost (the physical product) that are taken into account by the consumer market. The big change therefore for the consumer publisher is how to manage that changing perception of value and manage the transfer from being a print-based business to a digital-and-print business. At this point many publishers have started to re-evaluate their role in the publishing value chain and step back to explore again what they really are doing for their customers, getting back to first principles in order to understand how to direct and restructure their businesses.

This chapter looks at the specific changes in the consumer market with the development of ebooks and how this has already changed the activities of some of these publishers in areas like fiction publishing, while other areas, such as illustrated books, are waiting to see how these developments will pan out. It will also explore the different sorts of products available. Some of the wider issues of pricing, self-publishing, publishing structures and the activity of major technology-based competitors will be looked at in Part III of the book, which explores the critical challenges that publishers across all sectors need to face.

Development of ebook sales

We looked at the history of the technology in Part I of the book. But how did these ebooks get to consumers? The early ebooks were essentially available from the late 1990s, when early ebook vendors were emerging. These centred around various book programmes that took content from publishers and made it available in digital format. These vendors contacted publishers to ask them to work with them to produce ebooks. Often they were focused on particular areas, such as the academic arena, with the aim that aggregated collections could be sold to institutional libraries.

However, there were examples of companies that sought digital rights from the mainstream trade houses. There were four main problems:

- payment
- digitisation
- lack of devices
- retailing ebooks

First, the rights needed to be granted in some way and that might possibly involve payment: authors, after all, were entitled to royalties for their works and these were often covered in the contracts they had by the subsidiary rights for digital rights, so somehow these needed to be taken into account. This could pose a problem as the business models did not always accommodate this.

The second problem was the cost of transferring the texts into digital files, which, even with some of the workflow beginning to be in digital format, was still costly; broadly, the ebook vendors took on this cost, but it became, for most of them, a very expensive part of their operation and often their business models could not sustain it, so they either folded or had to ask for contributions from the publishers (who were, in any case, often beginning to see the possibilities of digitising for themselves and not handing it all over to third parties).

The third problem remained the issue of how the consumer could consume these titles without any really reasonably portable device to use. The final issue was quite how to sell titles to consumers: a variety of business models developed and different approaches to marketing these digital libraries, but they were difficult and the cost of producing the digital format in the first place was constantly a problem. So while some early ebook vendors do still exist, these early experiments in selling ebooks, particularly to the consumer market, broadly disappeared as the first generation of ebook vending.

Drivers of the growth of ebook market e-readers

E-readers, as we have seen, began to be widely available from around 2006, with Kindle really driving the sales from the end of 2007. One of the particular issues that Kindles cracked from the beginning was to ensure that the ability to purchase the book was seamless with the delivery to the device. Early ebook vendors could process payments and a book could be downloaded but this still might take time and would require somewhere in the procedure an internet connection to a computer that, in most cases, required a wire to connect. One of the beauties of e-readers was the ability to download books via wifi or 3G, allowing quick and easy access to books potentially from anywhere around the world.

What Amazon then did was connect the product with the device in a way that Sony, although it was first to the market, was not able to do. Amazon had the book listings and could simply ensure the Kindle connected effortlessly to their storefront so that, from browsing for a book through the ordering and paying for it, to the downloading of it onto the device (with an automatic back-up on Amazon itself) the customer could do it all in one place very quickly; with the additional benefits of Amazon's well-developed customer service approach it made the whole process of buying ebooks simple and problem free.

Most critical of all was the fact that Amazon already had customers, customers who bought books and had an established, often ongoing, relationship with Amazon. To convert existing customers to ebooks was always going to be easier than finding and encouraging a market to make the connection between buying a device and finding a marketplace; Amazon had customers predisposed to them and people to whom they could regularly market, keeping the Kindle high in the consciousness of customers when buying other items. The Kindle therefore was one of the key reasons why the ebook market was able to start to develop in a much more convincing way than it had before.

Case study: Early initiatives

Some notable events occurred around the development of ebooks for the consumer in the early stages.

Project Gutenberg

There were some public programmes that focused on digitising works that were out of copyright. Project Gutenberg is one of the most famous examples; it started as early as 1971 but gained momentum as digital publishing developed further. In its mission statement it says it aimed to 'encourage the creation and distribution of eBooks', with a vision of digitising important cultural works in order to create a lasting digital archive, focusing essentially on works in the public domain. Volunteers worked on the project (and continue to do so) digitising the works.

These books are available in the most open format possible so can be downloaded onto most computers and devices for free; they include most of the key works of classical literature that are out of copyright. The format is simple and not intended to do more than create a basic digital library; consumers may still want to buy classic works that are published by mainstream publishers in digital format for the selling points that they can bring (more hypertext linking to indexes, tables of content, additional material or annotations, better page layout, etc.).

To some extent Project Gutenberg was a catalyst in that it meant for those early adopters of ebook readers there was an extensive archive of material ready to download for free. This was important as it made the purchase of e-readers attractive – there were lots of books ready to go on them (in some cases now pre-loaded), though it also enshrined the notion for some consumers that if you invest in the hardware there are huge amounts of content available for free.

Rosetta Books

Another interesting development was the case that revolved around Rosetta Books. Rosetta Books still exists as an ebook site where you can buy a variety of trade books in e-format. Early in 2001 it made the headlines as it published important backlist books apparently without copyright agreement. The founder of the site was a literary agent who believed he held the rights to publish digital books by the authors whose print books were with various large publishing houses in the US.

The argument revolved around how far an existing contract for a book covered digital rights where they were not specifically stated. This was not around the subsidiary rights for publishing a title in digital format but really focused on the nature of what counted as volume rights – did a digital book count as well as a print book as a 'volume' or did it have to be a physical manifestation of a volume? Rosetta Books argued that the author had not signed over the rights to a digital book so had the right to publish it where they wanted. Random House took the company to court but Rosetta Books' position was upheld. This really only applied to older books; newer contracts were much clearer on this situation (and now are very precise), but it illustrates an issue that has continued to dog certain older titles from important literary estates.

Challenges for publishers

As customers took up the Kindle and started to buy ebooks, various challenges emerged, of which three were prevalent:

- how to price ebooks
- who built the ebook files
- which books were the most likely to be bought on a device

Prices

At first there was a considerable pressure from Amazon to price low; taking an approach similar to the music industry reasonably early on after the launch of the Kindle, Amazon did promote the idea of fixed prices for all books and wanted to set the bar at $9.99 for hardbacks in the US (normally sold upward of $20). Once you had bought the device and connected to Amazon to purchase everything very quickly, commoditising ebooks around cheapness and standard pricing appeared a good way to attract a growing market for the devices, even if it meant loss-leader price strategies. This was never actually achieved and perhaps Amazon was never going to be able to make it work, but it was a possibility that frightened publishers in the early days of Kindle in the US. It was clear ebook pricing was going to be treated much more fluidly by Amazon than print prices, and publishers felt less in control. It was one of the influences that led to the large publishers putting pressure on Amazon to accept an agency approach to publishing, another being the way Apple worked in relation to ebook sales, more of which we will explore in Chapter 12.

Digitisation by publishers

Once e-readers were more prevalent, it was clear by then that there were customers who would buy ebooks. Whereas early ebooks had been developed by third parties, there was a natural pressure on publishers themselves to ensure their books were available in ebook formats, ready for online retailers. It was not a huge difficulty for them to do this but it marked a change from the earlier arrangements, where conversion of files was shared between the vendors and the publishers. New books began to be automatically made available in ebook format and by 2010 most publishers were automatically producing ebooks as well as print books for much of their new narrative output.

The bigger question remained about how much of the archive to make available digitally, involving more complex conversion processes, but even this has become less of a problem more recently as publishers are broadly going through the process of digitising most of their main in-print backlist and considering releasing their out-of-print backlist in ebook format.

Types of books to digitise

It is a particular type of book that works most effectively on e-readers. Books that are broadly narrative in style, what is increasingly defined as long-form narrative, are especially well suited to e-readers. They do not involve a lot of visual material; they are not interactive or media rich. Basic ebook formats are not hugely sophisticated so are best left dealing with reasonably straightforward text; they also cannot cope with complex page design and in general do not preserve the page style at all, with readers navigating often in terms of locations more than with page numbers.

Simple ebooks often do not have interactive indexes or table of contents. For the free books mentioned above Amazon bolts on a table of contents, charging a small amount for its own 'premium' edition. However, these limitations in, for example, navigation or text style, do not especially matter if one is reading a novel designed to be read in one direction from beginning to end. Effective book marking and syncing to where one has read, with a couple of additional benefits such as a dictionary, highlighting or adding notes (in a rudimentary way), mean that the e-reader usually does enough for the reader. The overall benefits of long battery life, portability and the ability to store many books on one light device are compelling enough. So the long-form narrative, whether fiction or non-fiction, has proved to be very successful in ebook format. As such titles are not complex, and do not require a lot of effort in terms of checking ebook files and formatting, there is room for the price to be lower and in general publishers have accepted that point.

Genre publishing

What has also become apparent is that genre titles have been particularly successful, that is, books that clearly sit within a particular genre such as romance, horror or crime. Readers who especially enjoy accessing books in a particular genre may like to read lots of them but may not necessarily want hard copies stacking up. There may even be a tendency to regard these sorts of titles as more disposable. Consumers of Mills and Boon-style romances, for instance, tend to be keen to move on to the next title rather than dwell for any length of time on the last one they read; the style of selling for these books often reflects that (with new titles constantly being released and semi-subscription options to buying them). Genre therefore has an element of easy commoditisation about it; readers generally try out things within that genre, and with low prices there is less risk for the reader if a particular crime novelist for instance does not live up to their expectations.

The area of genre has two other aspects going for it that have made it successful for ebooks. The first is that it is very easy to categorise books that sit firmly within one genre; if they are easy to categorise they are easy to find in an internet environment. If one looks for horror titles on Amazon it does not take long to find the area and explore the books on offer. Browsing becomes easier if you are looking for a particular type of book that is simple to define.

And because of that the second phenomenon can occur: that of the growth of self-publishing authors. It is difficult to be discovered on Amazon, so if one can place one's books clearly in a particular well-defined part of the site there is more chance of being discovered. Titles that do not fit clear categories are much more difficult to publish in an internet environment without the sort of complex and costly promotion activity, developed with extensive experience of the workings of book marketing and PR, that publishers can put in place; this is much more of a challenge for new self-published people. Self-publishing, as we will see in more detail in Chapter 13, exists across all sorts of books, but niche titles do appear to be areas where it is easier to find some success, compared to, for example, self-publishing literary fiction.

The ebook business model

The growing market

With the market growing, the move into ebook selling has been an important development for publishers. None can afford to be left behind and while predictions of a swift switch into digital publishing away from print have not been realised, the growth of the ebook market has nevertheless been inexorable. Overall the digital market is growing, and in the consumer marketplace in the UK the annual rate of growth is often between 200 and 400 per cent, though this is slowing now the base figure of the market has grown. The trend for trade publishers who have strong lists in terms of narrative fiction and non-fiction has been to see the percentage of digital sales increase. This growth has been faster in the US – a large market and the early availability of e-readers have ensured this – but the growth in international markets is following. For some US publishers the percentage of digital sales for these sorts of books is coming close to 30 per cent, while a more standard percentage is around 15–20 per cent in the UK.

An important driver of market growth is critical mass, the availability of enough product in digital form to attract the market. This has been important to drive sales and also exploit the typical purchasing behaviour of a new e-reader owner; there is usually a large spike in sales at the point someone get a new e-reader as they load up their device with new products; this then evens out and slows quite considerably, so it is important to exploit this first rush of activity.

Publishers have digitised much of their key backlist in order for their titles to be available for purchase. While not every backlist book will necessarily be digitised, there has been an impetus to ensure titles are available in order to maximise ebook sales; some customers re-buy their favourite books in digital form, and some publishers have been able to reinvigorate the sales of their backlists by providing this new medium; in addition, new customers have discovered some older well-known titles that may have been difficult to track down in print form. In some cases this has led to a pricing dilemma, as it is often cheaper to purchase the paperback of an older title where stock is being sold off than the Kindle version.

With this growth there have been continuing problems around copyright for older titles, and for some time publishers had to focus on reviewing their contracts and, in some cases, renegotiating them (in a way that did not affect the specialist markets). Digitising backlist, however, is not the same as releasing new titles: the backlist titles have already, in theory, made their money or, at least it is hoped, broken even on their previous print sales; these books were published in the first instance without the expectation of a digital book – the ebook therefore represents a nice additional uplift on the title. The question that is more testing for publishers is how to manage the business model for the new titles.

Print supports digital

Given these growing numbers, the business model has yet to move on radically. Print sales still make up the majority of the market: publishers need to ensure they do continue to focus on these markets. The way publishers have often looked at the sales of digital versions of their books is as a sale on top of their existing print versions. The legacy of digital rights in the subsidiary rights part of the contract may be one reason for the continuation of this, while the other critical point is that digital books, sold as they are at cheaper prices (often considerably cheaper than the hardback), are not able to support the total cost of the book.

Therefore, digital sales are more often than not added onto a profit and loss account as an additional sale, with the print version – first in hardback, then in paperback – accounting for most of the costs. In many cases digital sales have been treated rather like a special deal sale, one which adds a bonus of money but does not have to carry the higher costs of creating the books. This means that while costs are saved on the digital sale in terms of printing and distribution, the costs of preparing the text (such as copyediting and cover design, for instance), marketing it (often very costly) and payment/royalties to the author (where very large advances can have a crippling effect on the book's profit and loss account) have to be covered by print sales. The high price of the hardback has traditionally supported some of these costs, with profits being made on the release of the paperback at a later stage.

The ebook, like the paperback, can bring in extra revenue that goes to the bottom line, but without a hardback launch in the first place the book may not be affordable. However, how far can this be sustainable when publishing an ebook at a lower price? If fewer people buy the print copies, particularly the hardbacks, the logic of the current business model would suggest that the hardback price might have to increase further to continue to support the rest of the formats.

The relationship between costs and prices therefore has been thrown into the air, with customers' perceptions of where they think costs lie adding a further layer of complexity for publishers when trying to price cost effectively, but still attractively, for the market. This problem is at the root of the business models for consumer books and the models have yet to adjust convincingly, unlike the specialist markets, where customers have always held a clearer understanding of the value of the content in relation to the price when assessing the worth of the material.

Pricing and the ebook intermediary

Pricing is distorted further by the sorts of deals the intermediary does on the different formats, if, like Amazon, it can offer the different formats (as opposed to digital-only stores). So, however carefully crafted a pricing and format policy might be by a publisher, if Amazon decides to discount the paperback considerably while the ebook is set at the publisher's price according to agency pricing (which we discuss in Chapter 12), the prices at which the book is available seem to go against logic. In the trade print books market customers have been used to a fairly consistent approach to pricing for many years and have reasonably fixed expectations. Customers do not like complex or illogical pricing and tend to blame the publisher.

Phasing

Different publishers take different approaches to this. Early on some publishers followed the strategy of phasing the release of the ebook so a hardback comes out first, with the ebook release following on later with the paperback. This can still be the case with titles that are publishing events, such as a large significant biography, or for books where the hardback is launched early as a beautiful object in terms of production quality.

However, for other titles, such as novels, it has proved too difficult to delay access to a key title to separate launch dates. Clearly there is a legacy of producing hardbacks of novels, with customers waiting patiently for the paperback to come out if they are not willing to pay the high price of the hardback. But this expectation is a little different in the digital arena: why wait to get at a book (a contradiction given that one of the aspects at the very root of digital reading is speed to market)? And while the hardback was available for keen print customers, albeit at a premium, if a reader is a complete convert to the digital environment they do not want to be penalised by having to wait for the ebook.

If it releases ebooks alongside hardbacks, though, how does the publisher then manage the release of the paperback? Some publishers have released the ebook at the same price as the hardback and at the same time, but then the price reduces if the book subsequently comes out in paperback. While there is a logic to this, nevertheless the price differential between a hardback and a paperback is clearly presented in the physical attributes of the books, while an ebook is the same at the higher price and at the lower price, a fact that could annoy customers.

A customer of an ebook, priced high at launch, is buying not only the book but the early opportunity to read the book: this is one of the reasons for buying the hardback. However, educating the customer about the reason for this sort of 'premium' around an ebook is more tricky as, again, the actual product itself does not change when the price does.

So the ebook format stretches the customer's traditional perceptions of books and how they are published; the basic premise of the issue remains the same: customers always paid more to get the product early, but the change in print format from a hardback to a paperback distracted the customer from this central point; so publishers have to work out how to get customers to step back and see this issue of timeliness transparently.

Digital-only imprints

With business models still needing to be rethought, the focus has been on versions of the same content available in both print and digital formats. However, there are digital-only products that are being developed by publishers. These include short stories or journalistic pieces (long-form journalism) that can be quickly signed up and developed; publishers have been asking their backlist authors to write for these digital imprints or encouraged new authors to become involved.

The advantage here for publishers is that they have something they can sell at a low price (creating a floor, as it were, for their longer works); they do not have to cover the costs of expensive book production, and they can market these assets (saving money) and agree reasonable terms with authors, who have not had to commit too much of their time or effort to produce the work. This also drives customers to explore more digital titles and the low price allows customers to buy in easily. Most of the major publishers have developed some sort of 'born digital' list of this sort and are increasingly exploring options for other ways to publish digital-only products.

Genre publishing has also become an arena for publishers to launch digital-only lists. For some, this is a way of capitalising on the growth of genre markets with low-priced books. For others, it is a way to break newer authors who may in the longer term become print authors.

Case study: Providing customer choice

Releasing ebooks in a phased way is not always the clear solution. Taking the opposite approach, some publishers have chosen, for specific titles, to make a splash, launching the title in several formats at once, to ensure complete availability and choice for the customer. There are ways of differentiating between the formats to encourage sales of each.

One famous example was the autobiography of Stephen Fry, which Penguin launched in the UK in September 2010. This was produced in five formats in the UK. The hardback book took the traditional approach, priced at £20. This still outsold the other formats, with sales around 400,000; launching in autumn to feed into the Christmas market clearly was important. The ebook was launched at the same price (though it came down later to match the paperback price) but only made up 10 per cent of the sales for all the editions taken together.

An enhanced ebook was also created, launched at £20; this included the ebook plus some audiovisual material specially commissioned for the book, together with more navigational tools, internet links and photos. This was available for all colour digital reading devices and could be bought direct from Penguin. Enhanced ebooks have to be treated slightly separately by Amazon; the basic-level Kindle itself cannot support audiovisual material, so that part of the book cannot be seen, but a Kindle app on an iPhone or iPad can view it (this is not an issue for Kindle Fire tablets).

The audio digital download was also launched, at £12.99. This was the second most successful of the formats; being read by Stephen Fry, it was always going to have a strong market, but it is worth noting that the audio download market is clearly a strong one for books and in many cases the audio rights are held by publishers.

Finally, there was an app (myfryapp) which was priced at £7.99 and which featured the same basic content in a digital environment but with visual indexing so the title could be read in a non-linear fashion, which made it very innovative; given the content was the same, the price was low in comparison to buying the book, reflecting the app market, which we will look at on p. 121.

Not many books can replicate a strategy of this sort and the success of the various elements can be difficult to measure: this sort of book was obviously going to sell enough for experiments like these to be affordable: this is not the case for many titles, especially in areas such as new fiction.

Issues for the print products

Despite all this, hardbacks do still sell and, while their sales are declining in some consumer areas, there are specific characteristics to hardbacks that are influential in their continued survival. Depending on the type of book, the hardback represents something substantial; a coffee table book has a particular physical presence; art books require large high-quality pictures; cookery books should be durable and, for some, easy to annotate. Hardbacks are more often chosen as a gift and hardback launches before Christmas can continue to do well.

New approaches are also taking print titles further. While the future of print titles is not something that can be explored in depth here, there is a growing trend toward the development of the book in terms of its beauty as an artefact. A biography can be launched as a beautiful and expensive hardback before it becomes available in paperback (e.g. Claire Tomalin's biography of Dickens); lush cookbooks by celebrities, providing a sense of lifestyle, often do not turn into paperbacks let alone ebooks (for instance some of Jamie Oliver's books). The deluxe print edition, with time spent on covers and production quality, is a growing genre. The collectable nature of physical books is appreciated. These are manifestations of a redefinition of print for some areas of publishing.

Problems with ebooks

There are also a few issues that need to be solved for ebooks:

- gifts can feel less meaningful if given as an ebook voucher compared to a selected physical object
- library loans become complicated
- sharing good reads with friends is a problem
- the second-hand market also has yet to be considered

Specific titles can be gifted via Amazon in certain markets. Amazon is also developing a lending service via subscription so you can borrow books; you can in theory lend a title to another Kindle for a certain amount of time, though it might feel cumbersome. There are also library lending services using open ebook formats. There are, therefore, technological ways around these problems, but the physicality of the print book is part of the reason why some of these issues can never be fully resolved.

Other digital products

Enhanced ebooks

Ebooks have always been essentially an electronic reproduction of the book. The nature of digital publishing in this environment is rather straightforward and does not really exploit the opportunities that digital publishing provides. Ebooks still follow a broadly narrative approach and are no different in that respect from the print version. However, the enhanced ebook can take this further, adding in a variety of multimedia elements from photography to video clips, adding value to the product. This enables some publishers to charge more than for the paperback or the plain ebook and, depending on the cost of the additional features, supports the cost of the cheaper editions. It allows some flexibility in product development, designing a strategy for keen readers or fans of a particular writer; it is similar in concept to the special features added to DVDs or collectors' editions, which contain added value.

Definitions

The term enhanced ebook is loosely used and can be seen as somewhat interchangeable with apps. Indeed many argue that the term enhanced ebook will not be used for much longer; the concept of the book will have moved a long way beyond a digital book with add-ons, which is what many see the enhanced ebook as today. However, the principle of 'a book with features' is still an important one and for the moment I will use this term to distinguish a certain type of media-rich book that occupies a middle ground between the ebook on one side and the app on the other. Indeed the distinction is necessary to differentiate between books which have additional materials linked to them (special features, audiovisual material etc.) but are still produced using ebook software rather than produced and delivered as an app.

In the longer term it may well be that all ebooks are more enhanced than a simple black and white digital version of the text. The development of the iBookstore and iPad Author means that it has become easier to produce multimedia books as standard. The enhanced ebook is a title that would sit within the iBookstore on Apple, as opposed to within the Appstore, where book apps would sit. This distinction is important – an enhanced ebook can include visual learning material, embedded video footage and audio files, yet does not necessarily need to be as complex or as potentially expensive to develop as an app.

Enhanced ebooks and tablets

For some areas of publishing this is where the tablet becomes important. The ability to view beautiful visual material on extremely high-resolution screens in a portable way is important for titles where the illustrations and artwork are key. These titles will not necessarily be labelled 'enhanced' ebooks but they are beyond the basic digital version of a fiction title. The illustrated book market has not yet moved in any major way into the digital environment, but this is coming. While the physical element will still play a part in the market, it is clear the growth of the tablet and related publishing software is providing an important opportunity.

However, these enhanced ebook titles at this stage do not necessarily do much that is genuinely interactive. We have seen that textbooks can have a layer of simple interaction where iBooks Author is used (rolling photo galleries, note making), but they are not as sophisticated or highly produced as app book products are. So enhanced ebooks do not take the format of the book that much further at this stage and there are not many of them to reflect any definite trends in pricing.

The business model essentially follows the print copy. Sometimes savings can be made, reproducing a lot more visual material than might be affordable for the print version with the cost of paper and print (subject of course to relevant rights clearance). If charges increase for downloading times, media-rich texts may also suffer if their files become large.

Enhanced ebook futures?

This middle ground may be where the direction of the digital publishing starts to change most actively. Some of the key questions that might indicate the future are:

- How flexible can these sorts of books become when compared with an app?
- Are the development costs more manageable in an enhanced ebook format than an app?
- What sort of product does the market want? An interactive app, or a book with extra material?
- How far is a title more discoverable if it is sold via a digital bookstore environment, dedicated to books, compared to an app marketplace?

- Do publishers have more control over the sale of an enhanced ebook compared to an app product?

This last question raises the issue of the policies of the marketplaces in which these products are sold. Enhanced ebooks can potentially be sold directly by a publisher; apps for iPads (or for Android) need to be sold through the proprietary app store. Will there be differences around sales commission, for instance, or in-app purchases? How will those marketplaces control and promote their different offerings? Google Play will have a different approach to Apple, and those will be important influences on publishers' decisions about what sort of product they produce. Apple has recently been reported to have rejected some titles from their app store in order to move them into the iBookstore; this might not be a major problem, may even be a very good idea, but it suggests that the publisher is at the mercy of a particular company's policy at a particular time. For publishers this represents a change in their business operations; these intermediaries will be influencing the sort of product they create and knowing their rules will be very important. These are all important considerations and ones that mean publishers need to bear in mind a wider range of distribution decisions for their content.

Book apps

The challenges of producing apps

The area of apps for books has, it seems, created much more of a stir for publishers as they consider whether to enter this marketplace and, if so, how they can manage it. Smart phones and tablets have developed an app culture offering highly interactive, visual material; it seems like there should be potential for developing exciting app books. However, the apps can cost varying amounts to develop, while the prices charged for general apps are low. Sales occur through one main intermediary who sets the policies for those sales. More third party developers are required in creating and administering the apps. Should publishers be getting into this marketplace, which differs so much from their traditional arena?

Other questions emerge. While Android-based devices continue to grow, research generally agrees that users of Apple devices spend more money than those with Android ones, so the focus of development has generally been getting apps into the Apple app store. However, that could mean missing out on an important part of the market. But if it is also to be sold for Android-based devices the product has to be built again; this does not necessarily have to mean building from scratch, but it can still be an additional cost.

Question of scale

There are various approaches to app publishing and the business models vary here; there is a big difference between a small-scale app and a large one, while prices can vary considerably. Some apps can be created reasonably cheaply if they are not too complex and broadly follow a developed template; this can then be tweaked for another product. Others are expensive and involve creating a considerable amount of new content to supplement any book content already available. There are consumer reference materials, for instance (such as photographic travel guides), that it makes sense to have in an app format allowing easy navigation in a variety of ways around a range of visual reference materials; other apps take an extremely sophisticated approach to the material (Faber and Faber solar system) and recast it and extend it by quite some margin beyond the original print version. Scale therefore is much wider ranging when producing an app than an ebook: a publisher could be producing anything from a quick quiz based on their books through to a complex and comprehensive multi-layered work, and with all sorts of pricing patterns to adopt.

Development strategies

The costs of developing an app can vary enormously and for some of the complex, higher-priced ones a partnership approach is the only way to afford it. In managing the development of apps various approaches have been taken:

- **Joint venture:** where an app is extremely expensive to produce (some can be well up to £100,000 where new material needs to be commissioned and detailed research undertaken as well as complex software development) it is unlikely a trade publisher would easily spend the money, and examples of the most sophisticated apps tend to have been developed as a joint venture or co-publishing deal where each party contributes a certain amount to the project (in time, services, content, money, etc.); for every sale made they will gain a share of the revenue. Disadvantages here are that control and ownership both over the product and over the ability to interact with Apple's app store can be lost for the publisher. Advantages however are the ability to produce high-quality content by involving partners who are expert at their different activities – whether producing audio files, specifically commissioned visuals, video content with actors, sophisticated GPS software, etc. The best people to deal with Apple may well be the developers rather than the publishers anyway.
- **Buy the services of a supplier:** paying the producer outright is the option that publishers would usually follow for less costly apps. They simply spec out their idea and pay a developer to produce it; here developers may be able to make use of their own software. The publisher then has complete control over the product.
- **Hybrid arrangements:** there are also hybrid models where developers offer a model which shares the profit. As an example, developers can cover the costs themselves, deal with Apple and own copyright of the app. They have fixed arrangements where they offer to the publishers a percentage of the revenue (the revenue left after the author has been paid their royalty). The publisher pays for the marketing of the product and manages the licence of the content from the copyright holder. There may be similar arrangements where developers have created a particular type of app template for which they have spent some time perfecting a certain unique type of navigation, or a way of integrating certain types of content, and this is used by a variety of publishers for their content. In these cases the developer still works as a partner rather than a supplier working to a publisher's spec. 'Made in Me' is an example of an app producer that has a story book app that can be personalised; this has formed the basis of different collaborations with stories held by different publishers.
- **Licensing:** a publisher can simply license its material into other apps in a rights deal. As we see later, these are not necessarily that straightforward but they do avoid any involvement in developing digital apps.

Business models

The basic app business model has, perhaps more than other digital books, released itself from any ties with the profit and loss of the print versions. An app stands alone and, while the myfryapp mentioned above did link to the book, many apps take a title and move quite some way from the print product, ensuring that the profit and loss account has to make sense without being an adjunct to a print book. Once a product is self-supporting the cost of development of the content has to be included, not just the cost of the format, so this has put pressure on app profit and loss accounts. It is one of the reasons that the emphasis of some publishers is on apps that exploit backlist materials, some of which may be owned outright by the publishers so the cost of the content is covered; and other titles will at least have paid for themselves in one format so there is no need to build in the cost of a large advance (as an example).

In terms of generating revenue, app models have developed in a variety of ways:

- **Paid for app:** this is clearly a straightforward single transaction similar to buying a book. In general most book apps currently take this approach (if they are not free), mimicking the book environment; however, other forms of payment are likely to become more popular.
- **The free app:** this is broadly for marketing and profile raising. Here the cost of development needs to be covered; the marketing aspect of the app may be worth it, to create a buzz and draw attention to the publisher's other activities (maybe its backlist), but it is difficult to measure in terms of sales success for other titles.
- **The freemium model:** the basic app is free but customers buy into additional material or services. This can cover the in-app purchase, where customers can agree to buy more material, and is increasingly popular. There are benefits: the app may be more attractive, overcoming some discoverability issues, while free; once engaged, purchasers may buy more access, which also helps the publisher get a better understanding of its customers. Publishers are usually confident of the quality of their content, so if they can get customers in to see it the purchase can follow.
- **In-app subscription:** this is also a common form of payment in the app marketplace and one that publishers may be able to use more effectively in the future as they experiment more with pricing. One of the trends is for consumers to pay a subscription for access and then expect content to be free once there, incurring no further costs; while there are questions about the devaluing of content (as we shall see in Chapter 12) this does mean the concept of a subscription is growing in currency if one can then follow up with enough content.

App pricing: the challenge of low prices

Pricing is, as ever, the central challenge. The average price for apps in general has its own dynamic and price points; book apps can be muddied by this more homogenous expectation around the price for apps. There are apps produced by specialist publishers that are able to sell at higher prices, but these do not require high exposure to a consumer market and can be marketed easily via the specialist publisher's existing direct marketing channels. The challenge is therefore in the consumer market.

The general consumer is used to buying apps at low prices; yet their expectation of the content is high, their experience with interactive content-rich apps in other sectors leading those expectations. In general the arena of the app is based on very high numbers at very low prices (micropayments almost), which is not a natural environment for publishers. Free apps proliferate in the market, though often as a way to engage customers to buy into something more. However, even the next step up is still cheap and there are several price points before one starts to reach the prices that match standard paperbacks.

So publishers have to consider whether they want to move down to meet the prices at the low end or try to establish a price band typical for book apps. A book can have a lot more content than a single-use app for a very specific task so the market may support higher costs, but an app over £10 is an oddity and the offer has to be extremely compelling. Faber and Faber have famously produced apps at around £15 which have proved successful. These generate some revenues for Apple at that high price and for that reason do stand out at times in some bestseller lists. However, these apps are very sophisticated and extremely expensive to produce; the actual development of the app and its architecture is costly, as is the creation of materials that needs to go into the app (for example commissioning film crews to film actors reading Shakespeare).

App price expectations

Publishers have a challenge to create an expectation of a book price within an app environment and they have to strike a balance between pricing at a price that customers will buy and covering the costs of development. If you look at apps at a higher price, such as the Faber and Faber titles made in association with Touchstone, the quality and sophistication is clear immediately; but they also take the book into new arenas; for example, in the case of their Shakespeare sonnets app, specially commissioned video clips of well-known actors reading the poems mean consumers may value this in a different way, perhaps more like buying a TV programme or short film. The problem is the publisher has to choose carefully to ensure its core market will buy at that price, while educating newer markets that some types of book apps are so sophisticated and so very different from standard apps that they have to be priced differently, even if the actual price is very similar to a normal book price.

In general, then, the app price is lower than the book price but for that lower price a lower-spec app is produced. It can still be interactive and highly visual but it may not be very sophisticated. The cost of producing it must be taken into account. The problem that this raises is that customers expect apps to do a lot once they pay for them. They can see the limitations in free or very low-priced apps, and do not necessarily expect much from them, but given the technological capabilities of apps (capabilities that customers expect simply because they have got used to technology) they expect apps of any sort to do a lot – so once a publisher is charging over £10 the expectation of technological wizardry for that app is immense. Here again the publisher is moving into a world where expectations and valuation of content are very different from the one they are used to. A customer for a hardback cookery book at £15 knows what to expect and the content is the main feature; but expectations of a £15 app would be very much higher.

Not enough apps have been produced yet to create a sense of how app pricing for books may settle, though one advantage of the apps market is that prices can be changed regularly and there is a lot more flexibility to test the market, promote special sales opportunities (e.g. free days for apps) and change pricing if necessary; so as a publisher observes a market it can manipulate the price much more easily and find the price point where enough people will buy while still supporting costs. Of course playing around with pricing too much is tiresome for customers and no one wants to find they have bought a book that was reduced in price immediately afterwards, but the opportunities for experimenting are much easier to manage than through a traditional book trade.

One area where book apps are increasing rapidly is the children's picture book market; one can see that well-known well-loved book characters make sense in an app environment where children can interact with their favourites. To some extent the content of the apps does not have to be extremely extensive and the pricing for children's picture books is not too far removed from low-priced apps, so the gap between a book and an app price is less distinct. These title have several attractions for publishers: they can be marketed internationally; high-quality visual material can be reproduced cost effectively and in any quantity; translations can be arranged easily (key for children's books).

Further challenges of the app market

There are some particular issues that publishers face with regard to the app market. These include:

- **Updating:** ebooks exist as a finished product once in the market and as they are reasonably straightforward they are not often affected by technological changes to devices. However, apps operate differently and with every new update in technology glitches can appear that need correcting to ensure the title still works. Providing updates and maybe additional material is something publishers need to consider; for other apps this tends to be considered as a free part of the service and so needs to be budgeted for in the original product. Updates can be a good way to present the product again to the customer and some publishers have noted increased sales to new customers when they have produced an update to their original product. However, this then raises other questions: do new editions need to be issued? If so, how often? These are questions that publishers have to resolve.

- **Competing in the app environment:** another aspect of apps is that, unlike the ebook, which still sits within a publishing environment, in this arena products may be competing with those produced by other sorts of entertainment industries. The quiz app, for instance, is not in the domain of book publishers alone and publishers have to consider whether they can really work within these newer marketplaces, with different competitors. In many cases, therefore, apps of this sort are often marketing tools, looking to drive sales of a brand name, whether in app or book environments, and care has to be taken over choices of products when deciding what to do.

- **Finding partners:** app developers will be working with all sorts of customers and may not always be focused just on book publishing (unlike the traditional suppliers that are more embedded into the book industry). They may well be working within games development and interactive media for a much wider environment. They can argue that book apps do need to go beyond the concept of the book in any case, but they are nevertheless working within a much wider entertainment industry. This can mean the low costs and tight profit margins that publishers often work to are not an attractive arena for them (compared to games manufacture, for instance). There are developers that work primarily with publishers and are able to offer smaller-scale opportunities for app development. App developers are proliferating and some are looking for content, so they will find links with publishers beneficial as they exploit the platform they are developing.

- **New market entrants:** some app developers will be doing their own publishing, finding their own authors and not going to a publisher at all. These latter groups are therefore developing business models that do not require them to fit a legacy of print products into their activity and they can do something new in an agile way, leaving behind the publishers, who have to redesign their large publishing structures. This is a very different supplier marketplace for publishers.
- **Discoverability:** the issue of discoverability is particularly important when selling apps. Publishers have to work hard at the continual promotion of the titles to maintain their presence in the app store. The category of book apps within the app store certainly helps a new title, mainly because there are not many book apps, so most book apps will feature in the bestseller lists for a while (as long as they can compete with Disney apps). However, within that, keeping your title to the fore requires constant effort, and as more books move into the area, further issues around discoverability emerge. Publishers have to monitor spikes in sales, perhaps after a good review comes out, and continuously market; watching rankings and trying to get the app noticed by Apple so it will feature on Apple's recommended and editor's picks lists are important. Overall, publishers are only beginning to understand the behaviour of customers in the app environment and this needs to be watched closely in order for them to work out how to manage app selling effectively.

Is an app worth it?

There are many considerations publishers need to be aware of when deciding whether to create an app. Even where one can be created cheaply, the publisher needs to be sure whether the app makes sense or not. There is an attraction to doing something exciting in the app marketplace, but as apps are such a challenge they really do have to be worth doing and make some sort of strategic sense.

The strategic objective needs to be clear. What is a publisher trying to achieve with an app? So, for instance, the app may need to make revenue, generating this by sales or access, in which case the costs needs to be balanced with the potential revenue. It may be that the app is more focused around marketing a product, in which case it is important to ensure there is a level of engagement with customers that may enable a publisher to assess its success. In some cases it may be purely strategic, to develop brand awareness for the company as a whole, or experiment with a format and price, in which case the break-even parameters may be a little different if profit can be put to one side.

Once the vision is clear, the type of development arrangement needs to be decided and clear objectives put in place for the arrangement, with detailed specifications and checks to ensure the project is managed effectively and does not try to do too much, go over budget or take too long.

Experience of working on multi-layered projects of this sort, developing new methods of communicating with different sorts of suppliers and building knowledge is important and takes time to develop, which explains why publishers are moving only slowing into this marketplace.

Apps are time consuming to set up but once fully in development can be produced quite quickly and can be made instantly available to the market once they are ready; the lead times and processes around marketing the product therefore are very different from traditional sales planning.

This expertise is not necessarily very different from the way specialist publishers have had to develop new project management techniques, but they have done so with the safe knowledge of a market ready for them; for consumer publishers the level of risk is much more difficult to quantify.

The impact of digital publishing on the wider consumer environment

Marketing and social media

This range of new product types emerging in the market poses challenges for marketing at just the point when the traditional approaches to marketing are changing. The activities within marketing departments are evolving rapidly in response to the sorts of structural changes that are taking place with the growth of digital products. Some argue that the marketing function will continue to grow in importance for a publishing house: where production spend is less, the marketing spend will need to grow to ensure discoverability for authors. It is a lot of hard work for a writer to undertake this aspect of publishing on their own, and marketing may be a compelling reason for them to choose a publisher above self-publishing.

In addition, as the number of sales personnel potentially declines with the decline of bookshops, marketing departments are becoming involved in negotiating deals and planning promotions with customers like Amazon. They have to develop greater expertise to deal with these sorts of key relationships. Reaching consumers in the traditional way of publishing generally meant creating some buzz and PR around a book in the form of reviews, events and awards, so driving consumer interest. Marketing needed to promote books to the key intermediaries, wholesalers and bookshops, in order to encourage these sellers to stock the books, making sure they had enough material with which to promote them while advertising books to get customers into bookshops in the first place.

Since the online marketplace can stock everything (the long tail), marketing has to expand its approach to focus not just on getting the book stocked on the shelves but also on discoverability of the book within the internet store. This challenge obviously exists for both print and ebooks. However, as more books move into a digital environment this can become more of a challenge and it is this that is changing the methods for marketing both print and ebooks. All sorts of techniques to develop discoverability are being explored, from posting animations or author conversations on YouTube to launching Twitter competitions and online games, for a new style of word-of-mouth marketing.

Marketing departments are rapidly developing expertise on the way to manage search engine optimisation, create good metadata in their material in order to facilitate keyword searches and ensure titles are highlighted as far as possible within online retail environments. They are also concentrating more closely on building direct relationships with certain groups of readers using social media. However, this requires skills in developing conversations and communities that have not traditionally formed a key part of the trade marketing activity.

Social media and content

Social media obviously play an important role in expanding marketing opportunities. A side effect of this is that, while social media are not the focus for monetising content for publishers, a considerable amount of content development of one sort or another is taking place on social media sites. Publishers have recognised the importance of using social media for marketing. Here are just some of the newer activities they will be engaging in:

- developing microsites for their key writers
- writing blogs for particular subject areas
- interacting with fan sites
- setting up competitions and events
- creating a buzz around Facebook sites and Twitter feeds

All of these require content, much of which needs to be created for these specific purposes. Some of this new content may come from authors (YouTube excerpts of key authors talking about their latest books or sample material loaded up early); some of this content may be being produced in house (such as reports on book events for blogs or other websites); and other content may be especially commissioned for the website, such as games to support a children's book series. Trying to create opportunities for customers to spread the word to their friends about good books themselves is critical, harnessing the power of word of mouth so they do the marketing for you – this becomes part of your 'earned' marketing.

In this environment all this additional content is free to the consumer. That could be seen to be diluting the offering (for instance, is this the sort of material which might go into an ebook?) but is an essential part of marketing for social media.

Social media for selling

One of the purposes of this sort of activity is to create a more direct relationship with the market. As the bookshops continue to decline and online stores dominate, publishers are looking for ways to get in touch with their markets directly to understand them better. Traditionally publishers have only needed a number of well-established, well-run relationships with key members of the trade rather than hundreds of individual relationships with individual customers. They need to learn the skills to get in direct contact with their customers from both a selling point of view and a product development point of view.

Starting conversations with their customer base has been a big driver. From the point of view of selling it is important that publishers begin to cultivate a customer base that they can approach directly. A publisher is not expecting to move much of its market into buying direct, but there are compelling reasons to try and tap some of the market at least. Amazon may claim a large part of its market and, unlike booksellers, who are dependent on publishers, Amazon is less so; it can put pressure on discounts. Getting sales knowledge from Amazon is a lot more difficult than via bookshops and in effect the publisher is further removed from the customer than previously. This is particularly noticeable in the change to ebooks. When they were delivering physical books daily to bookshops publishers could watch sales and stock patterns change at any time they wanted; they could also see more precisely where the sales were going. Now they are not able to watch sales patterns as closely and even when they get a report on downloads from Amazon the data may well not be as rich.

A further issue is around reviews and recommendations. Customers are less likely to read reviews in newspapers, which are suffering a decline of certain parts of the market where free news has replaced the need to buy a paper. For other parts of the market, reviews in newspapers remain key but they now need to compete with the continuous reviewing of customers on the internet, who may just be briefly recommending a title they enjoyed or setting up well-developed blogs and discussion forums. The marketing and PR department has to consider how to engage with these new voices.

Social media for new product development

Publishers are also beginning to use social media as a way to access more content, not just for further marketing purposes but potentially to source authors. This may be a way for publishers to manage the slush pile, using readers of interactive sites where new stories can be posted to help sort new book ideas; the ones that seem the most attractive to readers of the site move forward onto a list to be considered by publishers (authonomy is an example set up by HarperCollins). Here are, potentially, the roots to developing new sources of content for publishers. We will look at content development in Chapter 13. Where it may not be directly sourcing new authors, any discussion forum or recommendation site can provide a publisher with important research into the way at least some consumers behave in a digital environment. Publishers will only reach a certain group of users who participate actively in social media, but this can still provide some useful knowledge.

Change for bookshops

The use of social media for marketing has been important as bookshops decline. Exposure via bookshops has, up to now, been critical for a book title and marketing activity can promote large titles to audiences that may not necessarily have browsed in bookshops. There is research by Bowker PubTrack (carried out in 2007 and cited by Thompson) about the choices of book people make and how they quite often buy a book they had not planned to buy (some may have expected to buy something, for others the purchase might have been made entirely on impulse). A buyer might be inspired to buy something from browsing without knowing beforehand what specific title they would buy; the number of books customers bought that they did not necessarily intend to buy is an interesting statistic that shows how far browsing can affect sales. The bestsellers will be high in a customer's consciousness wherever they purchase, but for smaller titles, and particularly for gifts and highly illustrated books, where the customer is less usually looking for a specific title, the ability to sit beside a bestseller is important for attracting attention.

As intermediaries, the online shops are also less in the control of the publisher; publishers were able to organise promotions and shop fronts with bookshops to draw attention to particular titles and particular times; while deals are agreed with online bookshops, it is difficult to get the same impact. Amazon has also tried to keep conversations going and raise awareness of titles for customers specifically within the Kindle environment so that readers of ebooks are encouraged to interact explicitly with the online bookshop; this is done by recommending titles at the end of the book and creating an environment where there is rudimentary sharing of information with other readers of the book (allowing readers to read lines highlighted by other readers, for instance).

Bookshops are trying to develop their own internet presence; the large chains have sophisticated websites and some, like Barnes and Noble, have built successful online stores, but for others, such as Waterstones in the UK, it has been more of a challenge to create an online presence because Amazon had such a strong offering and online customers already. Independent shops that need to compete selling online books have options such as Hive from Gardners, a key bookshop distributor: here they can use the Gardners internet purchasing system and brand their own bookshop around it. Smaller bookshops are having to develop a greater community presence to maintain their business; they cannot afford to compete on discounts so need to develop other compelling reasons for customers to use them, whether it is by providing excellent individual service, reading group support or events (as examples).

With print being core to the bookshop business ebooks are a threat. However, it must be remembered that with the majority of sales still based in print, the bookshop is still an extremely important marketplace for a publisher even if it is competing with print distribution of supermarkets and online bookstores.

Bookshops do play an important part in showcasing titles and, in many ways, even where there is an ebook available the print title may be helping drive sales as a marketing tool, as the physical and visual impact is important; Amazon itself is aware of the power of the bookshop, providing a barcode scanner which means while they are in a shop browsing a customer can scan it into their Amazon app and purchase the title online. Meanwhile, where customers are not using bookshops but simply going online for ebooks, it becomes important for publishers to have some sort of direct relationship to build up the interest around new launches and keep customers aware of when a new title by their favourite author is due.

Publishers and the direct consumer sale

Some major publishers are developing the e-commerce aspects of their websites in order to develop the capacity to sell direct to their customers. Books can be sold in print form as well as downloaded, but the issues around compatibility mean they cannot sell a Kindle version and their systems are still not quite as smooth and as comprehensive as using an online bookshop. However, developing more expertise around e-selling may encourage at least a specific part of their market to buy direct, and with that sort of contact it is easier to profile customers and see who is buying their books. For the general market, customers will not necessarily know which publisher has the book they want, they may want titles across several publishers and they will stick with their tried and testing online marketplace. Publishers are also developing an online presence, setting up their own book communities. Anobii was set up by several major publishers to encourage reading and debating around titles, allowing users of the site to interact with each other alongside marketing activity. This particular site has been bought by

Sainsburys in the UK. The site still exists in an international environment, while in the UK the community element of Anobii has been built into the Sainsbury ebook retail site, thus combining a well-established retail brand and a social network site to attract book lovers.

Issues for digital browsing

Online sites are paying attention to ways of improving the browsing experience. Amazon has considered this aspect, organising its bookshop to try and build a browsing experience in various ways, including:

- the 'search inside' mechanism to get an idea of a title
- rankings from sales
- recommendations suggested by the Amazon algorithms
- recommendations based on connecting the title to other titles that were also bought by other customers at the same time
- reviews from other Amazon users, which themselves are ranked for usefulness

These are all innovative ways to try and develop the 'bookshop' experience but they do not quite substitute for the randomness of a purchase in a bookshop; nor does the sampling quite replicate the ability to flick through a whole book and get a sense of the length and structure of it.

Futurising the book

While we have seen how ebooks are developing as a new format, they have yet to develop as a new product. The enhanced ebook is moving in this direction but there are still many aspects of the digital book that are essentially those of a traditional book. The tablet is increasing the opportunities to develop illustrated titles, though these also tend to be recognisably a book. The app is taking the book into a new environment and experimenting much more effectively with the way of interacting with a book, perhaps through a game or with a recorded performance; ways of linking the book or story to something more personal or something the reader can manipulate to some extent have also been developed. But many would argue the starting point is still the traditional book.

However, the technology to make the book something much more again is developing, and companies are beginning to spend time futurising how books connect to each other or how a narrative develops much more interactively again, maybe through GPS links to a reader's actual location. Publishers at heart are creative and, with that, innovative. They have been innovative with content for a long time, even if innovations over format have been more limited up to now.

Publishers can see the opportunities to use an app environment to rethink the way the book works. These are examples of the different sorts of directions in which the book format can evolve within a digital environment:

- **Narrative form:** there are examples of products that have been moving to non-linear narrative forms – something that the children's apps have certainly been doing and some experiments in adult apps are now exploring. There are titles with multiple endings and ways for readers to interact and direct narratives (such as Profile and Inkle Studio's Frankenstein, where the reader is placed in conversation with Frankenstein).

- **Shared experiences:** another direction is to increase the connectivity of books, sharing reading experiences as you go and drawing elements of social media into the offering. Sharing writing too can build on this.
- **Curation:** in this arena editors can come up with much more creative ideas around content; they can curate new sorts of products or act as producers by bringing different content sets together and thinking of new ways to present them. New connections can evolve and readers can get a more holistic embedded experience.
- **Navigation and presentation:** for publishers there is suddenly a new space to explore ways to present things and overcome certain physical problems. For instance, an app can provide a new way to navigate a graphic novel, or stream in new content, or involve the reader much more closely. App developers are often looking for content to show off their exciting new presentation and content management tools.
- **New authoring approaches:** multiple concurrent narratives can be produced by different authors collaborating in interactive ways, taking over different elements or viewpoints of the story, adding to the content within real time, possibly responding to readers' interactions.

The cost of developing more sophisticated books, whether through highly visual elements or sophisticated software, is considerable. There are many stories, often covered in news features, of the complexity of delivering such projects, while the market itself is not big enough to justify them. These efforts, however, do try to take a different approach, rethinking the product and using technology to solve problems and create ideas, rather than simply transferring a book into a digital environment.

Many industry commentators can be quoted as saying that publishers need to see themselves as entertainers and from that point of view create new entertainment technologies rather than look at what book content they have and try to convert it into a digital product. If publishers can see what it is they really do – provide entertainment or share knowledge or create learning opportunities – they will be in a stronger position to move forward and not be trapped by the legacy of their print pasts.

So publishers need to extend their view of themselves. The term curating has been mentioned; it is currently popular, indicating the range of content a publisher might be employing, selecting and organising in order to create a new product. In this, digital convergence can be seen more clearly. A publisher may be dealing with anything from knowledge management and games development to e-learning and collaboration; it could be including anything from user-generated material to especially commissioned video footage in its products. The products of the future will not draw distinctions between these sorts of different applications of media.

Once this is recognised it throws up much wider opportunities to collaborate. Larger-scale partnerships can develop across a range of industries; a London app is being produced by involving audio tours, a museum, a publisher (Macmillan) and news archives. This is an example of digital products, that are born digital, driving an area of convergence for publishers – a programme on television can link to a book, which can bring together a community involved in a challenge. This can be a way for publishers to broaden their definition of themselves and ensure they are involved right at the centre of the new digital world, providing the content part of the package since it is content they are really good at.

Conclusion

The consumer marketplace, having lagged behind the specialist markets, as we have seen, has in the last few years been set alight by digital publishing opportunities. Models for straightforward ebooks have been developed and, while challenges remain (about pricing for example), the simple shift of format has proved reasonably straightforward. However, moves to adopt a more innovative approach to content with enhanced books and apps are not yet very widespread; publishers are being innovative and experimental but not on any large scale: they remain understandably cautious, given the cost of investment required, as they develop new types of products in the consumer marketplace. This is not just because of the nervousness of the publishers. Consumers themselves are just starting to explore new ways around stories, narrative and content in digital environments; but what will become critical for publishers is the need to understand the way the changing consumer will value this new approach to content in the future.

Further reading and resources

Books

Darnon, Robert. *The Case for Books*. Public Affairs, 2009.
Phillips, Angus. 'Do Books Have a Future?' Coda in *The Wiley Companion to the History of the Book*. Wiley Blackwell, 2007.
Thompson, John. *Merchants of Culture*. Polity Press, 2010.

Websites

authonomy.com – the HarperCollins site encouraging authors
www.anobii.com – a community book site, originally set up by a group of publishers and now being transferred to the ownership of Sainsbury; the Sainsbury's site can be found at www.sainsburysebook.co.uk
www.bookconsumer.com – for background to Bowker Pubtrack and its consumer book research
www.bookmarketing.co.uk – for research into the book publishing industry
www.bowker.co.uk – for background to Bowker and the various services it provides, including Pubtrack and consumer book research
www.goodreads.com – an Amazon-owned site for sharing reading experiences
www.shelfari.com – an Amazon-owned site for sharing reading experiences
www.tescoebooks.com/tescoweb/home.aspx – Tesco's UK ebook site
www.theliteraryplatform.com – a news site that covers developments in digital publishing, focusing on consumer publishing and showcasing new digital app and enhanced ebook products

Questions to consider

1 What sort of digital publishing strategy makes sense for the print backlist?
2 How do you attempt to overcome the issues of discoverability?
3 How successful are publishers at building brands?
4 If you were devising a digital strategy as a small independent publisher where would you start? What information would you like to have?
5 Is there a future for the 'enhanced ebook'?
6 What sort of apps do you think it makes sense for a publisher to engage in?
7 Take a selection of publisher websites and microsites. Which do you feel are the most effective at engaging the reader?
8 Do you think a publisher can really expect to create much of a direct relationship with its customers?
9 What is the future for bookshops and how can publishers work with them effectively?

Part III
Digital publishing issues

Introduction to Part III

Part III looks at the issues that are under continual scrutiny as digital models emerge. These issues cross over the different publishing sectors; they do not all necessarily impact on every sector to the same degree, but they all raise questions that publishers across fields are having to consider. They have also been grouped together because they remain very much open-ended discussions, constantly changing as the digital business environment speeds up. Because the digital world encompasses increasing levels of convergence, issues previously outside core publishing activities are impinging on publishers more explicitly: books are another form of entertainment and this now needs to be more clearly acknowledged as publishers compete with other sectors; the edges between types of digital environment are becoming more blurred; even the question 'what is a book?' has become a point of debate.

The brisk rate of change in the business environment for digital publishing has led to some unusual events that have, in the context of traditional publishing, been quite dramatic. One such event was the action by Google to mass-digitise a huge selection of titles following arrangements that had been made with some of the world's most famous libraries. This was viewed at the time by some as the freeing of information from where it lay undiscovered on dusty library shelves, while for others it was a mass raid on copyright and a threat to the rights of authors to own their creativity.

Another example has been the debates about various pricing mechanisms for digital products that have emerged with the advent of the large technology companies such as Amazon and Apple; courts have been investigating anti-competitive collusion among publishers, and publishers have accused Amazon of exploiting its monopoly position. These events continue to unfold and, while they touch different parts of publishing to a greater or lesser extent, they are important when examining the environment for digital publishing.

Issues such as these will continue to be debated and publishers are currently considering effective responses. They include:

- **Copyright:** copyright needs to be flexible enough to cope with the challenges of the digital age. Some question how far it is fit for purpose, while initiatives aim to ensure it can be effectively adapted.
- **Copyright infringement and piracy:** digital piracy is an issue for most publishers. The high value of reference information means it is a target, as are novels, where sheer quantity of sales are key. Enforcement is necessary but there arc other solutions as well to build a stronger legitimate marketplace for digital products.

- **Rights sales:** while digital rights release more opportunities for sales, they also mean more complexity.
- **Pricing:** digital pricing is more fluid than print pricing; the issues around agency and wholesale pricing may be short-term issues but the key is to understand the consumer response to pricing; the consumer is becoming much more of a player in the way digital pricing works.
- **Content developers:** the traditional publishing industry is under attack from new players entering the market for content as the nature of publishing is redefined; these players have money and powerful brands, and enter the content marketplace for different reasons. Can publishers compete?
- **Publishing structures:** as the industry has to re-evaluate what it is all about in the digital age, while some things remain constant, other aspects of a publisher's behaviour will have to change, and change quickly. Part III will take a look at the way new publishing structures might emerge from the traditional players in the longer term.

10 Copyright, piracy and other legal issues

This chapter introduces some of the main copyright and legal issues that need to be considered in the context of digital publishing. It aims to provide a brief introduction to each topic and outlines the background to some of the debates that continue to surface, with references at the end for further research.

The topics outlined are:

1 Copyright: fit for the digital age?
2 Issues around infringement: mass digitisation, protection with DRM and piracy
3 Contract considerations

Introduction

The emergence of digital products has led to a growing challenge for publishers operating in the digital environment. One of the most fundamental aspects of publishing that has come under scrutiny during the development and expansion of the internet has been the issue of copyright. Copyright has existed for hundreds of years and, while it operates differently in different countries, the basic principle of creators owning the right to their creation has come to form the basis of much of the way publishing business is done across the world. Copyright has been regarded as a way for creators of content to gain recognition for their work (an ongoing right to be seen as the creator) as well as to benefit commercially from their creation if they wish. For many this right is seen as important in encouraging creativity to continue; if creators know their work is protected in some form or other, they will continue to create, so enriching the intellectual, cultural and economic strength of their society.

One of the guiding principles of the World Wide Web since its inception has been the ability of everyone to connect and share information. There is a belief in the fundamental democracy represented by the fact the internet can facilitate openness and allow for engagement without boundaries. With Web 2.0 we can engage more directly with others across social media, for instance, whether by becoming involved in movements, recommending products or creating content. The growth in 'internet philosophy' books is testament to the involved nature of the debate, particularly in relation to free content. These questions can touch on copyright: should information be free? If so, is copyright limiting this sense of freedom? If work can be published and distributed very quickly and cheaply, does copyright remain an old-fashioned way of controlling the spread of content – indeed, is it a form of censorship in itself?

Publishers, as one of the stakeholders in the construct of copyright, are facing a growing debate about the relevance of copyright in the digital age. Copyright in the print book was reasonably clear. The creation was contained in a physical product, which made it easy to manage. However, a digital product is a lot more difficult to control as it can be distributed so easily and quickly. Most would argue easy access is a good thing: society should encourage the rapid and collaborative spread of research or provide educational materials to countries that cannot afford them. But managing content carefully, protecting creators and their rights are still important, even where the intention is for their content to be distributed openly and freely. There are also issues, such as infringement and piracy, which were already important but have become more complex with the rise of digital publishing. So the areas of copyright and legality are coming increasingly under scrutiny.

Copyright

Some key tenets of copyright

One of the key principles of copyright is that it needs to be clear who owns what. Creators need to clearly state that their creation is theirs and assert that it is not by someone else. Once they have clearly stated this, they can license the right to produce and publish their content to others if they wish, or even assign the right of the material itself to someone else (for instance where work is created as part of a job for which the employee is paid).

Another aspect of copyright is that it safeguards the integrity of the content: it is as the creator wanted it and has not been manipulated, changed or adapted in any way. This can be a critical issue for certain types of content (such as scientific material) and ensures quality of provenance. This can be important for users of that content, particularly where copies carrying possibly critical mistakes may be circulating easily around the internet. It is also important for the makers of content, providing some level of protection that their work will be distributed in the state they wish.

Publishers carry an important responsibility on behalf of authors to ensure they protect the copyright with which they are entrusted. Publishers are therefore pivotal in helping authors gain what they want from their creation – protection for their content and their reputation, as well as the opportunity to gain commercially from the work. The opportunity for digital content to be endlessly duplicated and to circulate continuously around the internet makes this more of a challenge for publishers.

Problems with the basis of copyright in the digital environment

Some see problems with copyright when adapted for the digital environment. Commentators raise the following questions:

- Is copyright essentially a mechanism for print?
- When content is so easily available is copyright adaptable?

- Does the commercial nuance to copyright contradict the essentially 'free' nature of the internet?
- Does copyright lead to too much control?

In the first case some feel that, as it has grown out of the print industry, copyright is not flexible enough to adapt to technology of a very different nature. It worked when production was limited, by the nature of printing, and the development of content was scarce – authors needed to make a living and publishers supported them in that. The print product was finite and distributed in a specific way. The internet instead opens up new ways of creating, spreading and using content.

Today content is abundant and, with low barriers to entry for publishing, access to it is easy; key aspects of the publishing value chain have changed. Business models for publishing and ways of controlling content are very different on the internet. Consumers too have changed, as has the pattern of supply and demand, so copyright is not necessarily the right construct to operate in this environment.

A creator has a right to gain from their creation and copyright provides a framework for that. Creators have made some sort of investment in that product, whether actual financial investment or time, and for that they should be entitled to reward. To continue to encourage investment in creativity creators need to be sure they can potentially gain reward for their work. The fact that copyright is bound up in the commercial arena is one of the reasons some people have turned away from copyright. As an example, many feel that research material should be distributed freely and easily, particularly now that it is easy and cheap to do so via the internet. Sharing leads to greater efficiency and valuable information should not be controlled by gatekeepers such as publishers through the licences they purchase from copyright holders. So some commentators believe copyright may not be adaptable enough to enable free and flexible use of content.

Ultimately, copyright gives authors a positive right to exploit their work and a negative right to prevent others from doing so without their consent. To some this smacks of a sort of control over information that stands in opposition to an ethos of digital democracy. Large publishing companies can, in effect, censor the marketplace in how they control the information they have; they may price the information too high, for instance, for some people to access it. For some of the internet commentators, this is seen as a way of slowing down progress. This may be a rather extreme argument in the case for leaving copyright behind. However, in the age of the internet flexible systems to distribute intellectual property in a variety of ways are required, whether by using copyright or by developing alternative or supplementary systems.

Does copyright need fixing?

There are those who believe that copyright is the way forward but it needs to be rethought radically. Some experts, such as Patry, the Senior Copyright Counsel at Google Inc., present the case for 'fixing' copyright to fit the new technological age. In their view, the sorts of changes to copyright that are needed are as follows:

- it needs a change of emphasis away from ownership to focus on access
- it needs the ability to encompass a much larger base of authors – as it were, the mass producers of a self-publishing age

- it needs to have broader definitions of aspects like 'fair use' to allow for freer distribution of material
- it needs to exploit opportunities for lots more smaller transactions rather than fewer larger ones

Points such as these are each debatable, and many argue that the current system is flexible enough and does not need to be rethought as drastically. With the right mechanisms in place, copyright can be an effective system for the internet age. For many authors the financial prospects for their work are important and copyright currently still appears to be the best way to exploit their work; the digital environment does not change the basic rights that authors have to own their content, and as such copyright is still an effective way to manage this. Nor does copyright prevent the free distribution of material, while by reinforcing the creator's rights of ownership it can still be valuable.

Copyright experts and organisations have been actively involved in developing effective ways to organise digital copyright. Indeed technology itself can be a friend to copyright, as we will see on p. 151, enabling it to be managed efficiently across territories, and helping to identify copyright holders accurately. Using technology to manage copyright is compatible with a fast-moving digital age. Those wanting to use copyright material can quickly and effectively get the required permission for that material at the point they need to use it, and pay for it seamlessly where payment is required. Indeed copyright may well, in this way, become cheaper to administer and cheaper to buy for users (micropayments are easier to manage digitally, for instance), while still satisfying the very relevant needs of authors.

Copyleft

Copyleft is viewed by some as an alternative approach to copyright. It is not entirely anti-copyright, in that it is still a form of licensing, but it is designed to allow the free distribution of material. It originated as a way to distribute software with the development, in 1989, of the GNU General Public Licence. It allows for people to use and adapt material as they want and for versions of the material to continue to be free even if they have been changed and adapted by other parties.

It is different from releasing the material entirely free into the public domain in that some terms remain; these focus on use, so, for instance, in terms of software it means that the source files must be available. It is regarded as a reciprocal licence as any adaptations have to carry the same terms (unlike a public domain product) and it is self-perpetuating as it continues down the line even after adaptations have been made.

Copyleft does have to be formally assigned to the material and there are layers of copyleft that can be applied, determining the sort of use that can be made of the material. Ultimately the aim is to create a way to distribute material for free and keep that freedom continuous, so discouraging users who might seek to develop proprietary versions for commercial use. That way companies cannot develop a monopoly over certain software solutions (for instance) and control marketplaces.

Open content and Creative Commons copyright licences

Open content is a term that is often applied to content that is available for reuse and redistribution, royalty-free. It was originally linked to a specific licence but is now more loosely applied, particularly in the context of open access material, where creators want to ensure content can be used in a non-restrictive way. In this way, open content is content which the user has the right to make more kinds of uses of than are normally permitted under the law, all at no cost to the user. Essentially it allows for the easy availability, copying and using of content. Forms of open licence can offer standardised ways to manage the copyright for information that is broadly available for use for free, but may still require some level of protection (e.g. from commercial exploitation for non-copyright holders).

Creative Commons copyright licences are an example of this. They were developed by Lawrence Lessig, Hal Abelson and Eric Eldrel, advocates of the free internet. These licences are managed from a base in California as a non-profit organisation; they allow authors of content to assign which rights they still want some control over and which rights they are happy to waive.

While one of the main aims of Creative Commons copyright licences is to ensure material can be distributed freely across the internet, another important aspect is the fact that many individuals can use Creative Commons licences easily; they make things straightforward for individuals to understand and apply. In the environment of digital sharing and social media this has an advantage; so, for instance, users of Flickr, the photo sharing website, often adopt a Creative Commons approach as they load their photos to determine their use. Individuals can easily take control of their intellectual property. The licences do not necessarily have to apply only to the digital environment but it is clear that this works well in the digital arena, where large quantities of information can be shared and distributed instantly and freely. Creative Commons creates a framework of flexible licences that can be adopted within the basic structure of copyright.

Licences are built up in three layers:

- a legal layer (legal code)
- a layer written in day-to-day language (the commons deed)
- a machine-readable layer, a standardised way to describe licences for software to read

There are six main types of Creative Commons licence that allow for different levels of control. At the heart of these six is the principle that the creation of the material must always be attributed to its creator so the author will get credit for their creativity and originality. At the basic level it can be simply assignment of attribution (with the acronym of CC BY), allowing the material to be adapted, changed and used, even commercially as long as credit is given to the original creator. Different licences allow for or exclude different activities, covering also the further licensing of material that has been used or adapted going forward, whether for commercial or non-commercial activities. They also provide tools to place works in the public domain, including the Public Domain Mark and CC0 tool, which allows creators to waive all rights (even those of attribution).

Critics see problems. There is no real control over the licence so it can easily be infringed. It is also rather inflexible in that it applies to a wide variety of media and products which can be a bit too generic. It can be difficult to protect moral rights (which is the basis of the attribution) really effectively, and if a derivative work that you allowed under your Creative Commons licence becomes subject to legal action, then you can be vulnerable. There are also issues around duration and compatibility with other systems which can affect websites carrying both standard copyright and Creative Commons material, for instance. However, there are examples of court cases where the strength of Creative Commons licences has been successfully tested.

As a way to empower individuals with the ability to control the use and dissemination of their work, particularly in open access environments, these licences can represent threats to publishers' own approaches to copyright and publishers need to engage with these systems in order to dovetail in with the variety of publishing mediums researchers may use in the future. There are examples of this; for instance, Bloomsbury Academic used Creative Commons licences for some of its titles in digital format.

Copyright infringement

In a digital age, copyright can prove difficult to protect from infringement. When dealing with print-only infringements it is easier to withdraw and destroy the relevant publications. The ease and speed with which content can be distributed means that even with an injunction it can be difficult to prevent the distribution of the material and more effort is required to track the copies across the internet in order to take them down.

Individual cases of copyright infringement can be and are dealt with where necessary in the digital environment, but there is one particular example in the last decade of a much larger-scale infringement which highlights some of the problems about the way copyright is sometimes viewed in a digital environment as the case study explores.

Digital rights management to prevent infringement

DRM can be an effective way to manage copyright and protect its use. It provides a reasonably robust way to ensure content is used in the way intended by copyright holders. The technology of DRM is reasonably cheap and straightforward, and it is effective at hiding complexity from users. It can be costly depending on the level of security required, while managing the exceptions that can exist within copyright regulations makes it complex. Piracy is another problem that copyright holders face, and to support the use of DRM in protecting copyright the US passed, as early as 1998, the Digital Millennium Copyright Act (DMCA) to impose criminal penalties on those who make available technologies designed primarily to overcome DRM protection.

However, there are aspects of DRM that are controversial. It can only provide a certain amount of protection against those determined to infringe copyright and there is no compelling evidence yet to support the notion that it prevents copyright theft in any major way. Instead it can be seen as hindering legitimate users as they find themselves prevented from using the content they have bought and believe they own in certain ways (e.g. for lending or shifting format); they may also find they have problems accessing their purchases if the DRM changes or is discontinued (for example if they cancel a subscription they may lose access to the archive of the editions they did pay for). Problems like these can appear to penalise legitimate purchase. There are several organisations that oppose DRM, citing the restrictions that it imposes on users and that it can represent a potentially dangerous level of control. Again, the issues of freedom and democracy on the internet surface.

Case study: Google and copyright infringement in mass digitisation programmes

One of the unexpected problems that publishers have faced is the interest shown by those outside the industry in the development of content. Mass digitisation of book archives has been one way to develop digital content quickly. However, dealing with content as a commodity in this way can cause problems, and one particular issue regarding copyright surfaced with Google, leading to debates around the Google settlement.

Briefly, in December 2004 Google announced that it had made arrangements with Harvard, Michigan, Stanford, Oxford and the New York Public Library to scan all the works held in their collections, thus digitising them. By scanning content from libraries in one big operation it was able to build up a database of materials for its books database (this has been variously named over the years, but currently Google Scholar, Google Books and Google Play all link to a books database). There were various reasons for this. It was enriching the search experience by providing greater depth of material. It also gained a large body of material that could be used for research into linguistic processing; natural language programming, for instance, is a research area for Google as it looks at ways to improve computer algorithms.

For the scholarly books it was focusing on in 2004 Google was scanning complete copies so that users could search across the whole work and across all works. The problem was that not all these books were out of copyright even if they were out of print (and some were still in print). Google took both out-of-copyright work and in-copyright work and argued that it was making it available under exemptions of 'fair use'. It showed that it was also adding value by collecting them together and providing a digital index for them. The underlying principle was that more content was good for everyone and no one could object to Google bringing works that were difficult to find into an environment where they could gain new life.

However, it looked as though Google was infringing copyright, and court cases followed in 2005 as publishers and authors said they had not been properly compensated for the use of their copyright. There were inherent problems with the variety of copyright regulations that different material was held under, depending on different countries. The Authors' Guild in America carried out a class action on behalf of authors and five large publishers, and the Association of American Publishers brought a lawsuit. While these were coming to court, libraries continued to join the Google programme: Google was carrying the cost of significant scanning and this was an attractive proposition.

Over subsequent years, settlements have been proposed, each raising certain problems while trying to reach some sort of agreement between Google and the industry. The first, in 2008, provided for payments to be made to authors and publishers for breaches of copyright, setting up business models for ongoing collection of and payment for relevant material and the establishment of a books rights registry paid for by Google to facilitate this; Google would then be free of liability.

However, this settlement contained many unresolved issues. Some felt Google would have a monopoly over the use of the material, even where only a preview of the book was available, and other companies providing databases across academic books would find it hard to compete against the sheer size of its database, much of it available for free. Certain aspects of Google's activity seem to support this as it often watermarks public domain works digitally, which can make it appear as if there is some issue of ownership. Where Google does charge other problems arise: for instance, it also sells the information back to libraries, even though those libraries own the books in the first place in print form.

The second settlement, proposed in 2009, expanded on the first, looking at the details around more flexible agreements on revenue models for authors, arrangements for orphan works (in copyright but where the copyright holder is currently untraceable) and foreign works. This was also rejected in 2011, again for a variety of reasons, such as the level of compensation to authors as well as issues of anti-trust. There was concern over the fact that Google would be released from any liability for certain future activities, not clearly defined at this stage. There was also the problem that rights holders would have to opt out of having their books appear within Google, rather than opting in.

Google argues that by putting books into its environment it is protecting copyright, supporting it and providing revenue as incentives for authors to continue creating and for publishers to sell books. However, putting the onus on the copyright holder to claim their right not to have their work infringed could be seen as counter to the spirit of copyright. Other issues remain: for instance, if a copyright holder opts out, Google still has a digital copy of their book in its archive: could that be regarded as a breach?

As more content is originated in a digital environment and more archives become digitised, this particular copyright problem for a mass digitisation project will be less likely to surface. Nevertheless, what this episode shows is that as content becomes more readily treated as a commodity, complexities arise. One of the issues it raises is that for copyright to be effective across the internet, more harmonisation needs to take place to overcome problems of working in different jurisdictions, when the information can originate from anywhere and be distributed anywhere.

Piracy

Print vs digital piracy

One of the important considerations for publishers is that they are not only protecting their own licence to publish but also protecting the author. Publishers undertake within the publishing contract to protect the copyright of authors, and it is important they continue to combat copyright infringement and to demonstrate clearly that they are doing this. For an increasing number of authors it is a key aspect of what a publisher can offer them. Indeed self-published authors, if they become successful, find that their work may readily be pirated; they see it as one of the benefits of working with publishers that they have the resources and knowledge to combat piracy.

Pirated print copies have always existed within the marketplace and publishers have always been vigilant in protecting copyright. In general the problem was limited to particular countries and the money that those markets represented did not cause too much worry for publishers. Ripped-off textbooks in developing economies where full priced books were difficult to afford did not impact the market in a major way. In countries where copyright may be regulated in a more lax way there was still a limit in terms of distribution and quantity as well as quality of pirated books. For the customer in well-developed markets, both the price and accessibility of the print version, when compared to the effort of finding and buying the pirate version, meant that in general customers purchased the legitimate product.

But digital books provide an easy way to distribute globally an exact copy of the actual book in unlimited quantity. In addition, there is a particular aspect of the internet which has nuanced the issue of piracy. File sharing, developing in the late 1990s particularly in the sharing of personal music libraries, has gained a certain credibility, tied in with the expectation that information should be, to some extent, free and the web should encourage sharing. Even if the public are more aware now of situations where they may be breaching copyright, there is still a feeling that if you do have to pay for content it should be reasonably cheap.

The changing nature of customers' relationship to their content and their sense of value in it is one of the aspects underpinning the issue of piracy. Where products are expensive (for instance educational textbooks in the US) and out of the range of some customers, they may well resort to piracy, since it is so much easier, in order to gain some sort of access to content they cannot otherwise afford.

Digital piracy has other attractions. It is much less easy to get caught compared to having to manage a physical product. Pirates can operate from a number of countries and shut down and start up new sites easily. They can make it very difficult for people to track them down as they may service customers in one country from a server in another country, with payment processing operating in a third. This is one of the reasons that sophisticated pirates may well be involved in wider criminal activities such as money laundering operations. Estimates of the money involved vary and they can be difficult to prove: some reports say that over 20 per cent of all ebooks downloaded to e-readers are pirated; one recent piece of research looked at the top ninety books on Amazon to find that around three million people search the internet daily for these titles, which could amount to around $3 billion annually: piracy happens at all price levels for all types of books.

Who is involved?

At one end of the scale, pirates will simply be individuals overcoming DRM to upload a textbook they happen to have bought to distribute for free over the internet. However, at the other, file sharing sites may offer well-developed subscription services for books that are carefully catalogued in order to pick up any slight variation in the way a title may be typed in; they can even carry advertising.

Meanwhile, the customers of pirated copies may be buying them in order to access content they cannot otherwise reach, maybe due to territoriality issues, or because they find the DRM mechanisms frustrating and off-putting. For others it is the ability to get things ahead of others, or to get them for free. There are examples too of users being thrilled by joining a pirate community and engaging in it in an almost competitive way. Meanwhile, some people may be buying a book assuming they are using a legitimate source. A customer's expectation that digital content is likely to be cheap adds to that problem.

How to combat piracy

The proliferation of sites and the cunning of the operators make it difficult for publishers to keep up with the pirates. However, there are measures they can take in tracking and taking down sites where pirated copies are available. Authors and publishers may spot that a book is available and make a note of the source. They can then issue the internet service provider (ISP) with a notice to say that it is hosting a site carrying illegal content. The ISP is obliged to take down the site once notified. The process can be quite involved, from identifying the hosting service and the legal jurisdiction in which it operates, to issuing and monitoring the appropriate take-down notices.

In the UK a copyright infringement portal has been set up by the Publishers Association to facilitate the formal approach to serving infringement notices. This portal has been responsible for taking down over 216,000 web pages in total and the numbers continue to grow. While this does not necessarily stop the sites popping up again in some other guise, it does cause disruption to the pirates' activity and it makes clearer to the more casual customer that the issue of copyright protection is to be taken seriously. Companies also exist like Attributor, which works with publishers to crawl cyberlockers and peer-to-peer sites to look for infringed copies. For more critical cases there may be months of building a criminal case against key perpetrators.

However, there are other things the industry is taking into account when considering how to combat piracy. One of the key ones, certainly to prevent the casual user from obtaining pirated copies, is to make the products available and attractive in their legitimate guise. This may be by

- ensuring access is easy across marketplaces and territories
- ensuring access is easy across platforms
- avoiding the use of heavy-handed DRM
- pricing effectively so that customers do not mind purchasing a legitimate copy

In all these the publisher is trying to make it easy for a customer to take the legal route.

There is also an element of educating consumers. They need to be aware that:

- the author, the individual, is being exploited – they are losing out (some consumers assume that it is only the interests of the 'wealthy publishers' they are affecting)
- some of those involved are serious, even dangerous, criminals
- there is an issue of consumer protection in the distribution of pirated copies

For some, the piracy of ebooks will never be as big a problem for the industry as it is for music, film and gaming industries, the nature of the product being a significant issue. Others also argue that piracy ultimately does not affect the legitimate users market. This seems unlikely in certain markets, such as the educational publishing environment; the more pirated copies of key texts are available, the greater the cost the legitimate products have to bear as they are sold in lower numbers. In the trade arena, however, it is widely suggested that piracy does not impact on the market unduly and may in fact encourage more sales of legitimate copies as word of mouth about good books spreads. Nevertheless, as ebook markets expand worldwide, and piracy continues to be reasonably easy, it is likely that its impact will increase considerably in the longer term.

Digital legislation

UK legislation

Activity within the digital environment affects many different aspects of society and the economy. So legislation is continuously being developed to cope with new challenges that affect anything from data protection to e-commerce. Various issues arise in relation to publishing and different pieces of legislation affect different aspects of publishing activity. For example, the 2000 e-commerce directive established that ISPs have a responsibility to stop illegal activity on their sites if it is brought to their attention, but individual countries comply with this directive differently, which can cause problems. For instance, obscenity laws differ between countries. What about jurisdiction issues when the server is in one country, the e-commerce activity in another and the customer in a third? When dealing with print products there is the expectation that one cannot control the distribution of second-hand copies; how does this adapt to the internet? Issues such as these need addressing in legislation.

Efforts have been made to move towards harmonisation across certain regions. One example is VAT in Europe: loopholes in VAT on the sale of products from different countries will be closed. Currently ebooks are subject to VAT but they can adopt the VAT rate of the country from which the retailer operates. Amazon operates via Luxembourg so can charge a lower VAT rate than in the UK, which means it can undercut the prices of UK-based firms. In the future the VAT rate where the customer is purchasing is the rate that will have to be applied, creating a fairer system across Europe. However, some countries charge lower rates of VAT on ebooks (just as the UK charges no VAT at all on print books), so harmonisation is not always possible. Here, as with the principles of copyright, the debates continue and legislation attempts to keep the laws on digital products relevant and enforceable.

The Digital Economy Act 2010 is one of the recent pieces of legislation in the UK intended to regulate digital media. One critical aspect of it is that it has focused on developing a system for tracking down and suing persistent copyright infringers. There are perceived weaknesses in the act, such as:

- who bears the cost of following these procedures
- how effective an appeals process might be
- whether innovation and creativity are genuinely supported or instead stifled

In 2011 the Hargreaves Report on Intellectual Property and Growth explored the relationship between copyright and the economy and competitiveness, looking at how far enforcement can impact copyright infringement and whether this has a detrimental effect on competitiveness. It set out a series of recommendations that included issues such as making it easier for organisations and individuals to manage licences and rights in an open and transparent way with a digital copyright exchange. Growing a legitimate market for rights trading is an important way to provide legal opportunities for obtaining information, discouraging illegal routes. Other recommendations included:

- provisions on orphan works
- specific suggestions with regard to particular types of intellectual property
- establishing international priorities
- emphasising the importance of education around copyright as a measure to protect from infringement

The Digital Copyright Exchange Feasibility Study was set up by the Intellectual Property Office in the UK, following the Hargreaves Report. It published two documents looking at the issue of managing copyright. The first report (Rights and Wrongs: Is Copyright Licensing Fit for Purpose for the Digital Age?) identified seven reasons why current licensing systems were not fit for purpose:

1   They were expensive (this refers to the process itself, not the prices being charged for the rights).
2   They were difficult to use
3   They were difficult to access
4   They were insufficiently transparent
5   They were siloed within individual media types (at a time when more and more digital content is mixed media and cross-media)
6   They were the victim of a misalignment of incentives between creators, rights owners, rights managers, rights users and end users
7   They were insufficiently international in focus and scope

The report went on to recommend that copyright licensing needed to be implemented across sectors and territories, and to do that the main issues that need resolving are:

- complexity of processes
- complexity of organisations
- repertoire imbalance between the digital and physical worlds (you cannot always find the things you want in a digital environment using legal methods, while a physical copy may well be easily available)
- the difficulty of finding out who owns what rights to what content in what country
- the difficulty of accurately paying to creators the fair share of revenues created by their copyright content
- the labour-intensiveness, expense and difficulty of licensing copyright for the high-volume, low-value transactions that characterise the digital world
- the lack of common standards and of a common language for sharing rights information across creative sectors and across national borders

This forms a useful checklist of the activity that has already started in order to harmonise licensing systems so that they can cope with future developments.

The second and final report from a the Digital Copyright Exchange Feasibility Study proposed an industry-led and industry-funded copyright hub, building on the work already underway to organise an efficient and responsive copyright licensing system. The hub would serve a number of functions, including:

- information and copyright education
- registries of rights
- a marketplace for rights-licensing solutions
- help with the orphan works problem

The report outlines the problems in more detail and looks at individual solutions for each point, as well as exploring ways the hub would improve each area and how it might be constructed.

Some US approaches

The emphasis of the Hargreaves Report was to draw back from enforcement as the main way of protecting copyright, but in the US stricter methods have been mooted to try and control piracy. Other content holders from the film and (to a lesser extent) music industries are driving this. While US law operates like that of the UK, where an ISP, once notified, must take down a site, there is a drive in the US to try and control access to websites outside the US that carry pirated content. One example was SOPA (Stop Online Piracy Act), proposed in 2012 to the House of Representatives Judiciary Committee to target these websites. This proposed law would have required American sites to take down links to identified sites outside the US. The payment processors too would be required to stop doing business with these non-US websites and ISPs would be required to block traffic to them using DNS filtering; particularly worrying at the time were the terms suggested, that this would need to be done within five days of notification. For many, including the founder of Google, this verged on censorship and it was regarded as a heavy-handed approach by the US to gain some sort of control over the world internet in relation to preventing piracy. For others it was simply too big in scope to be manageable and meant that even very well-established and clearly legitimate social media sites, where some sort of accidentally pirated content might be identified (e.g. within someone's Facebook page), could be vulnerable. This legislation faced challenges, and the political arena, where extensive lobbying, supported by considerable funding from key stakeholders, was very influential. In the end it was not pursued. Another example was PIPA (Protect IP), a milder version of SOPA; some interesting offshoots have emerged from that, such as Darrell Issa's OPEN idea, which posted up anti-piracy legislative proposals for the public to view and edit, so creating a more democratic approach to consultation and the creation of legislation.

Legislation and reviews will continue in these areas. They take the publisher's activity to the broader arena of creativity and the economy. Publishers have to monitor these debates constantly going forward in order to be ready with a response.

Harmonisation of rights systems and technical solutions

For all these topics we have looked at the issue of harmonisation surfaces. As the internet operates in a global environment, incompatibilities and conflicts between the laws and regulations of different countries or different standards cause complexity. The more these issues can be harmonised, the easier managing copyright and legal publishing issues will become, so reinforcing the effectiveness of copyright.

There are many movements and institutions looking at ways to standardise activity across borders and provide consistent information across technologies. As content is manipulated in more and more complex ways (for instance requiring micropayments for the use of small chunks of information), so the development of systems to cope with these is also critical. In addition, the sheer amount of content, since out-of-print content can become accessible again, requires some means of easy management across the wide variety of uses the internet has opened up. Centralised services that ease the use of licences, offer due diligence and help the user work within legal bounds will make it less likely that they will adopt illegal methods.

Examples of the sorts of projects that are being developed in publishing include:

- initiatives looking at providing better rights information for all stakeholders in the chain (from creators to users)
- automated or semi-automated platforms for rights trading where, for instance, gaining permission to use a diagram globally in an educational text for a negligible 'educational' fee could be much easier to manage, without needing costly human processing
- projects looking at standards for coding the information on, for example, licences, in databases compatible with others

Just a sample of such projects include:

- ONIX-PL, a standard for communicating publishers' licences to libraries
- Global Repertoire Database for music
- PLUS coalition to manage rights of photos
- ODRL open digital rights language for machine readable permissions agreements

There are projects bringing different registries together, such as ARROW, which is a tool to facilitate rights information management in any digitisation project involving text and/or images. It is particularly useful in relation to orphan works but it covers identifying rights holders on all works in or out of copyright and, if it is still commercially available, linking different registries together.

Another initiative is the Linked Content Coalition. This is a global content industry project that was approved by the EU in 2010; it aims to improve the management and communication of online copyright. Its remit is to develop a cross-media project focusing on working with various existing standards. It aims to create a framework for standards-based communications infrastructure so that businesses and individuals can manage and communicate their rights more effectively online.

Such projects need to be able to work across a range of business models (e.g. charging or free) and content types (visual or written), to be compatible across a variety of infrastructures and to ensure the barriers to entry are low enough for all stakeholders (usually down to the level of the individual who might be using one of these systems). Harmonisation is just one advantage. Building critical mass is also an important aspect to this. A collective licensing agency, for instance, may have more clout to act on behalf of all rights holders where problems arise. It is important to claim a right for all sorts of content that may have appeared lost or open to exploitation. For orphan works, for instance, initiatives like these represent a solution: they may have been seen as untouchable in the past, but now they can potentially be used and managed effectively, retaining money for copyright holders should they eventually emerge.

Other aspects of legal implications of the digital environment

While copyright is a very current debate, it is important to be aware that there are other issues with regard to the law that arise with the growth of the internet and can pose challenges to publishers. Issues of plagiarism and privacy take on new dimensions in a digital environment; individuals can easily post libellous material without due care or distribute personal information widely via social media. The explosion of information on the internet, the ability for anyone anywhere to publish material easily and the difficulty in regulating this has changed the environment for these aspects of the law. There is not the space to explore them here; for detail on these topics, see the references below. However, it is worth noting a couple of examples of where a publisher may need to review its position.

The first is the author contract, the basic outline of which remained broadly unchanged for many years. It contains various clauses that need consideration in light of digital products. We have seen that ebook definitions were needed within contracts with regard to volume rights, but there are also other areas that require clear distinction: for instance, an ebook is not strictly out of print so termination clauses that linked to books being out of print need to be adjusted. More care needs to be taken to cover aspects of ownership when books are being downloaded or transferred to be held in other databases or digital warehouses.

Another area for publishers to consider is developing new protocols to deal with problems that might arise. Information is much more freely distributed on the internet and can continue to be distributed ad infinitum once it is out there: where there is a case of defamation publishers need to develop a way of dealing with this; with a print copy it was easy to recall stock and limit further dissemination by pulping and reprinting a corrected version. How can this be managed in a digital environment?

Conclusion

The debate around copyright in the internet age continues and goes much wider than book publishing. Combating copyright infringement will remain a priority. However, the efforts made to ensure copyright is robust, together with developments around harmonisation and technical solutions to copyright management, should ensure that copyright remains one of the key frameworks within which publishers operate in the digital age. In this, as in other legal issues, publishers need to be leading the debates.

Further reading and resources

Books

Darnton, Robert. *The Case for Books*. Public Affairs, 2009. This contains two useful articles on the early stages of the Google settlement.

Fenwick, Trevor and Locks, Ian. *Copyright in the Digital Age*. Wildy, Simmonds and Hill, 2010.

Jones, Hugh and Benson, Christopher. *Publishing Law*. Routledge, 2011.

Lessig, Lawrence. *Free Culture: The Nature and Future of Creativity*. 2005; PDF available at www.free-culture.cc/freeculture.pdf under a Creative Commons licence.

Owen, Lynette (ed.). *Clarke's Publishing Agreements*, 8th edition. Bloomsbury Professional, 2010.

Patry, William. *How to Fix Copyright*. Oxford University Press, 2011.

Websites

www.arrow-net.eu – for the ARROW project

www.attributor.com – digital piracy solution provider with information on digital piracy trends

www.copyrightinfringementportal.com/index.php – copyright infringement portal run by the Publishers Association

www.creativecommons.org – the site for Creative Commons licences

www.editeur.org – EDItEUR is the international group coordinating development of the standards infrastructure for electronic commerce in the book, ebook and serials sectors

www.editeur.org/8/ONIX – information about ONIX

www.ipo.gov.uk – for the Hargreaves Report and the Digital Copyright Exchange Feasibility Study

www.linkedcontentcoalition.org – the Linked Content Coalition

www.publishers.org.uk/index.php?option=com_content&view=category&layout=blog&id=359&Itemid=1346 – copyright section on the Publishers Association web page

www.useplus.com/index.asp – Plus coalition

www.w3.org/community/odrl – ODRL

Questions to consider

1   Can you ever own an ebook in the same way as you may have owned a print book?
2   What are the benefits of maintaining robust copyright systems?
3   Do you think piracy has a significant effect on the market?
4   Many argue that making content easily accessible by legitimate means is an important part of preventing piracy, but how much will this market have to do to be attractive enough?
5   How far can technology provide the solution to copyright licensing?

11 Rights sales and new digital publishing opportunities

> We have seen how copyright is being re-evaluated given the changing environment and the move to digital environments. There are more specific aspects of rights sales that are impacted by the growth of digital products. Here we will look at:
>
> 1 The changing approach to territories
> 2 The challenges of digital products when selling rights
> 3 Key considerations for rights deals

Introduction

Territoriality is an area that has been debated more frequently following the ease of publishing across borders via the internet. Specialist publishing has tended to be global in scope but the consumer market has traditionally had a more territorial approach, and this is undergoing a shift. Publishers have been accustomed to buying print rights to particular territories: for instance, English language rights for the US might be separate from those for the UK and Commonwealth. Breaches in these rights, while possible, were less frequent given the limitations in the physical product. Products could be imported at lower prices but this did not really affect the market in a major way.

However, the ease of publishing into different territories via the internet has changed the approach. Controlling territorial limits can be difficult in a digital world. Publishers will control where they distribute their electronic products according to their rights agreements as far as they can. Some are particularly aware of a need to protect markets where they have dominated with their English language print editions; they want to avoid having cheap digital versions from outside their territory undercutting their own digital products. Sellers of digital books also try to abide by the rights agreements: Amazon, for example, do control what you can buy via their websites for different countries; it is also difficult to buy a US-only product on a UK Kindle. Technologically it is possible to manage territory rights.

The drive to global digital rights

Publishers can avoid these territory problems to some extent by owning global digital rights. There are benefits: if a publisher has global digital rights to a product, it can very easily distribute it to those markets in a way that may have been virtually impossible when it was distributing a physical product. Growth opportunities therefore exist where publishers can control global rights.

There is also some pressure from consumers. They expect it to be easy to access material across the internet; physical boundaries between territories make more sense than digital ones to customers, who can find it frustrating when they cannot access something easily. One example of what can go wrong is when Amazon realised they had been distributing illegally an ebook of an in-copyright work. George Orwell's *Nineteen Eighty-Four* is in copyright in many countries, including the UK until 2020 and the US until 2044, while in Australia, Canada and Russia it is out of copyright. In 2009 Amazon were selling on the US Kindle a copy at $0.99; when they realised they were distributing a version that was published by a company that had no US rights to the book (which had been loaded by the self-service system) they deleted the illegal edition from Kindles. Customers in Canada, who were able to have the edition, lost theirs too. The more interesting aspect that caused comment with this story was not the different copyright arrangements, but the fact Amazon could extract titles from Kindles that customers had legitimately purchased: they could, if they wished, impose a form of censorship controlling the products a customer thought they owned. While they were trying to enforce copyright laws, they broke their relationship with customers. They recognised the error straightaway and restored legitimate copies.

Problems like this will never quite go away as copyright regulations vary and cannot necessarily be easily harmonised; however, global digital rights do provide some solutions. Some trade publishers are aiming to gain global digital rights for all their new books. This may bring a change to the mainstream publishing scene as publishers change their models around the sorts of rights they want to purchase. Will print rights still be sold via territory, if the digital trend is towards global publishing rights?

Authors and agents may react differently to the offer to buy global digital rights. They may still want to have their print rights divided up to ensure they get the best option in each territory; if the digital rights are global there could be some interesting marketing dilemmas. Or there may be more deals on global rights for both print and digital products, allowing the larger companies to gain ground where they can offer the whole global package. Meanwhile some well-established authors will retain all their electronic rights to exploit themselves, maybe away from book publishers altogether: J. K. Rowling has worked with her agent to find web developers and producers, with sponsorship from Sony, for the Harry Potter digital site Pottermore (which is the only place where Harry Potter ebooks can be bought). Global digital rights make sense for many publishers but the topic does open up these further questions.

The challenges of digital products when selling rights

While global digital rights cover a publisher's right to publish the digital work, there are many opportunities for publishers to license on the material in a digital format which are covered by rights agreements. Any rights contracts can involve complexity but as content can be dealt with in many more ways in a digital environment, whether chunked into tiny fragments or distributed across many territories, the rights deals can face new levels of complexity. Some rights sales remain reasonably straightforward: translation or serial rights, for instance. But customers are innovating with all sorts of new product ideas and often deals have to become bespoke around the exact requirements of the customer.

The challenge for the rights expert is to think carefully about the implications of any digital rights deal so that they are sure they have covered any issues of, for example, competition or exclusivity when dealing with a product that may well be innovative and not tried and tested. This is as well as ensuring they are getting best value from the contract, something that can be difficult when the digital marketplace is unpredictable. The publisher wants to maximise revenue from a digital product that someone might be developing but it does not want to render it financially unviable by asking for too much.

When many of these products are new concepts it can be difficult to work out quite how much money they might make as well as to assess the level of importance of the content being licensed to that product, both of which are necessary in order to accurately value the content one is licensing.

Definitions

In the first instance one looks for definitions which could help with the rights arrangements; electronic publishing and multimedia are terms that vary and change; indeed the term multimedia is possibly used less than it was (when it was more clearly associated with the CD-ROM period of the 1990s). However, both terms are still used to some extent in contracts and there are some loose definitions focusing on the fact that electronic publishing tends to focus on one sort of content (i.e. book content) available in some form or other electronically (whether on a Kindle or on a smart phone etc.) while multimedia covers products that may integrate a variety of content types (sound, photo, video, text) seamlessly. Educational publishers producing web products integrated into an interactive whiteboard are examples of the latter, whereas a straightforward ebook – sold maybe via Kindle or iBookstore – is electronic publishing.

In certain areas the rights deals are reasonably straightforward. Selling the ebook rights is not especially complicated, for example. Licences to characters for games have been sold for a number of years and well-established rules and financial expectations apply. However, licensing content that may be delivered, for example, by an app in very small chunks in a daily digest that lasts for a certain amount of time before starting back at the beginning again is more complex; add to that the pricing model, where the first few digests are free before customers have to subscribe, and it becomes even more challenging. As products develop in complexity such definitions become less useful, and in many ways rights, once they step beyond the basic, often have to be sold on a product-by-product basis, with each product being considered individually when developing a rights deal.

General considerations

Various problems arise when looking at the sale of rights in a digital context, some of which have been reasonably well solved, others of which pose continuing challenges. Initially, it is important to double-check the contract to ensure that the publisher does have digital rights available to license on. New contracts will have these covered, even if not in detail regarding the exact range of products that could be included. Indeed the clauses currently tend to leave the digital section reasonably open ended, clearly recognising that the environment is moving so quickly that one cannot predict ahead all the sorts of digital uses that may become available for content. Old contracts, as we have seen, will not always have this covered in any effective manner and it may be safer to renegotiate them.

Another consideration is to ensure that the territories covered are clearly defined. Digital products can be distributed across boundaries much more easily than print products, yet, again as we have seen, the contract may only cover a certain territory for print and digital and so the reach of the digital product to which a publisher might be licensing content must clearly match what can be licensed under the contract; the contract may contain some sort of reassurance that the territories are ring-fenced.

Some of the early questions about how to license digital content have been settled. Electronic content has been licensed for a long time into databases (e.g. the big legal databases like Lexis Nexis) and in these cases the value of the content has become reasonably well established; arrangements for site licences too are often well established. Other early areas of debate, such as different applications of fair use or fair dealing within an electronic environment for material held in archives, have been broadly ironed out: for instance, there are generally accepted expectations of how much of a book can be viewed electronically for free before a user faces a pay wall (when, for instance, searching on Google books). Issues around inter-library loans and systems for downloading (but not retransmission) of material are also well established. In the latter case there are certain details in delivering digital information that have to be taken into account, such as the ownership of the material while it is being transferred (via broadband perhaps), or ownership of back-up material or stored material; in these instances usually fair use applies.

Other questions remain, however: for instance, should electronic copying be covered by a collective licensing arrangement as works for physical copying rather than being administered by individual publishers? This might at least counter arguments that publishers are preventing users using the work in the way they want or need to by administering their own rights too restrictively. In any case, the collective management of print photocopying has proved effective. Some publishers, both in the US and the UK, are opting in to collective copyright clearance systems, or allow an educational mandate to apply for certain materials and are monitoring how these are going.

Another area where publishers are looking for solutions is the use of published material in course packs; as we have seen, the opportunities for customers to create bespoke course packs are growing considerably. Publishers are keen to exploit rights to their content, so it is in their interests to make material available and ensure the copyright situation is easy to manage for users. Arrangements for digitising the material in the first place were early hurdles but increasingly all content is available in a digital format, so the focus is on creating infrastructure, often through joint ventures, to create systems that cover the copyright clearance too for users creating course packs. Publishers continue to face the problem that while they may own some of the material the user wants, they usually do not own it all, even when in a joint venture with others. The user may still have to compromise on their choice of materials. This can be off-putting. Third parties too are entering, such as Ingenta, offering web-publishing solutions, its focus being on providing better technology for users. There are other debates like this over abstracts and document delivery services which create challenges for publishers trying to license valuable content effectively.

The question of value in the new digital products

These general issues are a challenge but there are more specific considerations facing rights experts as they sell specific chunks of content for specific types of product, for instance into multimedia products. Content convergence is leading to products such as apps that may well contain book content, film content, animation, interviews and music. All these components need to be valued and measured in terms of both the amount of content within a product and its importance to that content. As we saw in Chapter 9, an electronic text of a poem for instance may be quite short compared to add-on commentary sections and video footage of it being performed, but if the app is about that poem the video footage only has value in relation to the inclusion of that poem. This convergence makes unpicking the rights around these various content chunks much more challenging.

Planning the deal: what do rights people have to bear in mind?

With these general points in mind, publishers, who are selling the rights for digital-only products, have to bear in mind a variety of issues when constructing a rights deal. The following issues are important for print products too but they require further attention when dealing with an unknown digital product:

- amount of content
- value of content
- technical specifications
- platform
- bundles
- option period
- compensation levels
- overlap with other digital products

Content and value

The amount of content and the value of the content are important considerations, as we have seen. As one puts a value on a chunk of content it needs to bear some understandable relation to the whole from which it was taken; that way prices for different sizes of content, as the content is cut in different ways, are in some way in line and not undercutting or conflicting with each other. It is not just a case of examining your own content in relation to the rest but also of assessing how far the added value provided by the other content enhances the saleability of your own content. For instance, your own content benefits from being available with other publishers' content in a major academic library-based database; in this case it is not in your interest to price your own content out of the picture. Seeing how a product is used is important for establishing relative value.

The other elements of content sold (e.g. photographs within the content that have their own permissions arrangements) need to be considered and sometimes those third parties need to be consulted. Ensuring the permissions for all these additional materials are cleared can be a large job. Publishers are having to rethink what they include to ensure they have the rights future proofed for products that they may license going forward; it may be that as they build the sort of asset management databases mentioned in Chapters 4 and 8 only those items with full global rights can be included (even if they do not, in the first instance, need more than simply UK rights).

Technical details

Each stage of the technical journey of the material also has to be taken into account, i.e. where it will be held, how it is transmitted, where it ends up being used. So it may be that when selling content for educational software, one needs to consider each type of hardware on which it is available. Or if material is available as an app, one needs to consider which operating systems it will use; and if it is available on more than one, whether the prices will be different. Sometimes an app on one platform is free while another is not; the apps may vary in sophistication and there could be differences between the iPad and the iPhone versions. If it is a game, is it downloaded or is it carried on a cartridge to put into a dedicated game console? If the latter, is it a handheld device or a TV-based system, etc.?

In relation to this you need to be aware of the robustness of the platform or at least systems in place to ensure that if the platform fails there is compensation in some way or other for lost revenue; or if the whole product fails, at least rights revert promptly. Therefore it can be important to have short licence periods too to ensure that rights are not tied up if new products are developed.

Bundles

Print and electronic bundles (quite widely available for certain specialist markets such as law) have caused their own problems; in the UK VAT is not charged on books but is charged for electronic products. So a publisher has to value the electronic component of a bundle in order to allocate a VATable element to the bundle. This can be open to abuse.

Option clauses and other contract arrangements

Defining the option period, usually a key part of a rights deal, is even more critical here as the length of time a technology company can take to develop a product varies; of course it can be quick, but if the company is slow to exploit the rights (perhaps it was not properly funded, as many new start-ups may not be) the publisher does not want to be locked in. Timeliness in relation to a particular type of technology or product is critical in a fast-moving marketplace. This leads on to the publisher being sure how far the company they license rights to is actually able to exploit the rights effectively; a publisher therefore has to develop new levels of knowhow to make these judgements and start to build experience around these. Rights experts usually know, for instance, which foreign language publishers will produce good translations and are well in touch with their local market; this sort of expertise needs to develop around new companies as well as new product types.

Where revenue expectations can be inflated by eager new technology companies, it is possible to consider compensation paid where revenue falls short, which may buy some insurance against working in a marketplace where it can be difficult to evaluate both the ability of the company to produce and effectively market the product and the eagerness of the market for it.

The usual sort of financial arrangements apply, so that a contract will be broadly based on a royalty arrangement. Net receipts are easy to define in the case of monitoring sales of a translated print copy; however, what they constitute may be less clear in terms of a complex app where other parties are also involved in taking a percentage of revenue (e.g. iBookstore). Understanding the way the app breaks down in price is key here: for instance, even the software may need to be valued in order to assess the price of the content.

With the proliferation of new product ideas, one might well be licensing the same content in several different ways for different platforms and uses. Rights managers need to ensure contracts are very tightly worded to allow this to happen, making clear to each person using rights the extent to which they can use them. They need to be clear on areas of overlap and also need to ensure they are not diluting their own content with too much exposure across new products, so devaluing it.

Conclusion

The area of rights is set to become much more involved and exciting in terms of finding new business opportunities. Publishers can potentially expand marketplaces if they develop more global rights deals. They can also potentially develop more wide-ranging rights deals with their content. If publishers continue to build on their expertise in content creation and development, so ensuring their longevity as an effective creative industry, understanding how they can value and manage that content most effectively is going to be critical.

Further reading and resources

Owen, Lynette (ed.). *Clarke's Publishing Agreements*, 8th edition. Bloomsbury Professional, 2010.
Owen, Lynette. *Selling Rights*. Routledge, 2011.
Upsall, Michael. *Content Licensing: Buying and Selling Digital Resources*. Chandos, 2009.

Questions to consider

1   Some predict that the breakdown of territories in terms of rights sales will lead to the domination by US publishers of the English language market. How far do you agree this might happen?
2   What considerations do you need to bear in mind in assessing the value of content when selling rights to small sections of it?
3   What new opportunities and what challenges do publishers face when selling rights for their digital content?

12 The pricing dilemma

This chapter explores some of the fundamental aspects of the underlying pricing models to show why pricing has become an important issue. It examines, in particular, one of the main areas of controversy that the industry is involved in today in the form of agency and wholesale pricing mechanisms. This issue is not likely to be a lasting one, but it is a good illustration of the sort of problems publishers face as digital business models change the environment in which they do business.

The chapter will look at:

1 Traditional price models for print and how it has been adapted
2 New digital products and consumer perceptions
3 Discounts and intermediaries' effect on pricing
4 Internet retailers and the price of digital books
5 The pressure to price low
6 New ways of buying: the challenge for specialist publishers
7 The effect for authors

Introduction

For those studying publishing, pricing used to be a reasonably straightforward issue. The principles behind book prices had not changed essentially for decades and, apart from market research when assessing new products to check pricing, or analysis to look at relationships between sales and price movements, pricing was not a particularly complex part of the publishing process. However, digital products have been posing huge pricing challenges for publishers. In each of the sector-specific areas in Part II we looked at the issue of pricing. For some areas digital pricing mechanisms are much more established than for others, but in all cases issues around pricing are affecting the digital business model.

Traditional pricing models

Pricing models for books in print, and particularly the price differentials between types of books, whether hardback or paperback, have remained reasonably static for many years. The prices themselves have increased, but the ethos behind these prices has remained similar since the rise of mass-market publications in the nineteenth century.

Essentially the prices of the hardback or library copies supported the first printings of the subsequent paperback, the higher cost of production and investment in the content reflected in the higher hardback price; in this way publishers could test the market and recoup some of the financial risk straightaway. In the nineteenth century, very cheap, often low-quality paperbacks could appear in many different sorts of editions after the first flush of success for a title; each would have its own slight price differentials and launch timings. Companies bought rights to print in paperback, or printed paperbacks once a title was out of copyright. Paperbacks developed in a much more distinct way with the introduction of the Penguin Library by Allen Lane, who launched a distinctive range of paperbacks designed to appeal to a growing affluent market; this market was interested in accessing good-quality material at a low price and the Penguin books were produced in a format designed to be easy to buy and distribute. This led to an increase in paperback houses and the mass-market paperback grew in strength throughout the twentieth century as production costs came down.

Hardback at a higher price continued to support the initial investment and the paperback followed aiming to capitalise on the success of a title; the basic hardback price and paperback prices tended to be linked in some way, and in many ways very stable, predictable price policies suited to the market were maintained. Even with the growing development of trade paperbacks (titles often going straight to paperback for certain mass markets, in a larger-format, slightly higher-priced version) this remained the basis of the pricing model.

The Net Book Agreement, which protected prices and which collapsed in the early 1990s, allowed for the first significant change in pricing for a long time, opening up heavy discounting for key titles within other outlets such as supermarkets and the possibility of special deals (like three for two). Nevertheless, the list price for these titles remained the same, based on the costs incurred by publishers.

The first run of hardbacks continued to support some of the up-front costs, like advances, making a subsequent paperback more sustainable; as we have noted, publishers have continued to treat a digital version as another sort of paperback, or as a special deal, bolted onto the main book, so that digital sales do not have to cover the up-front costs.

New digital format and customer perceptions

The entry of a new digital format has posed much greater problems. One of the basic questions has been: if the old prices were based on print products, how does one put a price on a digital product? One of the striking differences is that the old pricing models were developed over a long period of time, educating consumers as they developed. The basic principle of a high-priced hardback for first launch is accepted by consumers. However, it can be argued that this has embedded in the consumer consciousness an understanding of price based on physical attributes; this causes some of the problems for consumer expectations of price today.

To a consumer, the expensively produced hardback costs more because it is hardback; the paperback is cheaper as its production is cheaper. This does not adequately reflect the real issue around the hardback, which is to support some of the other risks taken on by the publisher (such as the advance or the cost of marketing, as we have mentioned); but it is still how the consumer views the main costs of a book. They can see too that printing a lot of stock and holding it in a warehouse is also a large investment in something physical. So consumers are very much focused on these sorts of costs when they consider the costs of the digital product. To many consumers it is reasonably simple: there is now no longer a need for publishers to spend money on printing, paper, binding, warehousing large inventories, packaging, shipping and postage. All those savings should simply mean the digital book is cheaper in a consumer's eyes.

There are additional considerations consumers have in mind. There is another purchase that has to be considered when buying ebooks – the e-reader itself. This is a costlier purchase. If people are to commit to that, that could well change their perception of the costs of the books they need to put on it. Consumers of information and entertainment today not only have a variety of competing options when getting their information and entertainment, but also have preconceptions about what all these different formats should cost; they are then applying their perceptions of one digital price model to another, in a way that did not happen when they dealt with physical products (a book, a CD and a DVD all had clear price points). So preconceptions about price may be shaped by other digital products (e.g. a music track or games app) or other digital services (e.g. a subscription to a service to watch unlimited films for 'free' or broadband, enabling internet access) that have very little to do with books. There is convergence within the consumer's mind across these entertainment products.

So publishers today face a challenge when pricing digital products. As we have seen, for certain aspects of the sector such as legal or academic there is an understanding of the intrinsic value of the information; while debates continue over certain issues, such as open access, the customer overall is not necessarily expecting low prices simply because of digital access. This, however, is not the same with markets focused on the consumer. The newer digital markets face these problems in perception and publishers need to consider how to re-educate consumers about the costs involved in publishing, particularly the unseen costs of marketing, PR, editorial and design work, and of course author royalties: publishers need to make these more visible. The publisher knows that the value is in the content of the work, nurtured and developed over a period of time by the author and the publisher. There is value in the very fact that the book has been written by a particular famous crime writer (for instance); that value is much more critical to the book's success than the cost of the paperback production.

Discounts and intermediaries' effect on pricing

Overlaid on this is the changing sales environment. The way publishers sell the physical product has changed with the growth of online retailers and this has become even more critical with the digital products on offer. The game changer in relation to the digital product is the involvement of the new key intermediaries such as Amazon and Apple in producing the devices needed for the digital products. These companies have control over the route to the reader as the devices are needed to get the ebooks. This has changed the sales environment for publishers and is having a significant effect on price. And, in addition, the way the publisher pays the intermediaries has come under scrutiny and has caused ongoing complications in the marketplace, as we will see on p. 167.

One hidden cost of publishing that consumers do not see is the amount that publishers pay intermediaries. Consumer publishing throughout the twentieth century focused primarily on selling titles through bookshops. These intermediaries were limited in number (independent bookshops, chains and wholesalers) and publishers could focus their attention on working with them to sell their titles to the general public. That meant they developed highly sophisticated relationships with the main distributors of their products and the direct relationship with the customer was less critical – that was fulfilled by the bookshop.

For this service the bookshops retained a percentage of every sale they made. This was also a factor in book pricing (one of which consumers are less aware). The seller of the books needs to make some revenue from the sale of the product as well, so an additional cost to cover that is also encompassed in the price. Booksellers have always had the problem that the lower the price of the book, the less margin there is for them to take away. While a publisher can sell bestsellers in vast quantities across all the sales channels it uses, and so can afford to allow big discounts, a small bookseller can only sell so many of that bestseller to their small customer base and so they need to recuperate as much as they can from that quantity. Publishers need to bear that in mind as they try to support the survival of bookshops, particularly as sales continue to leech into the digital marketplace. But making an allowance for the discount the bookseller gets is not limited to physical bookshops.

Consumers see that internet selling is easy and digital distribution saves the need for bookshops, so saving the publishers money, but, while bookshops suffer, it does not necessarily change the costs for the publisher. Even with internet sellers of the physical product, the intermediaries take a percentage. Sellers like Amazon demand quite a high percentage (higher than most independent bookshops) because they command a large market and can maximise sales quantities for successful books as well as make available titles that it would otherwise be difficult for customers to get. They can also decide on a price that may undercut the physical booksellers. This happens of course with the physical product as Amazon will routinely price lower than the publisher price and in some cases offer much heavier discounting for the customer.

Internet retailers and the price of digital books

However, the biggest challenge for bookshops and publishers alike is the digital product itself. The delivery of this direct to a device has meant the biggest change for the industry. Intermediaries delivering digital products expect to buy the products at a discount from the publishers as usual. However, some of the key intermediaries have a much greater interest in delivering digital products to their consumers because they are also selling the devices themselves. As we will see in Chapter 13, the ability to provide content for their devices is an important part of their strategy. Amazon and Apple are both companies for whom digital content is a critical part of driving the sales of their hardware. For Amazon, its development of the Kindle and its control over the software used for the ebook files on its device is an important way to gain market share. So it is very interested in making ebooks available that can be used on the Kindle, both to drive Kindle sales and to keep customers with Kindles buying products from them. Low-priced ebooks therefore are part of this strategy.

For newer players in the market such as Apple it is vital to attract customers to their products and so effective platforms for selling content are important, even if they do not always want and are not always able to control the price. Taking the case of Apple, it does not have book customers ready to convert to ebook customers as Amazon does;

however, it has consumers of its products from whom it wants to drive more usage of digital products, gaining revenue from any content sold and continuing to develop and maintain customer loyalty: digital books are key to this. While it is not necessarily instituting low book prices, Apple's experience with iTunes or low-priced apps suggests books are another commodity where low pricing is a more attractive option for it than higher price; putting pressure on book markets traditionally with high prices is not beyond them (as with their iTextbooks).

Publishers are therefore facing a marketplace that is much more unpredictable than before. The bookseller broadly operated within the confines of the publishing industry and played by the rules everyone within the industry understood. Now large global businesses are coming in from other sectors: Amazon admittedly started as a bookseller but is growing in stages to become an international retailer, software producer and hardware manufacturer; technology companies such as Google and Apple have moved into the bookselling arena, with a variety of different strategic imperatives and ways of operating.

Pressure to price low

Pressure therefore has come from consumers and from other competitors in the environment to bring prices low. Yet we know the cost of producing high-quality or very popular content is not negligible. Publishers in general have tended to price ebooks as an adjunct to the print version. Publishers have in the first instance tried to maintain prices similar to the print products, pricing a little below the standard paperback print edition.

However, as digital products gain ground it is unlikely to be possible to maintain this approach. The structure of publishing needs to be rethought, the economics of a book recast without the focus on the hardback print product supporting all the additional editions (print or digital). Publishers are looking at these issues; clearly a digital-only imprint will have had to take into account the lack of a hardback; but these currently tend to be low-risk initiatives based often on short material that may have a reasonably low royalty and marketing cost associated with it.

The pressure on price has been exacerbated by some other issues: free content readily available, territorial availability and piracy. The availability of free content, content that has been out of copyright but put into digital format such as the conversion of novels into EPUB formats from Project Gutenberg, has not helped publishers make a case for maintaining robust ebook prices; content can be and is available free, costing very little to convert and nothing to print or distribute. This influences consumers' expectation of what they can get in digital format.

More general aspects of undercutting price are also intensified by the digital format; books sold in other territories may be priced more cheaply; digital books can be easier to access from other countries where the prices may be cheaper, undercutting home markets; the drive towards a global price therefore is one consideration for publishers, but in all likelihood this will not push prices up but rather bring prices down. Piracy, too, has an influence on prices – customers are more accustomed to buying music in digital format now rather than file sharing and pirating copies, but that is partly because the prices are low in any case. So these factors also influence a drive to lower prices.

In terms of new launches, a look at the pricing across digital book sites shows that a variety of prices are available and the settled pattern for print pricing is not being copied

Case study: The wholesale vs agency pricing debate

The debate around the issue of agency pricing is likely to become less resonant soon as court cases and settlements sort out the main problems, but it is a useful case study in the way the industry has to face unexpected challenges. In the early days Amazon wanted to produce very cheap ebooks (cheap if based on a hardback price for a new launch) and even bought titles at a loss in order to promote cheap titles. This frightened publishers, who saw ebooks undercut their hardback prices on launch. Not all publishers launch an ebook on publication and there were experiments around phased pricing, like the films moving into the rental market and then onto DVD, as well as pricing and discounting. Amazon here continued to work as it always had as a physical wholesaler, buying titles at an agreed discount from a publisher and then effectively owning that 'stock' to sell on at whatever price it wanted; in this way it could undercut anyone else in price as it wanted, as long as it got enough profit for itself (or some other clear benefit where it sold a book as a loss leader). There are problems with that model for publishers: while physical stock was quantifiable, and so discounts were calculable for a finite number or period, ebook distribution was unlimited in number of sales, adding complexity; time-limited deals, of course, could still be managed, but negotiating these deals was more complicated.

Apple, moving into the market to push titles on its iBookstore, meanwhile adopted an approach to books that it already used with its app store. The creator of the content/app remains the seller at all times, while Apple creates the marketplace in which it operates: those sellers can price and market as they want, with Apple taking a cut of every sale made (broadly 30 per cent). Here Apple behaves as a sales agent taking a commission from each sale.

The difference between these models has set up a debate in the arena of consumer book pricing. The wholesale model follows the traditional bookshop approach whereby the intermediary buys the product at an agreed discount and sells it on at its own price – the stock is the intermediary's (until it needs to return any unsold and claim a credit back). Print book prices remained reasonably robust in this system as the bookshop would not want to reduce its own profit margin by marking prices down too far, though this was less of an issue for companies like Amazon.

In the agency model the seller remains in control of the product and the intermediary acts as an agent for the seller – taking a commission from the sale. There are legal aspects to this determining the difference in the relationship between the intermediary and the seller according to whether the arrangement is wholesale or agency. For some, the agency model makes sense as the publisher can retain control over the price, ensuring parity with other book products and making sure its sales are not undercut by excessive discounting by other parties. When the digital price seemed potentially to be in freefall, this sort of control became attractive to prevent ebooks becoming too cheap. This is all an issue while the ebooks market is in development and the main sales of a book remain the print sales; if ebooks at low prices lead to an equivalent increase in sales, then publishers will have less of a problem.

However, problems have arisen in various ways. One is the way the agency model works with Apple; it has certain controls that sellers have to abide by in order to sell from within its stores; some of these controls are around the issue of price and how far prices can be undercut by other companies/intermediaries. These have been highlighted as the agency model comes under scrutiny and competition problems have arisen.

The reason for this is that a group of the largest publishers forced Amazon to treat their ebook sales in terms of an agency model, rather than as wholesale product. This might have been to some extent forced on them with regard to the pricing guarantees required when making their books available on Apple. But it was also clear the publishers could have greater control over their prices and benefit by avoiding any heavy discounting planned by Amazon. The reason they could push Amazon to accept this is that they held the print titles hostage, suggesting that they would not let Amazon carry their key print titles if it did not use the agency model when selling their ebook products.

If you looked at books on Amazon by the publishers that adopted the agency model you would have seen a note stating that the publishers had set the price. This did not necessarily mean that those publishers which were too small to force the agency system on Amazon found their titles were sold at cut prices, nor that the big publishers automatically charged a very high price for theirs. There are clearly market forces at play as publishers price key backlist competitively. Amazon, too, while it will offer a lower price compared to the first launch of a hardback, is keen to capitalise on successful new launches and does not generally go too low with its price.

This has caused controversy. Not only is it interesting to see publishers able to wield some power with an intermediary if they have some critical mass of print and backlist, but, more critically, debates about price fixing and cartels have surfaced. The Office of Fair Trading in the UK started an investigation but it was closed once the whole matter had been set in motion by the EU. Various issues around the legal definitions of the models, together with the specific situation that Apple places its sellers in, are under scrutiny. Is Apple controlling prices by ensuring no one can undercut it? Is the consumer being cheated as prices cannot be set by Amazon so market conditions cannot be allowed to play out their course in a genuinely fair competitive environment? Are publishers ensuring prices cannot be competitive? Is Amazon itself operating a monopoly position, and so uncompetitive?

One of the key points of debate revolves around whether agency pricing has produced any obvious rise in ebook prices, and evidence to support this is difficult to find. Nevertheless it seems unlikely the agency model will persist in relation to Amazon. The US Department of Justice has also been investigating ebooks price fixing by US publishers. Different publishers and Apple are taking different approaches to the investigations within the EU and US as to whether to go to court or settle in some way or other. Some settlement agreements have been proposed, but even these are being assessed as to whether there is a breach of contract involved.

What has been of benefit, though, is that this has provided some breathing space for publishers. They have been pricing titles on Amazon and Apple and, for a while at least, created a perception that prices for newly launched ebooks hover around the £5–7 mark (with some lower), which may help create customer expectations that ebooks are not necessarily as low in price as a 79p track on iTunes. There has also been time to create digital-only lists and price points around short stories, which also may create a higher price point for longer-form narrative. Publishers are getting more used to creating ebook prices that do not have to bear a relation to the print product and so may be able to find their own level within an ebooks market without facing any preconceived expectations from customers.

in any way. But no publishers are pricing their ebooks extremely low. Apart from occasional, sometimes controversial, promotions (Ken Follett's latest book appeared for a period of time at 20p), the very cheap titles on Amazon are either short stories (from publishers) or self-published titles, with genre titles often priced low too.

New ways of buying

This might deal with the immediate problem of pricing ebooks, but there are more fundamental questions about the way content is valued as customers are buying content in new ways. These issues include:

- valuing component parts
- pricing aggregated content
- the challenge of new subscription models
- changing consumer purchasing habits

We have looked at rights sales issues, and pricing the components effectively is critical. Once content becomes more fragmented, the challenge is to price the chunks effectively to cater for a variety of purchase patterns whether they are sold in lots of small quantities or in larger groupings. If the product is bought in large aggregated slabs of content, the accumulated price of the chunks must not add up to too much; thus the individual component prices may end up small. But then if the product ends up mainly purchased in small chunks, due to their cheapness, parts of the content may not be used at all. This can lead to questions as to whether it is sustainable to keep producing these sections of content (e.g. in a journal) or whether they have a marketing value to attract customers looking for comprehensiveness, even if they are not used directly. So the relationships between the prices for different components or for different types of access need to be modelled carefully in a way that is new for publishers; other aspects of a product need to be valued as well, whether it be assessing the value of a diagram on a certain page or the importance of speed to market.

Pricing the aggregated content might seem a more straightforward proposition but the problem is that people can end up buying something they do not want alongside the things they do. If the prices become too high, they cannot be afforded. The payoff between individual titles, which used to be the way libraries could manage a budget, is not something that can be easily replicated in large digital databases.

The consumer is also growing used to new forms of subscription services. For other forms of entertainment, the content is the commodity and what consumers buy is access to the full library rather than any specific product. Once you have paid once (for access to an online juke box, for instance), paying again for the content can feel negative to many users.

Customers are becoming more used to buying in increments. If we take the app as an example, it may well be that customers can access the basic app for free and top it up with a purchase. Micropayments are becoming a standard way for consumers to purchase things. Topping up like this can also be seen, for instance, in Kindle, where the free editions quite often do not have a table of contents (one that you can click through to the right section). For certain things this can be quite useful (e.g. complete plays of Shakespeare are difficult to use if you have to scroll through the full text to find a play you want, or use the limited search facilities), so customers recognise that element of a product is useful and worth paying for; an index on top of that, if more searchability is useful, can be worth a little more and so the product range can build up to ones with click through to annotations and notes. In this sort of case it is not content that buyers are getting, but easier access to it. In this way a product becomes less free – but it still starts with content that is free to tempt you in, then if you are interested enough you'll pay a little more for an additional aspect of the book/service. This presents book publishers with more challenges. How can they work with this model for their content? Can they break their content up into chunks that make micropayments workable and profitable for a product that is less mass market?

The effects for authors

There are also considerations in relation to the author. Some of the main issues are around the changing value of their content:

- lower prices means they get less royalty unless they sell a lot more
- authors expect to earn more money since their content is more valuable now that the print is not part of the risk the publishers bear
- authors may expect more money from digital – as the costs in their eyes are lower, their share of the profit should be larger
- authors wanting to make a living out of publishing will find that where publishers are squeezed on price they cannot spend as much on authors – the fate of mid-list authors becomes a consideration here

These are issues that are already being raised by the industry: agents, for example, are pushing for higher digital rights deals. This will have to be addressed to some extent by publishers, and the economics of the publishing process may have to change in order to do this.

Conclusion

It might well be time to review pricing mechanisms. The costs of producing an ebook, as we know, are lower but not necessarily very much lower. In addition, the industry is still pricing based on supporting an infrastructure that it no longer needs (from print production systems to large warehouses). Pricing on this basis to support a legacy infrastructure will pose more problems when newer market entrants emerge that do not have that legacy and can effectively price and manage their risk purely within a digital environment.

There are possible opportunities in pricing, however, that the new digital environment enables. Digital-only imprints are developing rapidly and pricing low; these currently tend to be focused on particular genres (romance and crime, for instance) and the economic model for these is one that may be difficult to apply to other aspects of publishing. Prices can also be more fluid compared to print products. Consumers do not want to be confused, but prices can be adjusted up or down easily, whether in response to a day-long special deal available on Amazon or when a title moves into a new phase of its life cycle; this can enable publishers and/or intermediaries to capitalise on price points effectively. Understanding the movement of prices and sales in this way will become an important skill.

The changing behaviour of purchasers could also be an opportunity. It may well be that consumers buy more books for their e-reader than they did in print. There may be many reasons for this, such as ease of purchase and more impulse purchases with a quick click of a button on an e-reader. However, lower prices may make spontaneous purchases easier for customers, who feel they risk less with a lower price on an individual product and so end up buying more. When studying owners of iPhones compared to owners of Android phones, it can be seen that Apple users spend more money on average on products for their phones, even though there are more Android phone owners. Potentially these new ways of buying may increase the amount spent on titles in the longer term.

Further reading and resources

Books

Anderson, Chris. *The Long Tail*. Random House, 2006.
Thomspon, John. *Merchants of Culture*. Polity Press, 2010.

Websites

www.wsj.com – online wallstreetjournal has followed quite closely the debates over agency book pricing

Questions to consider

1   How can publishers develop a stronger customer awareness of the value and cost of their content?
2   What can be learnt from the agency and wholesale pricing issue?
3   What considerations does a publisher need to bear in mind when developing a pricing strategy for a book launched in both print and digital formats?
4   What pricing effects might digital-only imprints have on other titles?

13 Content and the new market players

The digital environment makes publishing content easy. Publishers, who traditionally were the experts at publishing, are finding new players in their space. In this chapter we will look at:

1 New content players: Google, Apple and Amazon
2 Self-publishing
3 Other sources of content: communities and agents

Introduction

Publishers have developed expertise in content; finding it, nurturing it, developing it and producing it. Publishers see this as one of the important aspects of their role. In the traditional publishing value chain, content is one of the points of scarcity. Publishers are able to find and nurture authors and put their work into a format that can be distributed as effectively as possible. The crafting of that content is helped along by publishers, whether editing content at an early stage or preparing the content for publication, with the aim of achieving high quality where possible. The process of selecting content in the first place also involves a level of quality assurance: this could be by peer review to ensure scientific articles are accurate and valuable; or through testing books in the marketplace, such as educational texts; or by understanding market trends and finding the best books to reflect the interests of different readers. Understanding and managing content therefore is the lifeblood of publishers.

However, the digital age has introduced certain changes into the environment that render some aspects of the publishing value chain less critical than before. Clearly the ease with which publishing can occur on the internet means that some of the value that publishers traditionally added has become something most individuals can undertake if they wish. Distribution, for instance, can be achieved reasonably easily for all sorts of material, whether an academic posting up research on open access sites or via individuals self-publishing with Kindle.

The content itself is no longer scarce either. Matching content and readers is much easier to do on the internet; though it is not necessarily always straightforward and can require a fair amount of effort, nevertheless it can be done in a way that was not possible before. And content itself is everywhere – easy to identify and easy to get. It may be unregulated content, it may be unformatted, unchecked, badly written or inaccurate, but it is at least available and anyone therefore can get involved in 'publishing' it in some way. We can all be publishers, whether we post something on a blog or publish something more carefully constructed for a specific use; we can even simply publish the fact that we 'like' a photo on Facebook. So publishing has become democratised and content is publishable by anyone.

While this might be seen as a threat – who needs publishers if you can do it yourself? – it is content that is still central. Good content more so. Publishers understand their content and what it can do and offer, and how it can be used and provided to readers effectively. The way content is valued is changing, however; this theme has come up throughout the book. Different types of content have different, sometimes new, roles to play in the digital environment. New large players are entering the content marketplace from other industry sectors driven by motives very different from those of publishers. At the other end of the scale, individuals are able to take control of their own content and publishers. These issues are having an effect on the environment within which publishers operate.

New content players

We have seen that there are various reasons for some of the ways content is being re-evaluated. This is in part influenced by large internet and technology companies moving into the arena of content, publishing with different goals in mind; these can have distorting effects on the way content is conceived. Google, Apple and Amazon are three key players that in some way or other are becoming involved in the content marketplace. We will briefly look at each one and the effect it is having.

Google and digitisation of content

We have already explored Google's desire to obtain access to a large amount of content in the section on the Google settlement (see the case study in Chapter 10). In the rush to content, its digitsation drive was by far the largest and most comprehensive attempt to gain a lot of content in one go. Some observers feel Google did it to gain a level of ownership over the content (for the non-copyright materials) by offering to cover the cost of digitising its services. It is expensive to digitise, however; as experiments in the early 2000s showed, it is difficult to develop a financial model that would make it self-sustaining; it is therefore difficult to digitise large quantities of archives without the sort of financial support available to a company like Google. Publishers obviously do digitise their backlist, but that is different from the wholesale digitising of vast archives.

However, there is a lack of selectivity in what is digitised (not only in relation to copyright). Google to some extent treats the content as a commodity – the more the better, without a need to distinguish between good or bad. The search engine distinguishes which content might be of interest by the search, and the user can then select as they want (in theory with the confidence that anything relevant is brought up by the search and so they won't miss anything critical), even if it means sifting through lots of records to find it; in this way a user may stumble on something significant they never expected. Of course this content has been, at some point, endorsed by the mere fact a publisher did publish it. But the principle is that the user is free to find and select without the 'censorship' of any intermediary.

So in the Google approach to content there are benefits for Google that are clear. It drives more searches on its site; Google also becomes more key to certain communities for research (e.g. the scholarly community for researching large archives) and more central to researchers' day-to-day work. This can help it in various ways: it directs those interested in buying an in-copyright book to publishers and other bookselling partners; it can sell an ebook to those interested in purchasing direct from the Google Play site (competing with other online sellers in many cases); or it can connect to key institutions via partnerships such as an initiative with the British Library, where Google will be digitising 250,000 out-of-copyright works from the 1700s to the 1870s.

This approach to content can be viewed from different angles. For Google and its supporters the ability to access content provides a ready rich source of material that is for the first time easy to get at. Material that would have gone out of print has been brought back to life and a highly sophisticated search engine makes it accessible, ensuring user-centred results with good levels of filtering. This represents the democratisation and freedom of content. Anyone can access it, not just a few academics (for instance) in a particular library; making content that, for instance, in the case of the British Library has been paid for by all of us and carefully curated at our expense and for our use, accessible for all to benefit from is a compelling argument. For owners of content that appears on the site, it can potentially drive more sales too.

But, as we have seen, there are downsides. Some commentators do not trust Google's motives; while the side effect can beneficial, Google's main aim is not really dedicated to the furtherance of publishing as a process of cultural enrichment. Google can appear to be getting much more control than was wanted in some cases and taking huge sweeping steps in the interests of accessibility. The value for the search is in quantity not in quality, so there is a risk that mass producing content can devalue it. This dilution of information quality is enhanced by the search, where hits and misses are all mixed up. And while a search engine can be sophisticated, a person's search is still only as good as their search terms, as they are using an engine which may in fact be distorted by the search algorithm designed to search for more of the same to suit you. There is also a slight risk of deteriorating copyright as the market is swamped with non-copyright material. Many argue, too, that we are always paying for content in some way or other, even if not explicitly.

Apple driving usage

Google has not been in the business of creating content so much as getting it from other arenas. It is, as such, not directly in the business of publishing. Apple, however, is much more involved in the process of publishing. We have seen its involvement in both selling content (with agency pricing) and creating platforms on which to publish content. Apple's aim to continue to produce high-quality hardware, creating trends and leading the market both in application and design, maintaining a lead through innovative software and hardware but ensuring it remains robust and trustworthy, allows it to price reasonably highly and maintain its higher-end products. In doing this it has managed to build a market that appears loyal to its devices and with a certain consumer demography that means, as we have seen, that its customers spend more money on their devices than those with equivalents. This makes Apple an important consideration. While Google develops its software for devices around Android, decisions for publishers continue to focus around building materials for Apple first and Android second.

However, with Apple, like Amazon, as we shall see in the next section, acting as an intermediary to the market, this can cause publishers problems in two key ways:

- controlling access to the market via its bookstore and app stores
- providing free tools for users to publish without the need for publishers

In the first case, publishers need to go via these stores for their books and apps to be made available on Apple products and they need to abide by Apple's rules – which can be changed quite quickly (such as the percentage levied on in-app purchases) or can cause limits to publishers' ability to negotiate elsewhere (e.g. on prices that must not be lower with other sellers). These rules can be subject to regulatory scrutiny and may well change again, but the key point is that the publishers are rarely in the driving seat in any arrangements and may have to change and adapt business models as quickly as Apple changes its own.

In the second situation, software such as Apple Author means individuals can make their own books and sell them direct via the Apple stores. Publishers can use these systems too and work with Apple to adopt this sort of software for their titles, but the more individuals produce their own school textbooks (for example), the more problems this can cause for the educational market by reducing the market. In any case many publishers will prefer to produce titles in proprietary software so they can manipulate the content in more sophisticated ways and are able therefore to sell the product elsewhere, but the costs of cheaper authored titles may well prove a problem, pushing prices up further.

Amazon and its publishing

This dependency on the intermediary to reach the market and having to play by its rules is a problem also with Amazon. Contracts are negotiated regularly between Amazon and publishers over the various sales arrangements for books and ebooks and, as we have seen, this can cause problems for publishers. It is important for the larger publishers to act together, therefore, as individually it can be difficult for them to have much clout against a large organisation like Amazon. However, while publishers can go elsewhere to sell their print books, if their books are not available in Kindle they lose access to a considerable portion of the market. While it is also in the interest of Amazon not to antagonise publishers, as they do want their content, it can also be quite robust in its negotiation.

Amazon, of these big three market entrants, is the one most actively engaged in publishing. It has arrangements with publishers to print Kindle titles, arrangements to publish its own print titles, as well as publishing activities directed at producing online content professionally (e.g. its purchase of Marshall Cavendish). Amazon's main publishing activities centre around genre publishing such as sci-fi and cult writings, with 47 North, mystery and thrillers with Thomas & Mercer and romance with Montlake Romance; it also has specific areas such as translated works with AmazonCrossing.

These are publishing divisions centred around publishing for ebooks but Amazon has been driving growth in self-publishing by allowing authors direct access to publishing titles within Kindle. This has been driven in various ways such as the Kindle Singles programme, where books longer than long-form journalism but shorter than most short books can be published; here it is encouraging everyone, not just individuals as yet unpublished, but well-established authors to participate – bypassing publishers for certain types of writing. This is tapping into one of the advantages of electronic publishing: the short story format is a difficult one for publishers as readers have proved to be less interested in them, so making a viable print book has been difficult. However, the cheaper ebooks make this possible.

Self-publishing

The area of publishing where Amazon's Kindle has made the most impact has been the self-publishing aspect, not just for short works but for full-length works via Kindle Direct Publishing (KDP). Amazon is not the only place for self-publishing but it has developed a self-publishing environment that has proved very successful. Having a ready marketplace also helps, and third party self-publishing sites will help authors get their books into the Kindle format as well as other ebook formats. While it does require some effort, it has proved to be a place where people can publish their own titles and make money from it. Kindle has a simple pricing structure where it takes a percentage of any sales and authors keep the rest and keep copyright. The titles will appear within categories on Amazon rankings and rise in the rankings as they are bought. Books that are difficult to categorise suffer. However, there is no other intervention with the book so the authors themselves need to ensure they are well edited (most self-published authors agree that a good edit is essential and something worth paying for as a service), produce cover artwork and do any additional marketing to help their title along up the rankings.

Many are not successful but some are, and the high-profile authors have generally become successful from Amazon's self-publishing programme rather than others. Kerry Wilkinson sold over 250,000 ebooks in six months for his crime fiction. Amanda Hocking is another example of someone who became very successful from her self-publishing activities. These particular examples are clearly the exception rather than the rule. Nevertheless, the barrier to entry is low – as long as they have some time to spend on getting things right and loading them up, anyone can have a go – if they are not successful, and after all many are not, it has not cost a large amount of investment. Even small sales can be satisfying, though to get to any quantity of sales can take a while. One hundred sales may seem a lot to an individual, but if each book is priced at £1.99 (a typical price for a self-publisher), at a 70 per cent royalty this leaves £140. It's nice to have but not necessarily the roots of a writing career.

For any self-publishers that are successful, there is still the attraction of going mainstream with publishing. In both the cases outlined above the authors subsequently found publishers to take them on. Certain features of self-publishing this way can ultimately put individuals off self-publishing. The attractiveness of a publisher for these high-profile authors is based around:

- good editing
- having the publisher deal with the technical side

- high-profile, professional, comprehensive marketing
- access to wider distribution routes
- being able to get some protection against piracy
- above all, being able to write instead of do all the other stuff

The self-publishing community

There is no doubt, however, that the self-publishing phenomenon has taken off with digital publishing. Amazon's KDP has helped develop a critical mass of self-publishers but the marketplace does not just involve individuals loading their files into KDP. There has been a proliferation of companies involved in helping individuals with as much or as little of the process as possible. With its roots in vanity publishing there are now many ways to publish directly, whether one wants to simply get easy digital print copies of titles or to buy in a variety of publishing services depending on specific need, from marketing to layout, from editing to levels of copyright protection.

Companies offering a variety of these services, such as lulu.com or matador.com, will also undertake the preparation of the ebook files so you do not have to manipulate the software and load the books into sales sites. They can manage bibliographic details and sales relationships as well, thereby taking the books wider than the Kindle-only products. However, this is an expensive and time-consuming process. Studies of self-publishing show that it can be a satisfying and effective way to publish, allowing authors much more freedom; they can avoid many of the frustrations of being published by a large publisher, who may not treat them as they hoped. Nevertheless, many also see that the attractions of being chosen by a publisher are still compelling: it can put its weight behind a book in production and marketing, allowing the writer just to write – which is one of the key things a publisher can offer an author.

A community has grown up around self-publishing, with many self-published or 'indie' authors providing guides and blogging on websites dedicated to showing you the best ways to market your book, keep a book's profile up in the rankings or get it well edited. This market is growing, and the numbers of readers and writers of self-published fiction are increasing, particularly on Amazon. Any changes in the Amazon business model would impact directly on this market, however, as the authors are dependent on Amazon.

One of the key things that the success of self-publishing counters is the argument that publishers know best what to publish. In the self-publishing environment the market can choose, and if a book is good, so it is felt, it will rise to the surface. Are so-called experts needed as gatekeepers or to arbitrate on the cultural importance of some books when the crowd can choose? Here there are arguments about the democracy of the internet, but it also raises issues about lack of selectivity, problems of trustworthiness, the need for some sort of curators/arbiters of culture.

It is noticeable, though, that the self-published books that are successful are those that have the characteristics of good books: good plot, well written, compelling characters, etc. This could be an argument for the fact that good books will still rise: there is no need for a publisher to select them. However, a lot of books have to be read for the good ones to rise to the surface. The recommendation/rankings software tries to help this process, but for some readers having titles selected by trusted sources (which could be via a reading group blog or by them being published alongside someone they recognise) rather than crowd rankings may mean they find more quickly the books they want to read.

Finding content: harnessing the power of the crowd

Finding new talent is also one of the traditional areas of expertise of publishers. The digital environment can facilitate ways to identify new content sources. Sites that bypass publishers, focusing on a model of crowd recommendation – writers can post up novels, or parts of novels, for others within the community to read, maybe comment on and ultimately recommend – encourage writers to continue with their work if there is enough positive reaction from the community.

Publishers are getting involved here too as they develop sites like authonomy that work in this way, with the possibility of those successful titles being creamed off and considered for publication. These are often small operations but they aim to provide a direct relationship with readers that is not just based on the purchase of a title.

Finding sources of content that may be cheaper than the traditional route is important. Though few would see this as the major strategic stimulus behind such sites, they do provide a way to access authors without agents. Agents remain key to the publishing environment, but publishers are always looking at ways to manage the 'slush pile' and digital options to encourage a certain level of market research are another tool for them. For some of these initiatives the impetus is setting a contractual arrangement with new writers that avoids some of the pitfalls of the potentially unearned advances and overpriced manuscripts at auction, which add considerably to the financial risk that publishers take on with new publishing.

Publishers are also getting involved by providing writing courses and advice services (such as those of Faber and Bloomsbury). In an effort to develop these relationships further many publishers are re-emphasising their interest in book events, creating and running all sorts of events, fairs, reading groups and educational activities to create an environment for loyal customers.

The agents

While the publishers seek ways to bypass the agent sometimes, the agents also see ways to bypass the publishers. Most agents have left publishing companies in order to avoid having to do the publishing, and instead to focus on the authors and the ideas. However, agents feel that the digital options for publishers should mean that authors get better deals for digital sales. As authors get used to models on Amazon and Apple for 70 per cent of the total revenue, so this increases an author's expectations of what they can get for digital sales – particularly digital-only sales. Some agents, too, feel that there should be clearer recognition of higher earning potential for authors within ebook contracts. Agents' roles are also expanding as they look at further ways to exploit the content they have on behalf of authors given the opportunities for digital products as the case study illustrates.

Threat from big name authors

It is worth reiterating, too, the threat to publishers from published authors, who can, once famous, go it alone. Pottermore, mentioned earlier, is an example of this but there are other cases where authors have launched digital versions themselves. Clearly a bestselling author with a large budget can produce something highly sophisticated and innovative; they may well employ experts from publishing and other industries

Case study: Odyssey editions

There are alternatives to publishers for disgruntled agents – as Andrew Wylie, the New York-based agent, showed in 2010. Infamous in the literary world, his agency has responsibility for several major estates, including those of Saul Bellow, Norman Mailer and Evelyn Waugh. These were the sorts of titles that had no clear digital rights within publishing contracts; the print publishers of these titles in general wanted to keep to a standard royalty rate of a digital subsidiary right, but the Wylie Agency, wanting more for the digital rights, decided to release these themselves. *Brideshead Revisited*, for instance, is available on Amazon in Kindle format, and Odyssey editions, the name of the imprint set up by Wylie, is given as the publisher. Publishers who had the print rights to these editions went back to Wylie to renegotiate and in many cases agreed to the higher-value arrangements. This has not proved standard practice but it does reflect the ease with which a publisher can be bypassed for titles that are already well established and well known.

(web developers, social media experts, etc.) to do it but they have put the investment in themselves, knowing that they are not taking a huge risk now that they are well known. The publisher took the risk when taking on the title when they were unknown.

Even authors and agents that are unknown may decide to withhold digital rights if they feel they can exploit these better themselves. Bloomsbury never did have the digital rights for Harry Potter. This leads to the question that many ask: publishers have a role in discovering and breaking new authors (with the help of agents), which they do very well, but if those authors (or maybe their agents) then do everything in the digital environment themselves once they are established, how does the publisher benefit from the risk it took to break the authors in the first place? Publishers will not want to see themselves as only the print outlet for an author. Self-publishing can happen therefore at both ends of the spectrum – new authors can emerge via self-published works, a publisher may take them on to invest further in them and then when they become extremely famous they can self-publish again. The role of publishers therefore gets squashed in between and the benefits of the low costs of taking on an unknown author, as well as the higher returns if they are successful, are eroded at both ends.

Conclusion

As we look at the changing nature of content we see both large and small market players emerging: huge conglomerates used to operating in markets well outside the traditional publishing arena and commanding huge investment capabilities at one end, with individuals taking risks and making their own success by exploiting the freedom that Web 2.0 allows for anyone to 'publish' at the other.

Publishers have to revise how they treat content and compete with others who have very different approaches to content. They need to re-evaluate their own role: what in the value chain can they offer where so much of what they used to offer has slipped away? Debates of this sort centre around the need for gatekeepers to help sift through the flood of information that is available, using editorial skills to select and bring to the surface 'good' content. Though does that debate hold as true for a ghost-written celebrity biography as for a Man Booker Prize winner? Publishers can add value because they understand the structure and intricacies of content; they know how to manage it effectively as well as preserve it. These sorts of skills may need to be reinforced with a consumer that is finding content in all sorts of other places within the digital environment. Publishers may need also to re-evaluate how they can ensure the quality of their content, as that may well be a defining feature of what they can sell.

Further reading and resources

Books

Baverstock, Alison. *The Naked Author: A Guide to Self Publishing*, A&C Black, 2011.
Keen, Andrew. *The Cult of the Amateur*. Currency, 2007.

Websites

There are many books and blogs on how to go about self-publishing. Some self-publishing sites include:
kdp.amazon.com/self-publishing/signin – takes you to the page on Kindle self-publishing
www.authonomy.com
www.completelynovel.com
www.faberacademy.co.uk – Faber is an example of a publisher diversifying to offer publishing services to the individual (Bloomsbury is another)
www.lulu.com
www.troubador.co.uk/matador.asp

Questions to consider

1   How should publishers respond to each of the big companies with regard to their approach to content?
2   What threat does self-publishing pose for publishers?
3   What are the benefits for authors of going to publishers rather than self-publishing?
4   What can publishers do to prevent lead authors going it alone once they are big enough?

14 Futurising publishing structures

Throughout the book we have seen how the digital environment has created huge challenges for publishers. Many commentators have concluded that publishers will need to reconfigure their traditional activities in order to face these challenges effectively. This final chapter looks at:

1 The changing elements of the value chain
2 Reorganising publishing structures in the specialist sector
3 Predicting change in the trade sector

Introduction

The development of the digital environment for publishing has brought about many changes for publishing, whether reorganising the production process around the digital workflow and asset management systems or reconfiguring the activity of a marketing department to integrate social media practices. There is an increasing pressure on price and new market entrants are staking claims on the publishing of content. Each aspect of publishing that we have explored in Part III of the book has led to the conclusion that publishing as an industry needs to rethink some of its fundamental behaviours. New business models need to be developed quickly. And where a business model changes, all the elements of that model may need review, from discounting and sales practices to royalties and content development.

There is the additional impact for those businesses that have not had to make any major structural changes in any regular way: the legacy they carry of an infrastructure, honed over decades to traditional publishing practice, means change is both costly and cumbersome to implement. Newer players in the market can benefit in various ways: they do not have to carry the costs of any old infrastructure; they can ignore part of the market altogether (e.g. the print market); they can be nimble either through the low entry costs if they operate at one end of the market (e.g. self-publishers) or by commanding huge funding for investment that outweighs the financial strength of many large publishing houses, as the large technology companies can.

The question is complicated further by the fact that that legacy is still necessary for the time being. Print books still represent the larger part of global sales and even as sales slow down they will continue to be significant; so retaining aspects of the traditional infrastructure is still relevant, whether promoting relationships with bookshops or ensuring warehouses operate effectively. Publishers therefore cannot throw out everything with the aim of reinventing themselves for the new digital age, yet many observers agree that tweaking at the edges is not going to be enough.

The changing value chain

Changes in the traditional value chain have been a theme throughout the book. Figure 14.1 shows a simple value chain for publishing. Finding the content, the development and production, then the promotion and distribution of that content are all aspects of the publishing value chain where the involvement of publisher is clear. The publishing structures that have developed for this are very effective in the print-only world. As we have seen, some of these aspects of the value chain are becoming redundant – warehouses, for instance, are not necessary for digital-only books. Also other sorts of companies can have more involvement in or access to aspects of the value chain, thus meaning that publishers are no longer unique in providing these services. As certain elements of the value chain are eroded, so the structure needs to adjust.

But it goes deeper. Internet commentators who promote democracy and freedom for distribution on the web can sometimes suggest that publishers are the enemies of their ideal for free information as they want to control the process; others, meanwhile, will see that there are still important roles that publishers need to play but they may have a different emphasis from the traditional value chain. So, for instance, when bookshops are playing less of a critical role in the distribution of information, and anyone can become an author if they wish, the importance of selecting, or curating, content of a suitable quality (for whatever genre) may be gaining ground, as is the focus on marketing in order to obtain maximum discoverability. So the value chain can be reoriented to some extent through this sort of nuance: good content selection and effective marketing. But the fact remains that competitors moving into the market will have different structures and different approaches to the value chain which are much more fluid; as the traditional business of publishing begins to break down, publishers are considering ways to re-engineer it at a more fundamental level.

Challenging and reorienting the traditional value chain

If one takes a simplified version of the value chain one can then examine each area and question its place in the digital publishing environment. Below are just some of the issues and questions that arise with each part of the chain. This is not intended to be a comprehensive discussion, but the list encompasses the debates that have arisen

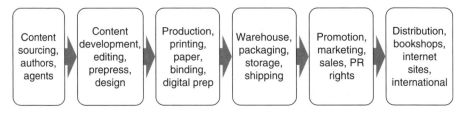

Figure 14.1 The publishing value chain.

throughout the book. It is, however, clear that each area can generate considerable debate about the role of publishers within that particular function:

- **Content sourcing:** authors can publish themselves and reach readers without much intervention – though they still need a digital intermediary such as Kindle Direct Publishing. Selecting and competing for good content therefore is changing. Publishing was always possible for an individual willing to pay for the individual components of the process and put in the time and effort required. However, economies of scale, extensive marketing departments with key networks and contacts gave publishing houses a lead. But things are getting easier and less expensive, enabling more people to do this, so the value chain is more exposed. Still publishers may provide the best and most direct route for customers to reach good-quality content.
- **Textual/structural work on content:** this still needs to take place, though it can be done without the need for publishers, using freelancers and communities to help self-correct. However, publishers may be the best at doing this given their experience – for some the beauty of having an editor work on a piece of writing is becoming clearer now that more poorly edited content is prevalent; whether editors ensure content is free from errors (so increasing its credibility), at one level, or work on the structure to make the content the best it can be, they add value. Editorial work can be done more quickly with digital methods. Speed to market is impeded by too much interaction with the text and if stages can be skipped (and fewer stages allow fewer mistakes to creep in), then digital puts pressure on this aspect of the chain.
- **Production:** various stages of production can take place without using traditional methods and the whole process can be managed more quickly. However, publishers have developed considerable expertise in managing digital content. Being able to manage content flexibly and to archive it for easy access in the future, make it discoverable with good metadata or repackage it in different ways, can, of course, be a huge advantage. For those involved in self-publishing the technology aspects of going digital without the help of experts can be time consuming and frustrating.
- **Distribution:** this can be physical and digital. Where physical products are needed, publishers are likely to be the best at doing this given their long experience and well-developed infrastructure, but digital distribution does not necessarily require a publisher given the various intermediaries that are available to use instead. As long as you pay for the technical help/software (or indeed use free systems such as open source blogs), distributing content digitally is easy. As the move to digital becomes more marked, the need for warehousing, for instance, will change; even for print books easier, just-in-time printing and local printing will mean warehouse strategies will change.
- **Global distribution:** the digital world brings everywhere closer as instant distribution globally is easy. This means the publishers who would add value by facilitating global distribution by selling rights or by shipping and selling physical books through a well-developed network of agents and international offices are less critical as these markets can be reached much more easily from one place. Nevertheless, discoverability remains an issue.
- **Sales:** bookshops are becoming less critical in the value chain given the pressure of getting cheaper print books from other intermediaries (from digital retailers

to supermarkets) and in terms of the ability to promote and distribute ebooks. Publishers need to develop new relationships quickly with the new digital intermediaries, while also developing direct engagement with customers. Clearly a publisher will not be able to have much of a direct relationship with all its customers across all its product lines, but this issue reflects the need publishers have to move beyond the very close relationships they have with bookshops (though they must maintain those too as a valuable source of sales and promotion) and recognise that if they don't do this they will lose more control over their marketplace. But all this throws the spotlight on the sales teams; they were the experts with the bookshops. With fewer bookshops sales functions are changing and integrating with marketing – as relationships with, for instance, Amazon need to be developed, relationships very different from the traditional bookshop relationship.

- **Marketing:** this can of course be done without the need for publishers. Much can be achieved using digital marketing practices now without large budgets. It is now possible for an individual to develop their own community of customers through successful blogs. It is a lot of work, however, and publishers have developed sophisticated ways to maximise discoverability within the digital environment as well as command impressive marketing budgets for big titles.

As these elements of the value chain change, so costs change – while production costs may come down due to less printing, the costs of marketing across so many more media can go up. Customer service departments have in many places grown as they take on more technical helpdesk roles to support specialist digital publications.

When you unpick the value chain in this way, even though it is not a comprehensive list of each stage, most of the key problems that publishers face surface. It also shows how far considerations related to the old value chain remain prevalent. New market entrants will be free of this history and in many ways able to create a value chain of their own according to their particular skills from a blank sheet.

The result is that existing publishers recognise the digital imperative is changing many aspects of the way they work and do business; they see they have to reorganise themselves to align with the changing market and review their publishing structure from the very roots. They need to look at what they can do, what they need to do and what they can't afford to do any more; and they need to work out how to plan and pay for it. Publishers may need to strip back the value chain, taking out the parts that are no longer relevant, and to reconfigure what it is they do add in light of the digital environment.

Reorganising publishing structures in the specialist sectors

In the specialist sectors publishing structures have already changed in all sorts of ways. Such companies have gone through a more measured pace of reconstruction compared to the trade arena, partly because while technology has moved quickly it has done so reasonably evenly; greater market understanding of the content has also helped make the transition a little more smooth, without the upheaval that brand new mass consumer technologies have brought to the consumer market. Many have managed effective transfer of their business operations to cope with the new digital challenges. They have already had to revisit their skills bases and reorganise around the new requirements of a digital industry.

This has been managed in a variety of ways, as we have seen. Many have had units for a number of years in different countries to prepare content and manage the digital warehouse or supply services such as e-inspection copy management or helpdesks. Internally departments have been changed so that, for instance, they can expand and reduce staff numbers quickly and efficiently depending on their workflow. Expertise to plan for and cost big projects, project management skills, capability in creating product specifications for outsourcing and commissioning technical expertise are all examples of new skills and roles that specialist companies have expanded. This has meant a shift from the traditional desk editorial departments and some of the commissioning roles have changed, often focused on ongoing management expertise of large projects, keeping a commercial eye on their development and maintenance. Ultimately the ability to form and reform teams appropriately as technology changes or new projects come into view is at the root of some of the structural changes that have been made.

Other areas have, however, not had to change so much. Sales teams may have to become more technically literate about the products they sell and new sales activities around selling them developed (e.g. in providing training), but the sales team relationship with key clients remains at the core of product sales. Marketing departments have needed to encompass more social media marketing techniques, but close relationships with customers already existed and so it has been easier to grow these links within their traditional marketing activity.

Predicting change in trade publishing

For trade, the digital changes have been long awaited but only recently become much more of a critical issue as finally the sales of consumer technology reached a tipping point. Much more suddenly, the industry is facing the same problems that faced the specialist market. It is not just a case of foretelling when digital books will supersede print, nor for how long print will last – these questions are too general and do not quite go to the heart of the issue, say many industry experts. A change in format with different discounting patterns is less the challenge than the questions being asked of the real role of publishers in the internet age and the recasting of the fundamental business model.

Commentators review these questions regularly and pick out different aspects for chief scrutiny. By way of an example, a review of recent articles covers a variety of topics. Joseph Esposito, publishing industry consultant, in one article explores the fact that ebooks are being priced according to what the market wants to pay, which changes the business model; but he sees that 'enhanced' ebooks are a way for publishers to add value, while marketing is becoming even more of a driver for the business given issues of discoverability.

Richard Nash, a US-based commentator and publisher, believes that currently publishers are not doing enough to reorient themselves; instead they are only doing enough to minimise short-term disruption. The agency pricing issue might be an example – playing with pricing does not necessarily fit the company out for what appears to be an inevitable lowering of prices. The company needs to review its cost base and publishing practices in order to manage this new low-price model that others will exploit if they do not. He explains that more entrepreneurial approaches are needed from within publishing to compete effectively with entrepreneurs moving into their space. Supply in print or digital forms is reasonably easy to solve, but demand needs to be more carefully understood: the changing consumer is demanding information specific to their needs. In the old publishing model consumers had to choose from the selections the publisher put before them, but that has been turned around. Consumers will look elsewhere for information if publishers are not giving it to them in the way they want it, when they want it, where they want it. According to Nash, new skills such as data mining – making things discoverable – are going to be valuable as content becomes one gigantic data set; meanwhile intermediaries are changing – the search intermediary is becoming more important than, for instance, the retail intermediary.

Michael Healy, a US book industry professional, recognises that currently content is optimised for consumption in traditional book form but now thought needs to be given to the way content is commissioned, edited and formatted. The publisher's role as curator and arbiter is important here. And here one should not read curation as only about high-level, culturally critical activity or sophisticated taste; celebrity biographies may have a role to play for a specific market in terms of providing enjoyment and interest. The actual nature of the book needs to be re-engineered and in the process new concepts explored around pricing models, for instance (as explored in Chapter 12) taking examples from other industries (such as all-in subscriptions – providing value-added services around free content). Healy is a proponent of the need for publishers to build some relationship with consumers – challenging though that is and maybe only of limited effect for a certain segment of the customer base – in order to watch reading patterns, which ultimately are where the change is coming from.

These are just three examples of commentators exploring publishing futures. One of the main messages that they share is that reinvention of publishing structures and the choices a publisher makes should not be based on the original value chain. Newer publishers aren't bothering with bookshops, so are not having to calculate in discounts. A publisher may still need bookshops but may need to think of them in a different way (for instance as key partners for reaching the reading community) in relation to the new value chain.

Another point in common between these commentaries is that it is the consumer that is changing – the way consumers consume any sort of entertainment is changing rapidly and books are bundled into that mix in a much more complex way. The range of readers is expanding: there are those who are using social networks to share and create books with strangers, while at the other end of the market there are those for whom very private enjoyment of a book away from everything is what is attractive. This wide spectrum is going to prove a challenge.

Conclusion

Opportunities exist for publishers according to all these commentators – for instance, Nash points to the fact that there is the chance to explore different sorts of narrative alongside the long form, while Healy believes trade publishers can develop certain niche markets and build brands to become reader-centred businesses. Publishers often say when asked about their future that they recognise that they are in the business of entertainment and of creating communities. They are becoming producers across different media; they see the centrality of the reader in all they do; they should be regarded as creative specialists and can rethink not just design and format, but products themselves. Publishers are not behind on these new ways of thinking about what they do.

Nevertheless, in all these cases, the basic structure of the publishing company needs to be considered – can the old functional departments still exist? Will departmental lines blur (for instance between commissioning and marketing as content is created for a website and a book), or will new structures be invented, ones that take a hub approach, pulling in expertise as required for a particular project centre? New structures will need to be designed to be more flexible about external partnerships. Those who invest in new capabilities before a well-defined market has come into view will be the most able to cope: they may be developing digital archives that can be easily exploited in various ways; or they may be reviewing the way they produce the print to reinvent its role in the publishing programme; or they may be building partnerships that can evolve; or, as we have seen with Penguin and Random House, consolidating to gain strength in a changing marketplace. Whatever strategy they adopt, they need to ensure they are organised in a way that means they can exploit the potential of digital publishing most effectively in the future.

Further reading and resources

These are three interesting articles from good commentators on the future of publishing. There are many more like this to be found in journals such as *Publishing Research Quarterly* and *Logos*.

Esposito, J. 'One World Publishing, Brought to You by the Internet'. *Publishing Research Quarterly* 27: 13–18 (2011).

Healy, Michael. 'Seeking Permanence in a Time of Turbulence'. *Logos* 22/2 (2011).

Nash, Richard. 'Publishing 2020'. *Publishing Research Quarterly* 26: 114–18 (2010). Nash is a well-known commentator on the area and you can find interesting video discussions with him on internet sites such as YouTube and Vimeo.

Darnton, Richard. *The Case for Books*. Public Affairs, 2009.

Questions to consider

1   What functions do you feel a publisher will need in place to manage increasing amounts of digital products? And what will it need less of in the future?

2   To what extent do you think specialist publishers are ready to face future challenges?

3   How might you reconfigure a publishing company to be able to adapt to the changing business environment?

4   What are the biggest threats and opportunities for publishers facing the digital publishing environment?

Final word

The digital environment continues to change at a rapid pace and the business of digital publishing is changing with it. Different sectors tell different stories and there is only room in an introduction like this to touch on some of the dilemmas they face. Each has its own particular challenges, but in each we can see a proactive approach to the opportunities on offer. Some sectors are further along the line of reinventing themselves than others. But also some changes are less seismic than perhaps was first thought – we are a long way from the death of print. We know also that issues such as discoverability are becoming critical to publishing, while other areas are taking on new dimensions, such as open access, and we need to see the implications of these.

The problem with a book like this is that things are changing so quickly along all aspects of the value chain that it is difficult to include everything and keep all these elements up to date. In any case, as digital business models continuously change, so learning about one way of doing things is fruitless. Rather, future employees in the industry need to be able to adapt quickly, understand the implications of strategies, be capable of experimentation, apply creativity to publishing solutions, be responsive to trends and quick to recognise when change is needed. This and more! And yet none of this is entirely new. Publishers have been entrepreneurial from the beginning and the industry has gone through periods of great change before now. The ability to spot good content, craft it for a marketplace, perfect methods of distribution, and communicate and celebrate the products has always been fundamental to publishing. So understanding how different models have developed and how they are evolving is important for seeing how things can continuously change but still be rooted in the skills and expertise that the industry has always had. Exploring the various responses to critical issues such as copyright or pricing is also important as a way of understanding what problems and opportunities exist moving forward.

From what we have seen, there is no doubt that the industry does need to look at ways to reorganise itself quickly in relation to the changing marketplace; in many cases it is well on the way to doing this, though in other aspects it is at the start of this process. More significantly, the industry needs to understand the changing consumer. Reading habits are changing in a fundamental way; consumer behaviour and consumer expectations are being altered by the digital world, so the industry does need to pay attention and understand how it can become focused on different sorts of readers. Publishers need to take this right to the point of reassessing how books work, moving from linearity to connectivity, understanding what level of involvement a reader wants with the content, whether it is a researcher annotating with additional notes or a fan engaging with others to write additional material (while still also catering for those who like the escapism and solitude of reading a good story). The consumer is much more in control now and publishers will need to continue to be much more sophisticated in understanding consumers' demands.

What is still a huge challenge for publishers is the fact they are operating increasingly in an environment where other companies, outside the traditional publishing industry, are influencing the way it behaves. In this way, the boundary of the marketplace in which they move has changed from one that was reasonably contained to one where they are at the mercy of other people's business models. It is this, in many ways, which is forcing the biggest change on the industry. Some criticise a company like Elsevier dominating a marketplace in the STM area, but that is not necessarily so different from the way Amazon could be said to dominate the internet retail space.

Is the behaviour of the publishing industry that we can see now as it comes to terms with these issues simply a route to a final goal, a fully transitioned digital publisher? Or should we, rather, see this as the way it is from now on; publishers will need to be constantly changing and innovating, continuously responsive to an environment that is continuously moving? In this case, publishers will need to be quick at adopting new methods of working in order to be agile in the digital age. As they move into these bigger digital environments, they may also need to spend more time explaining why they remain necessary. Publishers, who have traditionally been modest about their brand names and perhaps a little distant in their own direct contact with customers, need to assert themselves and explain what it is they do; and also continue to show, as they have always done, that they can do it extremely well.

Index